AF477560

Schooling in Western Europe

Schooling in Western Europe

The New Order and Its Adversaries

Ken Jones, Chomin Cunchillos, Richard Hatcher,
Nico Hirtt, Rosalind Innes, Samuel Johsua and
Jürgen Klausenitzer

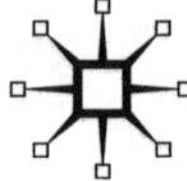

First published 2008 by
PALGRAVE MACMILLAN
Houndmills, Basingstoke, Hampshire RG21 6XS and
175 Fifth Avenue, New York, N.Y. 10010
Companies and representatives throughout the world

PALGRAVE MACMILLAN is the global academic imprint of the Palgrave Macmillan division of St. Martin's Press, LLC and of Palgrave Macmillan Ltd. Macmillan® is a registered trademark in the United States, United Kingdom and other countries. Palgrave is a registered trademark in the European Union and other countries.

ISBN-13: 978–0–230–55143–5   hardback
ISBN-10: 0–230–55143–2   hardback

This book is printed on paper suitable for recycling and made from fully managed and sustained forest sources. Logging, pulping and manufacturing processes are expected to conform to the environmental regulations of the country of origin.

A catalogue record for this book is available from the British Library.

A catalog record for this book is available from the Library of Congress.

10   9   8   7   6   5   4   3   2   1
17   16   15   14   13   12   11   10   09   08

Printed and bound in Great Britain by
CPI Antony Rowe, Chippenham and Eastbourne

Contents

Notes on the Contributors

Chomin Cunchillos writes on behalf of the Colectivo Baltasar Gracián. The Colectivo Baltasar Gracián (CBG) is a group of teachers in secondary schools in Madrid. The group has developed a way of working that combines research and political analysis, focusing on the Spanish education system. The CBG has a website – www.colectivobgracian.com – and publishes an electronic magazine, *Crisis*.

Jürgen Klausenitzer is an activist and education consultant. His work is frequently published in the German e-journal *Widersprüche* (www.widersprüche-zeitschrift.de).

Ken Jones is Professor of Education at Keele University and is a member of the education network of the European Social Forum. His book *Education in Britain* was published in 2003.

Nico Hirtt is a founding member of the 'Appel pour une école démocratique' (Belgium). He is the author of several books on the politics of education in Europe, including *Les nouveaux maîtres de l'école*, published in 2003.

Richard Hatcher is director of research in the Faculty of Education at the University of Central England in Birmingham and is part of the education network of the European Social Forum. He has written widely on education policy.

Rosalind Innes is an Australian feminist and social activist who has lived and worked in Italy for many years. She is a lecturer in English at the University of Basilicata.

Samuel Johsua is Professor of Education at the Université de Provence Aix-Marseille. He co-ordinates the educational agenda of the altermondialist organisation ATTAC. He published in 2003 *Une autre école est possible: manifeste pour une éducation émancipatrice*.

Abbreviations

ATTAC	Association pour la taxation des transactions pour l'aide aux citoyens
BERA	British Educational Research Association
BFS	Building Schools for the Future
CBI	Confederation of British Industry
CDU	German Christian Democratic Party
CERI	Centre for Educational Research and Innovation (OECD)
CGIL	General Confederation of Italian Labour
CISL	Italian Federation of Workers' Unions
COBAS	Committees at the Base (Italian workers' movement)
COBAS-Scuola	Committees at the Base, Education
CPE	First Employment Contract (France)
DES	Department for Education and Science
DfEE	Department for Education and Employment
DfES	Department for Education and Skills
EAZ	Education Action Zone
ERT	European Round Table
ETUC	European Trade Union Confederation
FEN	National Education Federation (trade union – France)
FSU	Common Federation of (Education) Unions (France)
GATS	General Agreement on Trade and Services
GEW	Education and Knowledge Union (Germany)
LGE	General Law on Education (Spain)
LOCE	Law on the Quality of Education (Spain)

LODE	Law on the Right to Education (Spain)
LOE	Organic Law on Education (Spain)
LOGSE	Law on the General Organisation of the Education System (Spain)
MEDEF	Movement of French Business
OECD	Organisation for Economic Co-operation and Development
OMC	Open Method of Co-ordination (EU)
NPM	New Public Management
NUT	National Union of Teachers
PCI	Italian Communist Party
PDS	Party of the Democratic Left (Germany)
PFI	Private Finance Initiative
PISA	Programme for International Student Assessment
PP	People's Party (Spain)
PRP	Performance-Related Pay
PSI	Italian Socialist Party
PSOE	Spanish Socialist Party
QAA	Qualifications and Assessment Authority
QCA	Qualifications and Curriculum Authority
SPD	German Social Democratic Party
STES-I	Confederation of Education Workers' Unions (Spain)
UIL	Italian Union of Labour
UNICE	Union of Industrial and Employers' Confederations of Europe
ZEP	Education Priority Zone (France)

1
An Emerging Order

We write in this book about the remaking of schooling in Western Europe, and the policy orthodoxy – promoted by supranational organisations, shared across frontiers – that is so powerful an influence upon it. We draw much from others who have worked in this field before us – from theorists who have analysed the scalar shift in policymaking from national to supranational level; from sociologists who have traced both the classic patterns of schooling's regulation and their new forms; and from those who have delineated the repertoire and discursive nuances of the new world order in education.[1] To this now-abundant literature, we bring something of our own. Our particular interest is in the contestation that attends supranational policy orthodoxy – how its arrival within the major countries of Western Europe has been the occasion for widespread criticism, discontent and mobilisation. This terrain, on which are fought out disputes central to the ways in which Europe's present is understood and its future imagined, has not been so well explored by researchers, even when their sympathies have been engaged by those who challenge the new order.

The vantage point from which we interpret these disputes, and make sense of the changes that are reshaping the school, does not stand outside the territory of contestation. Our own formation as teachers and researchers has been affected by participation in movements that have sought change at the level of the classroom and the school, as part of a much wider political and economic transformation. We are thus aware that educational change is better seen not as the simple realisation of a policy design but as an outcome of purposive activity (and conflict) at many levels, from the local to the international. More specifically, our book is influenced by the positions and actions of the social forces that have been mobilised against what we think oppositional social movements justly call the neo-liberal project. We take neo-liberalism – whose general features and educational impact we sketch in the pages that follow – to be best understood as an aggressive programme, that self-consciously sets for itself the goal of achieving change of an epochal kind; it aims to defeat the movements associated with an earlier phase of state-focused, welfare-orientated reform and to install a new systemic logic by means of which societies respond at every level – from individual to governmental – to free-market imperatives. Our book is organised around various instances of this process of combative transformation, in which policy redesign is always accompanied by a concern for political tactics, and in which the forcefulness of opposition is a significant variable in the success or failure of educational programmes.

We are protagonists as well as commentators, then, but protagonists on the part of movements that are now, despite occasional spectacular victories – France 2005 – primarily defensive ones. And since the neo-liberal programme has been the dominant agenda-setting force in the post-1990 educational landscape, to focus on its achievements is also to recognise the strategic and intellectual problems of those traditions against which it has been directed. The educational systems that it is seeking to transform were created, in part, by popular aspirations for increased equality and social citizenship; and to a significant, though never determining, extent, schools in Western Europe were for a period home to values and practices embodying solidarities of a sort resistant to the logic of the market, and strong enough even now to mobilise enduring protest. We owe our cultural and political formation to just such solidarities, and to this extent our book is grounded on the historic achievements of the last half-century. But we do not intend merely to celebrate a movement which in so many respects now finds itself on the defensive, an altermondialist optimism heavily qualified by a long succession of defeats. At the end of his book on social change in Western Europe the sociologist Colin Crouch acknowledged that 'the most energetic point of social power emerging in late twentieth century society was that of a globalising capitalism'. Surveying the opposition to capitalism's transforming energies, he noted 'the assembly of non-capitalist interests' embodied in the movements and institutions of the post-war era, and asked what is for us an essential question. Is this assembly 'simply a dead weight carried over from the past, or does it contain a potentiality for new action?'[2] It is with the exploration of this open question that our book is concerned, and our analysis and critique cut two ways: against a neo-liberalism whose programme promotes social and educational division while at the same time it narrows drastically the potential scope of education; and against a left that has not yet made sense of new conditions, nor created (in most instances) a credible basis for counter-mobilisation. It is from this double perspective-returned to in our concluding chapter – that we interpret policy shifts and political conflicts.

Then and now

For six decades, education in Western Europe has experienced continuous and accelerating expansion. In most of pre-war Europe, the elementary school – connected to no system of qualification – marked for most students the limits of their education; universities were in effect closed to all but a tiny minority. Since 1945, secondary education has developed, even in Southern Italy and rural Spain, to become universal – the countries where secondary education was poorly developed have caught up. Levels of certification are rising – with spectacular increases in the numbers of students taking public examinations. Access to higher education has been broadened to the point where it is possible to speak in some countries of the 'mass' university. And beyond the limits of a school and university system in which students pass an increasing part of their lives, governments project for their populations a future of 'lifelong learning'.[3]

In many respects, the pace of these developments has quickened over the last 15 years – it is in this period that the proportion of French students taking the baccalauréat has exceeded 60%, and in which the British government has set a target of 50% participation in higher education by 2010. At the same time, the requirements that policymakers place upon education are multiplying. Schools, colleges and universities are expected to take over many of the functions of the workplace as places where skills are developed and where the dispositions necessary for productive employment are formed. In societies that have become ethnically more diverse and economically more polarised, they are thought central to the management of cultural difference and the promotion of social inclusion. For students and for parents, they have taken on a new centrality, as providers of the credentials without which careers in the 'knowledge society' become hard to construct. In short, education – its demographic spread, its length and complexity, its importance to the lives of students– is more central to Western European societies than at any previous time.

In some senses, the developments of the last 15 years are a continuation of much earlier tendencies towards educational expansion and towards the inclusion of ever-larger sections of the population within formal education systems. But they have taken place in a new economic, social and political context, marked by a profound economic and financial restructuring, whose coherence can be grasped through the term 'neo-liberalism'. Economically, neo-liberalism involves the internationalisation of production systems, the free movement of capital across national frontiers, the centrality of financial interests, deindustrialisation and the growth of the service sector and privatisation; at the social level, it involves increasing polarisation of wealth and poverty – often of a racialised kind – and a growing mobility and precariousness among large sections of the workforce. Politically, there has been both a contraction of the state and an intensification of its focus. David Harvey's lucid presentation suggests the coherence of these processes:

> Neo-liberalism is in the first instance a theory of political economic practices that proposes that human well-being can best be advanced by liberating individual entrepreneurial freedom and skills within an institutional framework characterised by strong private property rights, free markets and free trade. The role of the state is to create and preserve an institutional framework appropriate to such practices ... If markets do not exist (in areas such as land, water, education, health care, social security, or environmental pollution) then they must be created, by state action if necessary. But beyond these tasks the state should not venture.[4]

In practice, Harvey makes clear, the state's role is far from the minimal one that pristine neo-liberalism suggests:

> The process of neo-liberalisation has ... entailed much 'creative destruction', not only of prior institutional frameworks and powers (even challenging traditional forms of state sovereignty) but also of divisions of labour, social relations, welfare provisions, technological mixes, ways of life and thought, reproductive activities, attachments to the land and habits of the heart.[5]

In this work of 'bringing all human action into the domain of the market', the role of the state – in destroying previous social arrangements and in creating the legal, social and political framework for the expansion of neo-liberalism – is crucial. Yet the capacities of the state are often disavowed by governments. It has become a policymaking orthodoxy to claim that governments have little power to halt or differently inflect the economic forces which shape contemporary societies – they must submit to free market globalisation and to the agenda of the institutions which further its projects. But at the same time, though acquiescent in relation to market trends, governments know they must in other ways be ceaselessly active, reshaping their social systems to respond to new exigencies – creating, in Tony Blair's words, 'a competitive basis of physical infrastructure and human skill' and managing the social conflicts attendant upon neo-liberal change.[6] The transformation of education is central to this reshaping, and has accordingly been placed at the centre of the agenda of national governments, and, increasingly, of the European Union itself. No aspect of education systems – from financing to forms of selection, from pedagogy to questions of management – is spared the critical scrutiny of governments committed to market-driven change.

In this book, we trace the impact of these processes on the school systems of England,[7] France, Germany, Italy and Spain. In each case, the effects are significant and continuing: it is possible to speak of a policy orthodoxy that affects all countries, and owes much to the interaction of the programmes of national governments with the work of international organisations – the European Union and the OECD, in particular – whose policy repertoire is growing in influence. But this orthodoxy is not, as it were, inscribed on blank and receptive surfaces. Its policies interact with national systems which bear the multiple marks of other social interests, and whose histories vary considerably. It combines in varying ways with already established conservative interests – business, the churches, educational hierarchies and philosophies. It confronts more (France) or less (England) organised opposition that draws from national traditions of educational reform and contestation. It has at its disposal state apparatuses whose competence and effectivity differ markedly from country to country. Thus, while it is possible to speak of a globalised policy agenda, this agenda – *pace* the influence of EU and OECD – takes different forms in different places – differences that we try to register throughout the chapters that follow. But in all cases, across very different national situations, there is one connecting thread: the new agenda has to work to defeat or assimilate the institutions, practices, values and social agents that were formed within an earlier educational order, and were shaped by reforming impulses of a markedly different kind. To make sense of contemporary educational conflicts, and of the difficulties that policy orthodoxy encounters, we need to sketch this earlier history.

Post-war reform

Difference and commonality: we will attempt to attend to both. Across the five countries, there are certainly common tendencies of development. 'Modernisation' – albeit belated in Spain and Southern Italy – has been their shared experience. Likewise, all have been affected to a greater or lesser degree by movements whose scope has been international: anti-fascism, 1968 – the *sessantotto* – and, in a different key, the complex of ideas and practices which has been called 'progressive education' or *Reformpedagogik*. But the tempo and extent of these influences differ widely from one country to another. The most important line of difference here separates those states where workers' movements were strengthened in the course of the conflict with fascism, from those where these movements suffered defeats on a scale which left them for a long period disorganised to the point where they could not play a significant role in the shaping of post-war settlements. France, Italy and England stand on one side of this line, the Germany of Adenauer and the Spain of Franco on the other. In all countries, the characteristic demands of the post-war period for expansion and greater equality were felt, but the pace at which they were answered, and the forms which the answers took, varied according to the relative capacities of popular and conservative interests. The resulting pattern of unevenness retains its force today.

We can nonetheless attempt to summarise the elements of a common history. Eric Hobsbawm calls the 1950s the start of capitalism's golden age, 'when even weak economies like the British flourished and grew'.[8] Production increased rapidly, and industrialisation brought about an epochal shift of population from rural to urban areas. Rising wages allowed higher levels of consumption, sustaining the long boom of the post-war period. State spending – military and social – was likewise both an effect of economic expansion and a means of supporting it. Education was part of this general movement. As Papadopoulos puts it, in his insider's history of the OECD, governments throughout Western Europe worked in the belief that 'more and better education (was) an end in itself and at the same time one of the most important factors in economic growth'. Between 1960 and 1980, education spending grew at an unprecedented speed: in France from 2.4% of GDP to 5%; in West Germany from 2.9% to 4.7%; in Italy from 3.6% to 4.4%; and in Britain from 4.3% to 5.6%. Even in Francoist Spain, the 1970 Ley General de Educación prompted a doubling of expenditure in this period to 2.6%.[9] Human capital theory – premised on the belief that educational investment increased productivity and stimulated economic growth – provided a rationale for this expansion,[10] but as Papadopoulos notes, there were other motivations too. The inclusive and progressivist rhetoric of these decades owed something to the terms of the post-war settlement, in which notions of democracy and social citizenship were prominent.

The Education Act passed by the British parliament in 1944 was the culmination of a long campaign by the labour movement for 'secondary education for all'. In the aftermath of fascism, the post-war constitution of the Italian Republic declared that education was a universal right, and guaranteed the intellectual freedom of teachers. In France, the 1946 constitution spoke of 'equal access' to education, training and culture; and the Langevin-Wallon report of 1947 had insisted that the task of education was a broad one – to construct 'the man, the citizen, the worker'.[11] Schooling was thus at the heart of 'a political project concerning the social tie' and became a means by which an educator-state could construct 'a public, national space'.[12]

This was the climate in which secondary education was expanded to involve groups new to secondary levels of education. In England, the school-leaving age was raised to 15 in 1947. In France the Berthoin reforms undertaken by the Fifth Republic in 1959 extended compulsory education to the age of 16. In Italy, where both industrialisation and mass scholarisation occurred at a relatively late point, the proportion of 14-year olds attending school rose from 20% in 1945 to 59% in 1962.[13] Accompanying these changes, which brought a new population into the secondary school, was a promise of equal opportunity, defined primarily in terms of access to schooling for working-class groups.

A second wave of reform

Almost from the beginning the legitimacy of the new educational systems was called into question by precisely those groups which had been addressed by the rhetoric of inclusive change. Expansion was to an important extent driven by demand – the demand of new sections of students and parents for higher levels of qualification. But from their view point, the systems of universal secondary education established after 1945 were restrictive, and the notion of equal opportunity on which they were based seemed largely of a formal character. 'Secondary education for all' meant no more than access for students of different social classes to types of school that differed widely and systematically in the type of progression to which they led. In the Italy of the 1960s, the numbers attending secondary school almost doubled, but – as Lumley argues – 'under the rhetoric of egalitarianism that proclaimed education as "a right for all" there was a strong current of meritocratic and technocratic thinking that clouded any perception of the emergence of new forms of discrimination and selection within the reformed secondary school'.[14] The English experience was similar: most secondary school students attended institutions from which they would enter the labour market with no qualifications; in the early 1960s, only some 20% took public examinations at 16. In France, following Berthoin, the establishment in 1963 of the *carte scolaire* – linking school attendance to place of residence – marked an attempt to promote social mixing. The creation in the same year of *collèges d'enseignement secondaire* for 11- to 15-year olds brought together under one roof three different types of education, from pre-*lycéen* to pre-vocational. There was little possibility of student transfer between these streams, however, and there were vastly different prospects for the different student groups.[15] In West Germany, the numbers attending the *Gymnasium* – the academic secondary school – doubled between 1965 and 1970, without a significant lessening of the institution's social selectivity.[16] The class basis of these separatist arrangements was plainly demonstrated by sociological research in several countries,[17] and was unattractive to parents, whose ambitions were not for secondary education *per se* but for access to particular types of credentials. Nor did it satisfy the social democratic parties and teachers' organisations which, pushed from below, were radicalising their policies to call for a single form of unified secondary education, and in some cases to reinterpret educational opportunity less in terms of formal access than of outcome. 'The average woman or negro [*sic*] or proletarian or rural dweller should have the same level of educational attainment as the average male, white, white-collar suburbanite,' wrote the English sociologist and policy adviser A.H. Halsey; 'if not, there has been injustice'.[18]

Under these pressures, educational reform began to assume in some countries a new character, based on comprehensive (i.e. formally non-selective) secondary schooling, and expanded access to publicly recognised qualifications. This was the tendency of English reform after 1965, and was later embodied in Italy in the form of the *scuola media unificata*; Roberto Moscati suggests that in this period the discourse of education reform in Italy centred 'more or less consciously (on) the social division of labour and the class structure of society'.[19] The aftermath of 1968 stimulated a similar project in France. Such influence was strong enough, in France, Italy and England to inhibit the programmes of the right: Gaullism and Christian Democracy presided over the period of reform, and even English Conservatism abandoned for a while its commitment to selective schooling.

Changes in institutional form were accompanied by a modification of school cultures. Policymakers began to recognise that quantitative expansion was not enough: there needed also to be changes in curriculum and in pedagogy. According to Papadopoulos, 'public authorities were forced to shift their attention to how, coping beyond numbers, their educational offerings could be made relevant to the diversified needs of their vastly expanded and variegated clientèle.'[20] This 'quest for relevance and equality' may often have been fostered by institutions of the central state – in England, the Schools Council, entrusted with curriculum development, was founded in 1963. But in the context of the later 1960s, it was shaped also by other interests, whose force we need to recognise if we are to make full sense of the conflicts that now attend neo-liberal change. Between 1968 and 1974, a series of working-class protests and emerging social movements challenged inequalities, claimed rights of participation, demanded recognition and asserted militant identities. In this context, large numbers of teachers, recruited from the generation of 1968, came to think of the school as an institution where democracy, cultural recognition and equal opportunity could serve as central principles. The ideas of Freire became internationally known, the Bolshevik educators of the early 1920s were rediscovered and the (Tuscan) School of Barbiana's critique of established education was widely emulated.[21] The demands of social movements for children's rights, their acute perceptions of the ways in which education served to perpetuate class inequalities at the same time as it proclaimed education for all and their scathing critique of elite and commodified cultures did not provide the norms of the school system. Nor were they entirely coherent in themselves: in contrast to an earlier generation of reformers, the new left of the 1970s was inclined to see the school as an ideological state apparatus, functional to capitalism – yet this did not prevent its immersion in projects aimed at bettering the education of working-class students.

Despite, or perhaps because of, these difficulties, new movements for educational change exercised nonetheless a diffused and potent influence. In all the five countries in this study– including, at a later point, Spain – teachers sought to develop through localised initiatives an education practice that could transform the ways in which schooling connected to the majority of its students. We discuss the sweeping course – and eventual exhaustion – of these developments in a later chapter. Here it is enough to note how they deepened the project of reform: an agenda for schooling should include questions of ideology as well as institutional form, and be attentive to the content of education as much as to questions of access to its higher levels. It needed to be alert to the identities and tacit knowledges of excluded groups and critical of the vested interests embodied in the official curriculum that had 'emptied education of its potential as a means of realisation', preferring abstract slogans of educational freedom to concrete interest in 'society and its needs'.[22] Such an approach, localised and sympathetic to subordinate cultures, expressed even in its weaker forms an attitude towards education which stood at a distance from economic demands.

These cultural shifts and institutional preferences established a school system that was in some ways resistant to the logic of capital and was thus a provocation to the educational right. The emphasis on child-centred learning in English primary education, for instance, seemed to the Thatcherite policy activists of the 1980s to entail an institutionalised indifference to economic 'requirements'; likewise, to the authors of the EU's Reiffers report in the 1990s the 'fashionable' and non-selective 'utopias' of an earlier period had disconnected education from 'societies, which do not work that way'.[23] But the impact of radical reform – understood as the opening up of higher levels of education and qualification to the mass of students, linked to curriculum change and an emancipatory conception of pedagogy – was in reality more limited than the polemics against it suggested. Despite the verve and energy of alternative or critical educational projects, the curricula and pedagogies developed in earlier periods remained dominant. This was illustrated very clearly by the problems stemming from the French Haby directive of 1975, which instructed *collèges* to organise teaching on an unstreamed basis: schools had neither the finances nor the curricular and pedagogic resources to do so in a generally successful way. It was a similar set of problems which led the Italian employers' organisation, the *Confindustria*, to note the failure of the school system to rise above local initiative and to 'capitalise from the ... experimental programmes it produces'.[24]

Enduring obstacles

Alongside these limitations, there persisted structural inequalities, underpinned by powerful social interests. These were especially clear in Spain and West Germany. Throughout what was in other countries a heyday of reform, the Franco government presided over a highly centralised system in which, despite population change, the number of children receiving pre-school education and compulsory basic education hardly changed between 1940 and 1960, and the number of state secondary schools grew only from 113 to 119; in 1975 only 70% of 14-year olds attended school. Religious interests dominated: more students enrolled in – mainly religious – private schools than in the underfunded state sector. From this base, the Church was in a powerful position to shape the system of the post-Franco period, while the public schools 'lacked both quality and infrastructure'.[25]

West Germany, like Spain, lacked the shaping influence of a strong working-class movement. Post-war education preserved the elitist structure of earlier decades: in the 1950s only 11% of the age cohort were enrolled in the *Gymnasium*, a tiny minority of whom (2%) were from working-class backgrounds. The expansion of the 1960s increased the size of the *Gymnasium*'s intake, without significantly altering its class composition.[26] Nor, in Germany, was the second wave of post-war reform as strong as in other countries. There was certainly a quantitative expansion: by the 1990s the period of compulsory education in Germany was, in most *Länder*, 13 years, the longest of all the five countries in this study.[27] But institutional change was limited and the system continued to be 'based on the idea of grading down all those pupils who can't cope with the standards set by historically evolved curricula and inflexible teaching methods'.[28] Inclusive secondary schools – *Gesamtschulen* – were established in some *Länder*, but these few institutions functioned more as the fourth strand in a differentiated system than as genuine comprehensives. Reform pedagogy became more prominent, especially in elementary schools, and, as in other countries, teachers' curricular and pedagogic autonomy increased. But these changes were not long lasting. The prospects for opening up the spaces of the school to radical experiment were reduced by the 1972 *Radikalenerlaß* law of the Brandt government, 'which soon developed into a weapon against radical students seeking state employment'.[29] The SPD governments of Brandt and Schmidt balked at the confrontation with conservative *Länder* that a thoroughgoing project of school reform would have entailed. Instead, changes focused on the development of a segregated system of post-secondary education, in which – alongside the academic *Gymnasium* – a strong vocational track was established, compulsory for those leaving school at 16, linking school and workplace-based learning and giving a powerful voice to business interests.

Educational change in Spain and Germany was more limited than in other countries. But this does not mean that in England, France and Italy egalitarian reform was fully accomplished. Between 1945 and 1980 education provision expanded and inequalities of access to secondary education were very much reduced. But at other points in the system – access to advanced secondary education and to universities – class-based inequalities remained strong and in some cases actually increased, as middle-class families mobilised their cultural resources to secure the success of their children (see chapter 5). Moreover, within apparently unified systems of primary and secondary education, a variety of formal and informal systems operated – school traditions and reputations, neighbourhood-based admissions policies, setting and streaming within schools – in which these class-based distinctions were codified. The result was that 'children from lower social backgrounds did not experience an increase in their educational opportunities until higher groups had fully satisfied their demand for it';[30] and when opportunities were at last presented – for instance in higher education – working-class students discovered that there were new hierarchies in which they were not well placed: nearly half the students in the 'top five' British universities were educated in private schools; in Italy, university completion rates were strongly conditioned by students' class background.[31] To this considerable extent, the promise of opportunity made by post-war reform was contradicted by persisting, and in some cases strengthening, patterns of inequality. As French researchers noted, a rise in average levels of attainment disguised increasing and class-related polarities between the most and the least successful students, and access to the most prestigious sectors of higher education – the *grandes écoles* – had become by the 1980s more closely connected to class origins than in earlier decades.[32] (Likewise, in Germany, while equality of opportunity increased in terms of access to middle-level examinations, opportunity at the level of higher education became more unequal.[33])

Alongside these intractable social problems, the reforming movements of the 1960s and 1970s faced other difficulties, connected to entrenched and politically powerful institutions that were hostile to the project of creating uniform, public systems of schooling. In all countries, there remained strong vestiges of this *ancien régime*. Nothing in the reforms of the period threatened the position of the elite English private schools (named 'public schools') whose fee-paying students continued to dominate the most prestigious universities and supply the cadre of the English ruling class. Far from dying away in the 1960s, these schools carried out a successful process of renewal, abandoning their more primitive features (beating, fagging, compulsory military training) and – with substantial funding from industry to support science education – emphasising academic attainment above character formation. Students in the private sector comprised only 7% of the total school population, but by 1980 nearly a third of students obtaining three or more 'A' levels – the 18+ examination which was a pre-requisite for university entrance – were privately educated. Alongside this sector, there still existed a large number of selective state schools, which had survived a process of comprehensive reform that had been left to localised initiative rather than national legislation.

Secular hierarchies of this sort were intertwined with religious influences: Christian organisations retained a privileged educational place. The 1944 reforms in England rested upon an accommodation with the Church of England and with Catholicism, in which operational control of a large sector of primary and secondary education remained with the churches. In France, the state reached a similar agreement with Catholic schools. In 1945, religious schools in France had depended for survival upon the limited resources of the Church; its teachers were likely to be members of religious orders. But with the Church–State concordat of 1959 assuring for them a subsidised future, the schools underwent a process of transformation, an old order adapting, as in England, to new circumstances. Teaching was professionalised and to an extent laicised; the curriculum was aligned with that of the public sector. Socially, too, their function changed. Though more likely than in England to be attended, at least temporarily, by working-class students, the higher levels of French private schooling were dominated by the children of *cadres supérieures*: as Dutercq comments, educational Catholicism frequently finds that it has no space for 'the poorest, the most vulnerable, the marginalised and those receiving state benefit'.[34] It came to serve instead as an alternative for many families to a public sector perceived as prone to violence, plagued by cultural diversity and academic failure.[35] In Italy, the constitution ruled out an accommodation of the French or English sort, but the Lateran pacts – made under Mussolini – enabled Church access to children in state schools. In addition Catholic organisations maintained an extensive network of kindergartens, *doposcuole* and child-orientated welfare activities – part of what Ginsborg terms the 'myriad world of Catholic associationism'.[36]

Problems of reform

The movements driving forward the second wave of educational reform were motivated by deep and attractive commitments, to social justice and to inclusivity. Whether measured in terms of rising levels of formal achievement, or according to less precise but possibly more revealing cultural indicators, their achievements were significant and their influence on a generation of teachers considerable. The slogans with which they were associated – equal opportunity, social desegregation, curricular transformation and an education based on the needs of learners – still have a contemporary resonance. But the weaknesses of the systems that they had helped assemble were also great. Following its 1970s apogee, the reforming movement everywhere faced difficulties that could not be ascribed only to the influence of remaining bastions of privilege. As we shall see, this was especially clear in England, where principles of 'child-centred education' had received probably a stronger level of government approval than in other countries. 'Educashun isn't Working', the 1979 election slogan of Thatcher's Conservatives, exploited a vein of popular discontent with the achievements of reform, which extended beyond the increasingly numerous think tanks and campaigning groups of the right. To many, the reforming project seemed to have failed: its egalitarian promise had been fulfilled only partially; the pedagogic changes with which it was associated were implicated, so critics alleged, in a fall in standards; the school seemed to have become more a site for the production of social and cultural problems than a means of resolving them. Likewise in France, the successful campaigns of the Catholic Church and the right against the integrationist Savary legislation of 1983–4 catalysed a wider movement of discontent: at their height, these protests merged with a vehement rejection on the part of some intellectuals of the basic character of school reform. ('All education in the proper sense is now forbidden', wrote Jean-François Revel in response to the Legrand reforms of the early 1980s – thus initiating a line of critique that has endured into the twenty-first century.[37]) The *scuola media unificata* also appeared to be in crisis. 'Italian schools,' wrote the authors of *Red Bologna* in 1976, 'need total reconstruction ... nothing more can be achieved by isolated reforms.'[38] Yet it was in just such a piecemeal struggle that the energies of the educational and social movements of the 1970s were consumed. With the flagging of these energies, it became clear that the scale of Italian education had changed, but not its nature. Despite a formal system of equal opportunity and a vast expansion of higher education, class-based differences in student performance persisted on a spectacular scale.[39]

The post-1976 turn

How did the difficulties of the reforming project result not in its refinement or further deepening, but in its replacement by an alternative programme, to which questions of social and educational equality were not at all central? The explanation for this reorientation, in which the educational compasses of all our countries have come eventually to point in the same direction, lies outside the school. The long economic boom of *les trentes glorieuses* ended in 1973 with a recession which reduced industrial production in advanced capitalist countries by 10%. There were further severe slumps in 1974–5, 1980–2 and at the end of the 1980s.

Unemployment rose from a Western European average of 1.5% in the 1960s to 4.2% in the 1970s. By 1993 unemployment rates in the European Community had risen to 11%.[40] At the same time, the extremes of wealth and poverty both grew. Poverty, according to one French researcher, became a 'caste-like situation', a long-term prison inhabited by the young, the unemployed, the de-skilled and the downsized.[41] In 1979 an estimated 10% of British children lived in poverty – that is, in households whose income was less than half the national average; by 1993, the proportion had risen to 33%. Meanwhile, the increasing wealth of the richest section of the population was reflected in the significant expansion of private education.[42] For the public sector the immediate consequence of recession was that expenditure slowed considerably, and in some cases came to a complete stop. In Britain and in Germany, public expenditure on education as a share of GDP declined between 1980 and 1993. Only in Spain, which after the Franco years was engaged in a programme to raise spending towards Western European norms, did funding for education substantially increase, and even there government expenditure was not high enough to squeeze out a private sector which remained a central component of mass education.[43]

The slump of the mid-1970s, however, was more than a resumption of the boom-bust cycles of capitalist development. In Hobsbawm's words, 'conjunctural fluctuations coincided with structural upheavals'.[44] The closing down of unproductive units became a permanent process of deindustrialisation. The movement of capital in search of profit led to the elimination of government checks on financial transfers and to a substantial and lasting constraint on the autonomy of nation states. The conflicts attendant upon the closure of industrial plants translated very soon into a war against the post-war settlement of employment security and welfare rights. The 'probabilities of a reliable and decent wage through manual work have been radically decreased for substantial parts of the working class,' wrote Paul Willis, in relation to England, and 'the threat of its removal has become a permanent condition for all workers'; thus 'the pride, depth and independence of a collective industrial tradition' gave way to 'the indignities of flexible and obedient labour'.[45] Willis, insisting on a perspective 'from below', highlighted the consequences of this reversal for working-class youth, and charted a post-1980 history of ever-tighter regulation. Papadopoulos, writing – as it were – from above, is more cautious and elliptical:

> The combination of resource constraints, high unemployment and demographic downturn had a direct input on the demand for education

as well as on the perception of its role and its contribution to social and economic development. Coinciding with the advent of conservative governments in a large number of (OECD) member countries, it brought a dramatic change in the political context of education. Continued growth could no longer be taken for granted either as a feasible or even a desirable objective. Constraints on public spending were particularly telling. As one of the major components of public budgets, education had to share the burden of restraint ... Resource limitations raised new questions about the setting of priority objectives, in contrast to the earlier situation where a multiplicity of educational objectives could be pursued more or less simultaneously. This scramble for priorities among different interest groups sharpened the political conflicts around education.[46]

The implications of even this guarded analysis are clear enough: with the economic restructuring that began in the mid-1970s, education embarked on a long and still-unfinished process of remaking. In this process, the forms taken by the school system in the post-war decades were subjected to fundamental and hostile scrutiny. The mixed and imprecise objectives associated with equal opportunity and the type of human capital theory that flourished in the long boom began to be set aside. Educational expansion was no longer thought to contribute *per se* to economic growth. Notions of education as an investment in human capital continued to be influential, but now 'in the more refined form of micro-economic analyses of the economic significance of individual segments of potential labour power in terms of profitability', with a view to guiding investment towards sectors 'with a favourable cost benefit factor'.[47] In short, government outlooks on education became more economised – increasingly dedicated to servicing the requirements of a new stage of capitalist development, at a low cost and with maximum efficiency; in Blair's words, 'for years education was a social cause; today it is an economic imperative.'[48] After 1975, when governments evaluated education, it tended to be through the prism of (restructured) economic priorities. Such a shift had far-reaching political consequences, since it could not be accomplished without confronting those social forces that had shaped the terms of the post-war settlement, and continued to exercise an influence over the values and everyday practices of schooling. Political conflicts did indeed 'sharpen', to use Papadopoulos's term, and have continued to sharpen since.

England and after

Even before 1979, debates in some countries had anticipated the new priorities. England was a pioneer in this respect, and its experience – inspirational for some, but for others a kind of educational spectre haunting Europe – will be a reference point to which we will frequently turn. By the mid-1970s, the Labour Government had succeeded in cooling the industrial conflicts of 1972–4 and in defeating the left of the Labour Party. An IMF loan had allowed the government to escape financial crisis, at the expense of a programme of structural adjustment that required an end to public sector expansion. In this context, the government – prompted by its civil service – began a process of reasserting control of those social institutions that it felt were out of step with its new policies. Education was first among them. 'The national mood and government policies', noted a paper on education prepared for the prime minister, 'have changed in the face of hard and irreducible economic facts.'[49] Motivated thus, Labour initiated a disavowal of the post-war settlement. What Labour began, post-1979, Thatcherite Conservatism developed, presenting the problems of schooling as a condensation of the worst effects of post-war history: bureaucracy stifled enterprise; parental rights of school choice were denied; and the unaccountable corporatist power of teachers fuelled demands for funding, drove down standards, politicised the curriculum and created a gulf between what parents and business wanted from the school and what education actually provided. Conservatism's solutions to these multiple problems involved three diverse elements. The first was marketisation – or (more strictly, since no monetary exchange takes place between provider and consumer) 'quasi-marketisation' – an accumulating set of reforms – analysed in chapter 4 – that strengthened competition and differentiation within the school system, empowered middle-class parents with 'school choice' and, via the decentralisation of financial control, created a new class of school managers. Marketisation was linked to a second element, that of stronger central regulation – the reshaping of teacher training, currricula and pedagogy so as to raise levels of examination performance and re-focus education on economic objectives. The third was an approach to social cohesion that emphasised English tradition and heritage, and sought to manage cultural diversity and changes in gender roles by a reassertion of an archaic national identity.

This mélange of neo-liberal and neo-conservative themes – of transnational economic imperatives mixed with concerns located in the preservation of a national polity – was never fully coherent: the economisation of educational processes and objectives was incompatible with the project of restoring irreparably damaged traditions. These difficulties stemmed from fundamental tensions in the social basis and ideological perspectives not just of Conservatism but of other sections of the European right (see chapter 7), which was never *en masse* comfortable with the neo-liberal turn of the 1970s. Nevertheless, the multiple repertoire of English Conservatism served an important political purpose. It allowed Thatcher's government to link the populist energies of regressive campaigners – whose standards of excellence were the grammar school and the traditional curriculum – to a modernising critique of education's post-war failings, whose fundamental claim was that the school was out of step with economic needs. Thatcherism thus confronted teachers, trade unions and the left with a kind of war on all fronts: national regulations and newly empowered school managements weakened union influence in the workplace; media campaigns attacked child-centred and radical classroom practice; market-friendly legislation undermined local comprehensive systems; politically and ideologically, this was a set of challenges to which defenders of the still-incomplete process of post-war reform had great difficulty in responding.

In the verve of its attack on the post-war settlement, if not in the refinement of its policies, English Conservatism led the way, opening possibilities for educational change which many governments sought in some sense to emulate. But this did not mean that England simply provided a blueprint for the rest of Europe, and nowhere was the pace and aggression of Conservatism immediately or completely replicated. Italy's political crisis was such that a project of institutional transformation could not break through – though demand-led growth and the campaigns of the student movement led to the massification of higher education. In Germany, the already-close alignment of education with business priorities, as well as the continuing influence of the humanist traditions embodied in the concept of *Bildung*, seemed for a long period to guard it against an emergent neo-liberal critique.

In Spain and in France, the pattern of change was more complex. The 1980s in Spain were a period in which a 40-year West European experience of reform and reaction was telescoped into a single decade. Post-Franco education expanded very rapidly. Movements of pedagogic renewal and for the democratisation of schools flourished; national movements in the Basque Country and Catalonia weakened the hold of the central state.[50] But these shifts were not decisive. The 1978 constitution sought less to recognise national rights than to absorb them within a general principle of regionalisation – a decentralisation which later 'served as a bridgehead of marketisation and which diffused the impact of class struggle on the central state through the dispersion of the management of public affairs'.[51] The Spanish Socialist Party's (PSOE) education law of 1985 – the Law on the Right to Education (LODE) – was likewise ambivalent. On the one hand, it fostered democratisation – establishing a principle of election for school governors and managers. On the other, it accepted in the name of educational freedom and resource constraint an agreement with the religious sector that installed private, usually Catholic, education at the heart of the Spanish system. A base for liberalisation was thus assured, with the 'critical support' of much of the left.

In France, the Mitterrand government was committed in this period to expansion: as education spending fell in England, it rose in France, even in the austerity years of the mid-1980s; in the 1980s, nursery education grew substantially, and between 1985 and 1990 the number of *lycéens* rose by 50%. Governments adopted an 80% target for the proportion of students completing a *baccalauréat* of some sort – thus taking democratisation beyond the level of the *collège*.[52] But this was an expansion qualified by sharp internecine criticism, in particular by attacks on a child-centred pedagogy that – according to a 'republican left' – downgraded questions of access to knowledge and left students adrift among the inadequate resources of subordinate cultures.[53] These criticisms of the ways in which the reforms of the later post-war years had treated the 'relationship to knowledge' created significant divisions between different wings of the reform movement; they were accompanied by a shift in educational governance that further problematised the tradition of *étatiste* reform. Via decentralisation, control of primary education passed to the *communes*, of *collèges* to the *départements* and of *lycées* to the *régions*. These debates and innovations were not immediate signs of a spreading Thatcherism; but they did constitute a set of discursive and institutional changes that at a later point would be articulated with stronger neo-liberal themes, in a much clearer, and contested, attempt to break with reformist histories.

Neo-liberalism takes stronger shape

The neo-liberal transformation of the school is a process, not an event. Its pace and rhythm have differed from country to country. They have been hastened or retarded not only by the extent of explicit resistance, but by the value systems and embedded practices existing within each nation state. Reshaping these values and practices around an authoritative orthodoxy has required a war of attrition, or – to adapt Rudi Dutschke's expression – a long and deliberate march, on the part of neo-liberalism, through the institutions. In the language of the World Bank and the OECD, this is a process of 'strategic incrementalism', a strategy whose modes of operation we discuss in chapter 2.[54] By the late 1990s, stimulated by the Maastricht treaty, and spurred on by international organisations – such as the OECD – which were by then much more specific in their policy recommendations, the process of transformation arrived at a new stage, brought about by the joint work of governments of left and right – of Gonzales and Aznar, Major and Blair, D'Alema and Berlusconi, and Jospin and Raffarin. Although their detailed labour of law-making and administrative decree has by no means created a common system of schooling, it has nevertheless elaborated the rough and improvised project of the 1980s new right, and made it possible to codify not only the general principles of neo-liberalism, but also its operational features, as they are applied in, and inflected by, national situations.

We have already sketched the general features of neo-liberalism. We now want to highlight some more of its implications for education, and at the same time to outline the way in which these are treated in the chapters that follow. Richard Johnson and Deborah Steinberg argue that New Labour project in Britain entails 'the deepening and extending of neo-liberal social relations and individualism ... the bringing of all spheres of social life into market and commodity relations and ... the expansion of these relations globally'.[55] In their reading, Blair attempted a new phase of restructuring, in which governments and corporations embarked upon three distinct but related clusters of transformations – of 'labour and the ... economy, of citizenship and subjectivity, of management and state power'. Each of these inter-woven clusters requires substantial educational involvement.

In relation to labour, governments have a vision of a European future in which conceptions of a knowledge economy play a defining role: individual and collective competitiveness depend more and more on the continual acquisition of new competences; human capital and systems of education and training become central to economic outcomes. These notions – analysed further in chapter 2 – provide new norms of policy, often counterposed to educational cultures and disciplinary conceptions of knowledge and thought to be outdated.[56] Thus, in France, the Thélot Committee recommended to the government that instead of striving to meet the target of 80% success in the *baccalauréat*, the school should concentrate on ensuring that students acquired 'the competences necessary ... for personal life and for successful (social) integration.'[57]

From this perspective, the school needed to take over from the workplace many of the functions of apprenticeship, abandoning in the process any tendency towards providing a mass general education. Others have noted that the economising agenda goes beyond the question of vocational skills. Remaking labour power involves not just competences, but dispositions. The tendency towards merging study with training for employment, or with employment itself, contributes to the creation of a new social subject – a category of student-worker whose studies are extended, who possesses 'employability' and generic skills, who cannot expect job security and must anticipate being 'multiply deployed across a range of sites'.[58] For the school to contribute to the making of such a subject requires an emphasis on such qualities as flexibility, adaptability and creativity. These are qualities that are strongly gendered. The requirements made of the growing female workforce in many sectors and at different levels of service and professional employment involved a demand for 'emotional intelligence', communicational capacity and adaptability to change that corresponded to what Johnson and Walkerdine call 'women's tutored expertise in empathy and personal reinvention'. It is qualities of this sort which new curricula emphasise, and as they do so, the gender identities of an earlier period are problematised.[59]

The requirements of 'labour and the economy' elide into Johnson and Steinberg's second 'cluster of transformations', that of 'citizenship and subjectivity'. Besides resubjectivising pupils in the name of economic need, schools must also respond to an expanding list of other priorities – including health, sex, citizenship, sports and, in some cases, religion. Many of these tasks are carried out in the name of reconciling or controlling tensions that are thought to threaten European societies, and these tensions are increasingly described in racialised or religious terms. In an article on anti-Muslim racism in Europe, Liz Fekete writes of an attempt by states to 'steer "race relations" policy away from multi-culturalism towards monoculturalism and cultural homogenisation'. In each country, she notes, a debate about national identity has

> coalesced around a pattern of events and themes specific to that country; new policy directions have been grafted on to the approaches traditionally adopted towards minority communities. Each nation moves towards the assimilationist model in a way that is consonant with the myths upon which that nation has been built. In the Netherlands, the theme of the national debate has been 'standards and values'; in Sweden and Norway, cultural barriers to inclusion; in the UK, 'community cohesion'; in France, the principle of state

secularism; in Germany, the primacy of the 'Leitkultur' (leading culture); in Denmark, the 'intolerant culture' amongst immigrants that prevents integration; in Spain, public safety and crime. But even though the terms through which the debate is entered differ, it is always linked back to immigrant communities and cultures and the threat that multicultural policies pose to core values, cultural homogeneity and social cohesion.[60]

The French Stasi Committee, which deliberated on the wearing of the '*voile*' by (a small number of) Muslim girls, expressed this sense of threat in especially dramatic terms – extremist groups were 'pushing young people towards a rejection of France and its values'[61] – but it is embodied in many other measures too, from Labour's introduction of citizenship classes in England, to the concern of the Spanish right with tradition and national unity: 'multi-culturalism is precisely what splits society,' said Aznar.[62] Just as significantly, this securitised discourse provides a means by which educational crises are understood by those who experience them daily: 'It feels as though we're raising criminals and terrorists here', said a teacher at a multi-racial Berlin Hauptschule whose staff were demanding its closure on the grounds that teaching there was no longer possible.[63]

The subjectivities desired by policy thus include social as well as economic attributes – a combination we explore further in chapter 8 on students and in chapter 9 on teachers. Alongside them is the last of the clusters of transformation to which Johnson and Steinberg refer – 'state power and management'.[64] As with changes in the demands made of labour, institutional reform in this area began in the later 1970s; its typical form was grasped at an early point by Nicos Poulantzas, who noted the emergence of 'networks of a semi-public or para-public character' that paralleled the organisations of the state and served to protect the state's operations from popular-democratic control.[65] As Poulantzas implies, these networks related to what was in some respects a statist project. Much has been made of 'decentralisation' and 'privatisation' as if they were measures that somehow rendered education systems newly autonomous and beyond the reach of the state. In fact, for such a system to supplant previous educational *régimes*, the active support of governments is required; and its functioning thereafter is tightly connected to state objectives. The new state forms analysed by Poulantzas depend upon that combination of decentralised operational management and detailed central regulation which has been termed the 'new public management' (NPM).[66] In this 'institutional renewal of public sector institutions',[67] operational decentralisation in a competitive environment is meant to produce efficiencies. Stronger central direction, based on highly specific and inflexible expectations of school outputs, connects educational processes to governmental purposes. The introduction of quasi-market relationships between institutions, and also of elements of privatisation, serves both to inscribe such principles in the everyday functioning of the system, and – in the latter case – to begin the process of establishing an entry point within education for profit-seeking businesses. The whole *ensemble* – which we analyse in chapter 3 on privatisation and chapter 4 on governance – is legitimated by reference to the higher standards it will produce and to the interests of national competitiveness.

These clusters of transformation map onto a pattern of educational provision that is both expanded and differentiated. OECD statistics show a steady lengthening of the period of formal education, and some countries – Spain in the1990s, England since 2001 – have experienced absolute increases in spending.[68] But there is no overall intention of replicating the growth rates and spending levels of the 1970s; private input must increase and public spending must be cost-effective. The rule of more from less applies: in the words of the Deutsche Bank, 'an appreciable improvement in the quality of educational outcomes is not necessarily linked to an increase in educational expenditure'.[69] Nor are educational resources equally available. The policy turn advocated by expert opinion is presented as desirable and practicable for entire populations, but this universalism is in practice heavily qualified by differentiation and inequality, reflecting the effects of the knowledge economy itself. Phillip Brown points out that the American and British economies, for instance, 'are characterised by enclaves of "knowledge work" along large swathes of low-waged, low-skilled jobs'.[70] This fundamental disparity structures educational provision. On the one hand, at higher levels, competition becomes more intense: there are 'too many contestants chasing too few prized jobs',[71] and the acquisition of the credentials that underpin individual success in the labour market becomes for the middle class an absolute and often desperate priority. On the other hand, there is the problem of those who are in practice 'excluded from the knowledge society because they do not have at their disposal the means to participate in it'.[72] Though they share common anxieties, the gap between these two social categories is stark, in terms both of provision and outcome, and the inability or in some cases the explicit refusal of policy to address it is a defining feature of the new system.[73] Governments seek undoubtedly to *manage* social difference, through educational and social programmes of many kinds, but the idea that high levels of inequality are both objectionable and eradicable has no place in policy. In the coded language of Thélot, 'the idea of success for all must not be misunderstood. It does not at all mean that the school must ensure that all its pupils achieve the highest possible level of qualification. That would be an illusory goal for individuals as well as an absurdity in social terms, since educational qualifications would no longer be linked, even vaguely, to employment structures'.[74]

Challenging the new

From one perspective, the new supranational paradigm has the status of something like an ideal type devised by policymakers: nowhere is it completely realised, and it often serves more as normative exhortation than as concrete description. To that extent, those researchers who draw attention to the continuing role of 'national and historical factors' in shaping education systems in nation states have much in favour of their case.[75] All the same, such a judgement tends to overlook the force and direction of change, the dynamic of which is generated at the international level, by a political class which has fought a common struggle, against working-class and public-sector interests, to turn the societies of Western Europe in a market-friendly direction and has developed – as chapter 2 will demonstrate – a unified sense of the next steps in educational transformation.

Notes

1. Our full debts are recorded in the notes that follow. Specifically, in relation to the themes mentioned here, we would cite the work of Roger Dale, Christian Laval, Louis Weber and their colleagues – *Le nouvel ordre éducatif mondial* (Paris: Nouveaux Regards/Syllepse, 2002); of sociologists working in the quantitative tradition, whose findings are summarised in Colin Crouch, *Social Change in Western Europe* (Oxford: Oxford University Press, 1998); and, in relation to new forms of regulation, Agnès van Zanten and Stephen Ball.
2. Crouch, *Social Change in Western Europe*, p. 425.
3. Our focus, throughout the book, is on the school – the set of institutions through which compulsory education is organised. As historians have made clear, the school has always been just one part of a wider system of formal and informal learning. Contemporary education policy also sees the school in this way, and we discuss the implications of this perspective in a later chapter. In many ways, however, the school retains a distinct character, and it remains possible to speak, discretely, of the social relations of schooling – in terms of the school's governance and regulation, in terms of the identities of teachers, managers, parents and students, and in terms of the kinds of tasks it is charged with addressing and the kinds of conflict that attend it.

4. David Harvey, *A Brief History of Neoliberalism* (Oxford: Oxford University Press, 2005) p. 2.

5. Ibid., p. 3.

6. For a classic statement of this dual responsibility, see Tony Blair, 'The Power of the Message', *New Statesman* 29, September 1995, p. 15.

7. 'England' rather than 'Britain' – there are significant differences between the education systems of England, Northern Ireland, Scotland and Wales which lack of space prevents us from covering here. For an attempt at such coverage see Ken Jones, *Education in Britain* (Cambridge, Polity Press, 2003).

8. E.J. Hobsbawm, *Age of Extremes: the short twentieth century 1914–1991* (London: Michael Joseph, 1994) p. 274.

9. A. Wolf, *Does Education Matter? myths about education and economic growth* (Harmondsworth: Penguin, 2002).

10. See, e.g., Gary Becker, *Human Capital: a theoretical and empirical analysis with special reference to education* (New York: Columbia University Press, 1964).

11. Quoted in Louis Weber, *OMC, AGS: Vers la privatisation de la société* (Paris: Syllepse, 2003) p. 105.

12. Claude Lelièvre, 'The French Model of the Educator State', *Journal of Education Policy* 15.1, pp. 5–10, p. 7, 2000.

13. OECD, *Reviews of National Education Policies for Education: Italy* (Paris: OECD, 1998) p. 40. See also the work of Daniele Checchi, who demonstrates the ways in which the Italian education system continues to lag behind those of England, France and Germany, in terms of secondary educational attainment – *The Italian Educational System: family background and social stratification* (Università degli Studi diMilano: Dipartimento di Economica Politica e Aziendale, 2003).

14. Robert Lumley, *States of Emergency: cultures of revolt in Italy from 1968 to 1978* (London: Verso, 1990) p. 53.

15. Jean-Louis Derouet, 'Lower Secondary Education in France; from uniformity to institutional autonomy' in *Education in France: continuity and change in the Mitterrand years 1981–1985*, ed. A. Corbett and B. Moon (London: Routledge, 1996).

16. Hanna Ostermann and Ute Schmidt, 'Education, Training and the Workplace' in *Modern Germany: politics, society and culture*, ed. P. James (London: Routledge, 1998).

17. E.g., INED, *La Population et l'Enseignement* (Paris: PUF, 1970); B. Jackson and D. Marsden, *Education and the Working Class* (London: Routledge and Kegan Paul, 1962).

18. A.H. Halsey (ed.), *Educational Priority: EPA problems and priorities*, vol. 1 (London: HMSO, 1972) p. 8.

19. R. Moscati, 'The Changing Policy of Education in Italy', *Journal of Modern Italian Studies* 3.1, pp. 55–73, 1998.

20. G. Papadopoulos, *Education 1960–1990: the OECD perspective* (Paris: OECD, 1994) p. 59.

21. Paolo Freire, *Pedagogy of the Oppressed* (Harmondsworth: Penguin, 1972); Daniel Lindenberg, *L'internationale communiste et l'école de classe* (Paris: Maspero, 1970); School of Barbiana, *Letter to a Teacher* (Harmondsworth: Penguin, 1969).

22. G. Murdock, 'The Politics of Culture' in *Education or Domination?* ed. D. Holly (London: Arrow Books, 1974), p. 101; Scuola di Barbiana, *Lettere a una Professoressa* (Firenze: L.E.F., 1967) p. 112.

23. Reiffers Report (Report of the Study Group on Education and Training) *Accomplishing Europe through Education and Training* (Luxemburg: European Commission, 1996) p. 71.

24. Confindustria, *Verso la scuola del 2000. Co-operare e Competere: le proposte di Confindustria* (Document presented by Carlo Callieri, vice-president of the Confindustria to Luigi Berlinguer, Minister of Education, 30 April 1998), www.confindustria.it.

25. J-L Bernal, 'Parental Choice, Social Class and Market Forces: the consequences of privatisation of public services in education', *Journal of Education Policy* 20 (6) p. 787, 2005.

26. H-J Hahn, *Education and Society in Germany* (Oxford: Berg, 1998) p. 115.

27. Though there is now occurring a readjustment, across all *Länder*, to 12 years.

28. P. Seidl (1972) quoted in Hahn, *Education and Society in Germany*, p. 127.

29. Hahn, *Education and Society in Germany*, p. 127.

30. Crouch, *Social Change in Western Europe*, p. 239.

31. Tony Edwards and Sally Tomlinson, *Selection isn't Working: diversity, standards and inequality in secondary education* (London: Catalyst, 2002); Checchi, *Italian Educational System*.

32. Marie Duru-Bellat, *Les inégalités sociales à l'école: genèse et mythes* (Paris: PUF, 2002).

33. Rainer Geissler, *Die Sozialstruktur Deutschlands* (Opladen: Westdeutscher Verlag, 1996) p. 259 ff.

34. Yves Dutercq, 'Administration de l'éducation: nouveau contexte, nouvelles perspectives', *Revue Française de Pédagogie* 130, janvier–mars 2000, pp. 143–70.

35. Choukri Ben-Ayed, 'L'enseignement privé en France' in *L'école: l'état des savoirs*, ed. A. van Zanten (Paris: éditions la découverte, 2000).

36. Paul Ginsborg, *A History of Contemporary Italy: society and politics 1943–1988* (Harmondsworth: Penguin Books, 1990) p. 170.

37. Quoted in Antoine Prost, 'The Educational Maelstrom' in *The Mitterrand Experiment: continuity and change in Modern France*, ed. G. Ross, S. Hoffman and S. Malzacher (Cambridge: Polity Press, 1987) p. 233.

38. Max Jäggi, Roger Müller and Sil Schmid, *Red Bologna* (London: Writers and Readers, 1977) p. 112.

39. Ginsborg, *History of Contemporary Italy*, p. 232.

40. Hobsbawm, *Age of Extremes*, pp. 405–7.

41. Serge Milano, *La Pauvreté Absolue* (Paris: Hachette Litterature, 2001) cited in Timothy B. Smith, *France in Crisis: welfare, inequality and globalisation since 1980* (Cambridge: Cambridge University Press, 2004) p. 193.

42. Jones, *Education in Britain*, p. 112.

43. Wolf, *Does Education Matter?* For Germany, Rainer Block, and Klaus Klemm, *Lohnt sich Schule* (Hamburg, 1997) p. 20.

44. Hobsbawm, *Age of Extremes*, p. 413.

45. Paul Willis, 'Footsoldiers of Modernity: The dialectics of cultural consumption and the 21st-century school', *Harvard Educational Review* 78 (3) pp. 390–416, p. 397, 2003.

46. Papadopoulos, *Education 1960–1990*, p. 141.

47. Jürgen Klausenitzer, 'PISA – Some Open Questions about the OECD's Education Policy', *Widersprüche 85* September 2002 (Bielefeld, Kleine Verlag) pp. 55–69.
48. Tony Blair, *Speech to National Association of Head Teachers*, 1 May 2004.
49. Department of Education and Science, *School Education in England: problems and initiatives* (London: DES, 1976) quoted in Ken Jones, *Beyond Progressive Education* (London: Macmillan 1983) p. 72.
50. Pauli Davila Balsera (2005) 'The Educational System and National Identities: the case of Spain in the twentieth century', *History of Education* 34.1 pp. 23–40.
51. Carlos Prieto del Campo, 'A Spanish Spring?' *New Left Review* 31 Jan/Feb 2005, pp. 42–68, p. 53.
52. Anne Corbett, 'Secular, Free and Compulsory: republican values in French education' in Corbett and Moon, *Education in France*, pp. 5–21.
53. A position particularly associated with Education Minister Jean-Pierre Chèvenement. See J.M. de Queiroz, 'Pédagogie et Pédagogues contre le Savoir' in van Zanten, *L'école: l'état des savoirs*, pp. 375–80.
54. See OECD, *Governance in Transition: public management reforms in OECD countries* (Paris: OECD, 1995) p. 84.
55. Richard Johnson and Deborah Lynn Steinberg, 'Distinctiveness and Difference within New Labour', in *Blairism and the War of Persuasion: labour's passive revolution*, ed. D. Steinberg and R. Johnson (London: Lawrence and Wishart, 2004) p. 9.
56. It should be noted though that at *élite* level, education systems continue to prize traditional forms of knowledge: head teachers of English public schools, for instance, are openly sceptical of the value of competence-based qualifications; in Spain, the Law on the General Organisation of the Education System (LOGSE) of 1990 called into a being a curriculum whose elevation of 'active learning' and attitudinal objectives above disciplinary objectives served to increase the attractiveness of private education.
57. Luc Brunner and Martine Laronche, 'Ce que va proposer le rapport Thélot pour réformer l'école', *Le Monde*, 25 August 2004. The report in question is that of the committee charged with responsibility for the 'national debate' on education in France.
58. See Marc Bousquet and Tiziana Terranova, 'Recomposing the University', *Mute* 28, Summer/Autumn 2004, www.metamute.com.
59. Richard Johnson and Valerie Walkerdine, 'Transformations under Pressure: new labour, class, gender and young women' in Steinberg and Johnson, *Blairism and the War of Persuasion*, pp. 114–133, p. 117.
60. Liz Fekete, 'Anti-Muslim Racism and the European Security State', *Race & Class* 46 (1) 2004, 3–29, p. 18.
61. Stasi Report (2003), quoted in Sharif Gemie, 'Stasi's Republic: the school and the "veil"': December 2001–March 2004 in *Modern and Contemporary France*, vol. 12, no. 3, pp. 387–97, p. 391.
62. *European Race Bulletin*, no. 4 (2002), quoted in Fekete, 'Anti-Muslim Racism and the European Security State', p. 19.
63. 'No Solution other than Police Presence for Unruly Berlin School', *Deutsche Welle* 1 April 2006, www.dw-world.de.
64. Johnson and Steinberg, 'Distinctiveness and Difference within New Labour', p. 8.

65. Nicos Poulantzas, *State, Power, Socialism* (London: NLB, 1978).
66. NPM is discussed in more detail in chap. 4. See also John Clarke and Janet Newman, *The Managerial State* (London: Sage, 1997).
67. OECD, *Governance in Transition: public management reforms in OECD countries* (Paris: OECD, 1995) p. 7.
68. For Spain, see OECD, *Education at a Glance*, Paris: OECD, 2002, pp. 145–53; for England, DfES, *Departmental Annual Report 2004* (London: DfES, 2004).
69. Deutsche Bank-Research, *Mehr Wachstum für Deutschland*, 2003, p. 7.
70. Phillip Brown, 'The Opportunity Trap: Education and Employment in a Global Economy', *European Educational Research Journal* 2.1, 2003, pp. 141–79, p. 150. See also Crouch, op. cit., chap. 8.
71. Brown, 'The Opportunity Trap', p. 152.
72. Reiffers Report, 'Accomplishing Europe through Education and Training', quoted in Nico Hirtt, Im Schatten der Unternehmerlobby, Die Bildungspolitik der Europaischen Kommission, in *Widersprüche* 83 (Bielefeld: Kleine Verlag, 1996) pp. 37–51.
73. 'From 1986 to 1999, the 10% of students experiencing the least schooling saw investment in their education increase from 2850 to 165000 francs. The 10% receiving the most schooling received extra investment in the range of 254,000–438, 000 francs.' Pierre Merle, *La Démocratisation de l'Enseignment* (Paris: La Découverte, 2002) p. 91.
74. Thélot, quoted in Nathalie Duceux, 'Du rapport Thélot à la loi Fillon', *Critique Communiste*, 174 Hiver (Paris: LCR, 2004) pp. 12–22.
75. See, for example, Andy Green, Alison Wolf and Tom Leney, *Convergence and Divergence in European Education and Training Systems* (London: Institute of Education, 1999).

2
The Europeanisation of Schooling

The European Union

In 2001, Anders Hingel, head of the education policy unit at the European Commission's Directorate-General for Education and Culture, observed the gathering coherence of the section's work. He observed a novel development: rather than 'holding forth on their [national] differences', education officials were 'beginning to give thought to common objectives'. Something new was taking place: 'common principles of education' were being agreed to between member states, 'leading logically' to something quite momentous, 'a *European Model of Education*'.[1] This chapter, which shares Hingel's appreciation of the significance of current events, is about the emergence of this model of education, as it is expressed through the policies and discourses of the European Union. We aim to trace the origins and trajectory of the model, to sketch its terms (which draw much, if not all, from the international policy orthodoxy discussed in chapter 1), to identify its impact on the EU's member states and to discuss its problems.

In the early phases of European integration, education played no part. It was the responsibility of national governments, not of European institutions. The 1957 Treaty of Rome, the founding document of the European Economic Community (EEC), made just a single mention of education, in the form of a reference to vocational training. The Brussels Treaty of 1965 was equally indifferent, but began a process that eventually enabled the coordination of policy – it created an executive body, the Commission, and a Council of Ministers. EEC ministers of education met for the first time in 1971 and by 1974, there existed a community education committee made up of the permanent representatives of member states. In 1976, emerging from this slow consolidation of executive competences came a resolution from the Council, the first relating to 'co-operation in the field of education'. It proposed a modest programme – research, the collection of statistics and the beginnings of projects aimed at strengthening through educational mobility a conception of European citizenship. Subsequently, the programme was elaborated: the *Eurydice* research and information network was set up in 1980; programmes such as *Erasmus* and *Leonardo* aiming at questions of educational mobility, were established and acquired a considerable reach: by 2001, more than 200,000 university students were participating in *Erasmus* programmes which enabled them to spend part of their course at a university in another EU country.[2]

Initiatives like these were intended primarily at achieving a sense of 'Europeanness' – among policymakers and among educational communities – in a Europe still influenced by a 'social model' that sought to combine economic growth with relatively high levels of social protection. Though the initiatives were mainly cultural in character, they were not entirely so – they contributed to the mobility of labour and in some respects to the harmonisation of qualifications, and to this extent they related to labour market issues. In the later 1980s, however, the terms of the relationship between the cultural and the economic began to change, at the same time as the social model itself was being re-examined. 'Following the Reagan-Thatcher period,' write Laval and Weber, 'there developed a tendency to view education as an economic tool, at the service of the economy and its competitiveness.'[3] Competitiveness itself entailed increased labour-market flexibility, in relation to a workforce intended to be leaner, more mobile, better trained, and more tightly managed than labour had become in the period of the long boom. It was in this context that the Single European Act (1986) emphasised the importance of 'human resource development'. Even so, for a period in the late 1980s, the early years of the Delors presidency of the Commission, the emphasis on liberalisation and competitiveness was to some extent obscured by Delors's advocacy of a social Europe in which questions of cohesion and quality of life were prominent. Beyond Delors, the social model lived on in EU discourse and in the hopes of the European TUC; but in practice the Treaty of Maastricht (1992), and its creation of Monetary Union – a Central Bank – and financial 'convergence criteria' for the euro, established a market-driven dynamic at the centre of Europe and the rethinking of education policy and education governance was significantly reconfigured in the terms that it provided.

This rethinking did not only involve an economisation at the level of the content of education policy; it also has had substantial political effects. These turn, first, upon the reconfigured relationship between EU policy and that of member states: the principle of subsidiarity, whereby member states retain exclusive control of national educational systems, has been drastically modified. Secondly, they impact upon political relationships within individual member states: governments pursuing within their own territories the EU's educational programme come into conflict with blocs of social forces committed to the principles, institutions and practices associated with previous, broadly egalitarian, types of reform. The text of the Maastricht Treaty reflected the lingering influence of these national pasts. Although it was more explicit than earlier treaties about the EU's interest in the creation of high-quality systems of education and training, Maastricht also recognised that the organisation and content of education remained the responsibility of member states. This principle of non-harmonisation was, according to Ertl, the 'letter' of Maastricht, and represented the price paid for including education in the treaty at all, when several states (including Britain and Germany) were 'very concerned about the possible effects of its incorporation'.[4] But it was a principle which became increasingly compromised.

Following Maastricht, the European Council of Ministers of Education increased in significance, and education acquired its own EU Directorate-General and Commissioner. Alongside institutional strengthening, there was a marked shift in the EU's understandings of the scope of education policy. The Commission White Papers of the mid-1990s helped diffuse a new policy orthodoxy, within a European frame of reference. *Growth, Competitiveness, Employment* – the 'Jacques Delors White Paper' of 1993–4 – placed education and training at the centre of a 'new mode of development', and called for the sector to adapt itself accordingly. Other publications – including the Reiffers Report cited in chapter 1 – elaborated this approach in more detailed and critical terms: existing education and training systems ignored the requirements of competitiveness; they failed to produce enterprising individuals; they offered elites too academic an education; they provided a mass education that was insufficiently vocational.[5] Through discursive efforts like these the necessity of change was established, and the organisation and content of education were established as matters for coordinated strategic discussion.[6]

The European Council (Heads of State) meeting in Lisbon in 2000 marked a new stage in the process of EU involvement at a detailed level of education policy. The Council declared that the EU, facing the challenges of globalisation and of a burgeoning knowledge economy, must, by 2010, transform itself into 'the most competitive and dynamic knowledge economy in the world'.[7] Education systems were placed unequivocally at the centre of this transformation, and at the same time the time-honoured principle of 'subsidiarity' was definitively modified: in Dale's formulation, the locus of policymaking was 'upscaled' from a national to a European level.[8] 'Never before', according to the Council, 'had systems of education and training been recognised as central to economic and social strategy and to the future of the EU.'[9] They were now too significant to be left to the haphazard and variegated process of nationally determined change. 'European policy in the field of education and training', stated the Portuguese Presidency, 'must look beyond the incremental reform of existing systems. It must also take as its objectives the construction of a European educational space of lifelong education and training, and the emergence of a knowledge society'.[10] In this context, it would be advisable to adopt 'a European framework that defines fundamental new educational competences ... competences in IT, in foreign languages, in technological culture, in entrepreneurial spirit and social skills.'[11] Through the Lisbon discussions, and those of the Council meetings that followed, the governments of the member countries thus transferred to the European level the power to settle large-scale questions relating to the orientation of education systems. In the Commission's words:

> We must certainly preserve the differences in system and structure which reflect the identities of the countries and regions of Europe, but we must equally recognise that our principal objectives, and the results at which we all aim, are remarkably similar ... No member is in a position to accomplish such goals alone. Our societies, like our economies, are today too interdependent to make such an option realistic'.[12]

Hingel suggested that the effect of Lisbon was 'revolutionary': it provided the EU, for the first time, with an over-arching common objective for education and training systems.[13] Viviane Reding, then EU Commissioner for Education and Training added to this evaluation a telling adjective: Lisbon had brought about 'a silent revolution'.[14] The term was perhaps more significant than Reding intended. As with many EU policies, it is difficult to see the Lisbon programme as possessing a popular mandate, and no 'great debate', nor public controversy, attended its (silent) emergence. It is rather the outcome of top-level steering, based on a matrix of understandings and prescriptions, which the EU shares with a range of other international policy organisations, from the World Bank to the OECD, but which is only problematically related to the concerns and ambitions of earlier programmes of reform. To locate the inspirations of the Lisbon turn, as well as to dispute its premises, we need to examine the themes and arguments of this matrix.

Knowledge, human capital, lifelong learning

For the EU, as for other international organisations, the economy is not everything. It is possible to find in its publications traces of a traditional, inclusive humanism. 'The main aim of education', stated the 1995 White Paper,' is to help each individual to fulfill his/her own potential, and to become a complete human being, not a tool for the economy.' Statements like these are infrequent, however – EU documents are not inclined to counterpose the educational and the economic. Much more likely is the attempt to merge the economic with the social in a term which straddles both domains. 'Social inclusion', an integral part of EU policy discourse, combines two emphases – the first that Europe must become globally competitive and the second that it must address problems of unemployment, exclusion and social cohesion.[15] The link between these positions is always heavily underscored: competitiveness is the way to reducing unemployment; higher standards of education are the means to economic success; and inclusion involves paid work. In the Lisbon Declaration, promises of economic growth, job creation, social cohesion and sustainability are likewise interwoven, so that the EU can claim legitimacy both as the defender of the social model in new, globalised circumstances and as the more effective heir of earlier, failed or incomplete programmes of reform. The work programme that followed Lisbon sought to put into practice inclusive themes, urging governments on towards the improvement of mass education, with increased access to upper-secondary education and lower levels of illiteracy.

But however much the social dimension is stressed, the logic of EU policy begins elsewhere. Like the other organisations that contribute to global policy orthodoxy, the EU takes as the starting point of its reflections on education and training a particular given: the extreme volatility of the global economy and the heightened state of competition which globalisation has brought about. It is from such a perspective that the World Bank notes that companies must make maximum use of the productivity gains that can accrue from technological innovation and the more efficient and flexible use of labour power. Employers

> seeing local markets more exposed to global competition, are requiring production processes that are much faster, ensure higher quality outputs more reliably, accommodate greater variety and continuous innovation, and cut costs relentlessly, as wafer-thin profit margins drive win-or-die outcomes.[16]

It is in this context – of an economy whose 'commanding processes' are productivity and competitiveness[17] – that there has developed what Jessop calls an 'increasingly dominant and hegemonic discourse' centred on the 'knowledge-based economy'. Descriptively, the term refers to a post-industrial economy where 'knowledge is at the heart of value added', where the workforce is increasingly concentrated in services and communications and where the sources of innovation are increasingly derived from large-scale research and development.[18] Concretising this in relation to Europe, the Kok Report estimates that up to 30% of the working population will in future be working directly in the production and diffusion of knowledge in the manufacturing, service, financial and creative industries. In political use however, the term has a much wider resonance. In education, for instance, the incessant efforts to redefine, in the name of the knowledge-based economy, the purposes, locations and practices of learning are more than just proposals for technical reform. They provide a master narrative of change that is an essential part of a 'broader struggle over political, intellectual and moral leadership'.[19] This narrative underpins policy's offensives against the archaism of established systems and definitions. The meaning of 'education' must itself be shifted, with 'lifelong learning' rather than 'formal schooling' providing the framework in which change is sought. In the course of the shift, the 'grammar of schooling' is remade: learning pathways are individualised; the value of formal academic qualifications is called into question; the boundaries between formal and informal learning become porous; and learning becomes continuous, from cradle to grave. The school becomes just one moment in this process, to whose overall objectives it must adapt itself.

Moreover, to produce in the workforce the required qualities of innovation and flexibility, a new appreciation of education's outcomes is needed; human capital formation must be measured not only – as it was in the 1960s – in terms of formal certification or quantitative experience of schooling but also now of personal capacities and dispositions. Thus the OECD specifies characteristics that 'allow a person to build, manage and deploy human capital'. These characteristics, 'which are seen today as qualities that are just as important as disciplinary knowledge', include

(1) The ability to acquire and develop skills. This includes the ability to learn, to identify one's learning needs and to manage one's learning activity.
(2) The ability to find the best place to utilise these skills. This includes career planning, job search skills, and the ability to blend working and personal objectives.
(3) Personal characteristics (like trustworthiness) which make people more attractive as employees, because they are more likely to deploy their skills productively. Motivational characteristics are likely to be central.[20]

The notion of employability thus takes on a wider meaning, and comes to refer to questions of disposition, as well as diplomas. Governments must 'create an environment conducive to the acquisition of skills and competences' of this kind ... so that the benefits of new technology are exploited and costs minimised'.[21] The problem, for business interests, is that education systems 'have not sufficiently adapted to the technological revolution which is unfolding before our very eyes' (ERT)[22] – a problem which is all the more serious because of what the World Bank calls 'the short "shelf life" of knowledge, skills, and occupations'. Since the value of knowledge is subject to rapid depreciation, a growing importance is attached to 'the regular updating of individual capacities and qualifications' (World Bank 2002).[23] Hence the OECD's emphasis on 'learning how to learn' and the contrast that the World Bank draws between 'traditional industries' in which skills remain constant over time, and 'the knowledge economy, in which change is so rapid that workers constantly need to acquire new skills.[24] The kind of worker who will be valued is one capable of moving from one role to another within a company, of learning new work practices, of multi-tasking within the space of a day or a week, and of adapting quickly to the demands of different occupational cultures.

Once acquired, employability must be constantly renewed. In this kind of learning, social and economic adaptability are key – with adaptability becoming individualised. The worker him/herself tends to become responsible for updating his knowledge and skills in an environment where these are changing very rapidly. This individualisation – at the heart of knowledge societies, says policy orthodoxy, 'the main actor is the individual',[25] – is a means both of pressuring the worker, or future worker, to seek out the kinds of education which are most useful in terms of employability and at the same time of pressuring educational institutions, through the interaction of supply and demand, to prioritise the same objectives. As the International Labour Organisation makes clear, it is a matter of establishing 'education systems that are organised around demand, which respond to the real and immediate needs of business, rather than systems that are organised around supply, which tend to rest on the priorities established by public sector organisations, and by established educational institutions'.[26] The redesign of post-compulsory education, in particular, is based on two linked principles, that 'individuals are best placed to choose what they need to learn and how they want to improve their skills' and that 'costs should be shared by all the actors concerned'.[27] Along the road of lifelong learning, there are tolls to pay.

Europe's problems

These understandings permeate EU thinking to the core, but they link more to a sense of troubled urgency than to one of accomplishment. David-Pascal Dion, of the European Commission's Directorate of Education and Culture, writes of the 'failure' of the EU project, attributing it to Europe's 'outdated economic institutions'. Making the EU the most competitive knowledge-based economy in the world requires the optimal functioning of education and training systems. These, according to Dion, are 'crucial factors for the formation and use of human capital' which in turn 'is a key driver of economic prosperity through higher earnings and productivity as well as of social welfare'. But Europe is not the first in the field. Globalisation entails an intensification of economic competition, but 'many of the most profitable opportunities have already been seized by the United States', which has used its leadership in ICT to dominate the knowledge-based economy.[28] In comparison with the United States, the EU's per capita GDP is low (only about 70% of US figures) and its rate of productivity growth is weaker. The EU's 'stock' of human capital is lower in quantity and quality than that of the United States: to use a rough measure, one-third of the economically active population in the United States has a degree, compared to one-fifth in the EU. There is insufficient knowledge creation (through a lack of R&D investment), insufficient knowledge diffusion (because of low levels of educational attainment and achievement) and – with insufficient rates of innovation – poor knowledge application. Without 'human capital investment in all these areas', economic efficiency cannot be revitalised and the social model will consequently be undermined.[29] Hence, Dion argues, the pressing importance of institutional reform.

Solutions?

The Lisbon summit set the scene for such reform, translating the general terms of knowledge-society discourse into a common, European-level 'work programme'. Subsequent Council meetings, in Stockholm (2001) and Barcelona (2002) elaborated this work. At Stockholm, ministers of education decided on three strategic objectives, relating to 'quality', 'access' and 'opening education to the outside world'. At Barcelona, these were further refined into 13 'concrete objectives': 'quality' involved among other things 'developing the competences required for the knowledge society'; 'access' emphasised active citizenship, equal opportunity and social cohesion; 'the outside world' was translated as 'the world of work', with a particular emphasis on developing the 'spirit of enterprise'.[30] Accompanying this work of definition was a ten-year programme of implementation, involving annual European-level reviews of progress made by member states, benchmarked against 16 'quality indicators' developed by the Commission;[31] at the same time the Commission began the work of identifying 'new basic competences' and 'future objectives of national education systems' in the knowledge society.[32]

The initial quality indicators relate to attainment, participation, completion rates, the monitoring of education and questions of resources; but as Roger Dale comments, the agreement of national governments to involve their education systems in such a process is as significant as the substantive issues on which progress reviews are focused.[33] Formally, the EU has no legal capacity to intervene in the structure, organisation and content of education in the member states; it came therefore to make use of a new policy instrument, the Open Method of Co-ordination (OMC), a device which took the development of EU policy to a new level, based on 'conscious efforts to develop new supranational forms of education'.[34] By this means, a decisive shift in the EU's position on educational governance was made – a turn towards detailed specification, target setting and monitoring which took the Commission beyond its previous powers and constitutional authority.

In the words of the EU presidency after Lisbon, the OMC is a means of 'spreading best practice and achieving greater convergence towards the EU's main goals'. It does so not through the establishment of binding legal obligations, but through 'soft law' – a dense proliferation of recommendations, resolutions, reports, action plans through which intergovernmental relations are strengthened and a common purpose developed.[35] This work is formally specified in terms of 'guidelines', combined with short, medium and long-term timetables; national and European 'objectives'; 'indicators' that can measure progress towards objectives; 'benchmarks' that summarise average levels of European performance; and monitoring, evaluation and peer review activities that provide further glue for the process of policy consolidation.[36]

Despite frequent references to 'the needs of different member states', the OMC effectively shifts the locus of agenda setting away from national governments, at the same time as it attempts to bypass the awkward constitutional issues involved in the subsumption of national diversity within a common European programme. As Alexiadou puts it, the 'OMC will radically challenge how education policy is governed in the EU ... since member states will no longer enjoy exclusive sovereignty over education policy'. In place of exclusivity, she envisages a 'complex system of multi-level governance', in which the OMC will be a powerful normative force.[37]

This system appears to be taking shape. Certainly, there is evidence of the OMC's normative effect. However soft its touch, it reaches deeply and significantly into the educational practice of member states, those which are in the rearguard of reform and especially those in Eastern Europe. The 2005 Progress Report made to the Commission by the Spanish government, for instance, acknowledged the EC work programme as a strong influence on the education legislation of the Zapatero government. The German report suggested that the European agenda could provide a means of eliding the policy differences between *Länder*. On behalf of France it was stressed that 'the Lisbon strategy was a factor in the overall shift of public policy in France with regard to education and training', and claimed that recent legislation was 'working from European thinking regarding basic skills'.[38] To a French audience, government institutions maintained the same story. When the *Haut Conseil de l'Education* presented its recommendations for the curriculum to be reconstituted on the basis of a common basic core (*socle commun*), it sought to support its case by referring to the strategies for education and training developed by the EU.[39]

The OMC thus provides means for the firmer establishment of a European model of education, not least because its choice of particular benchmarks and indicators has the effect both of describing European education, and of bringing a particular, and selective, version of it into being. The terms of this version are formally pluralist: 'sustainable growth', 'more and better jobs' and 'social cohesion' can all be found there. But in practice the dominant term is 'competitiveness'; as Dale puts it, any contradictions between economic and social discourses are likely to be resolved in favour of the former; challenges to the EU's established *acquis* of internal market and monetary union will be avoided.[40] In this way, the OMC provides governments with a further weapon for use against national traditions that have been shaped, at least in part, by social forces seeking other objectives than economisation.

After Lisbon

Since 2000, the economic/social 'balance' of the objectives announced at Lisbon has been further tilted towards the side of a particular kind of economics. The European Trade Union Confederation, a strong supporter of Lisbon, claims – perhaps ingenuously, as if it has identified a new development – that structural reform has become a codeword for deregulation and weakening workers' rights, with minimal social welfare and constant employer demands for labour flexibility.[41] Certainly, business organisations such as the employers' lobby UNICE, have lobbied hard to confirm such tendencies.[42] But they are hardly absent, either, from the EU's intrinsic dynamic: the EU constitution drafted in 2003 plainly aimed at the further concentration of power in the institutions of the EU, and at the inscription of liberalisation, deregulation and a market-based regime at the heart of the EU.[43] The presidency of José Manuel Barroso has also made clear its preference for the liberalisation of public services.

From the viewpoint provided by this commitment to an accelerating process of liberalisation, the Commission is dissatisfied with the progress made since Lisbon. The declaration of March 2000 was a ringing one; EU discourse is in its own terms rich and copious, with a well-developed sense of economic, social and educational purpose. But this does not mean that it can achieve an easy transformation of European education. The provisional balance sheet of Lisbon drawn up by the Commission in 2004 amounted to a catalogue of deep-seated problems. Private investment in education, especially higher education, is too low – five times smaller, proportionally, than that of the United States. School failure remains high – the target of 90% of students leaving school in 2010 with a diploma will not be met, even if the threshold of certification is lowered to 'basic skill' level. Vocational training is out of step with employers' needs. Higher education has not been restructured along lines that strongly differentiate the elite from the mass university, and student mobility across national frontiers is too restricted for a European market in higher education to be envisaged. The scope of life-long learning is also restricted: it is too much centred on providing a second chance for those who have failed at school, and lacks the capacity to contribute to adaptability and retraining in the workforce.[44]

Underlying these complaints is a sense of the recalcitrance of the existing educational order: weak private sectors, underdeveloped training systems, high rates of failure and insufficiently differentiated approaches to higher education are legacies that are hard to sweep away or transform; and national governments are often incapable – for reasons of competence, or political calculation – of dealing with them. The Commission's response to the resulting *impasses* takes the form of an attempt to intensify the process of a centralising Europeanisation. Acknowledging the – almost outdated – truism that 'the priorities guiding reform ... are defined by each country in relation to its own particular conditions and constraints', it simultaneously asserts that 'it is essential ... that from now on these national choices take fully into account the common objectives fixed at the European level in the framework of the Lisbon strategy.' Each state should establish clear short-and medium-term reforming strategies, and thus work towards realising the Lisbon objectives. A 'high-level' group should evaluate the implementation of national-level strategies, and identify where further work is needed.

All this is proposed in the name of defending the social model: Europe should not aim to be competitive, said the Kok Report, by initiating a 'race to lower real wage and non-wage costs' and by undermining their 'systems of social cohesion and partnership in the workplace'.[45] But to many, the race seemed already to have begun – hence the votes in France and the Netherlands against the constitution, and the Europe-wide protests in 2005 against the EU's Bolkestein directive that would have liberalised and commodified the provision of public services. It is possible – in the manner of the British press – to dismiss such movements without analysis, as the result of a 'drift to the demagogic and blindly nationalist extremes of right and left', but it is more productive to identify what their emergence suggests not just about the problems of governance and economics that beset the post-Lisbon project, but also about its social and political fault-lines.[46]

One of the major fault-lines traverses the idea of a knowledge-based economy. As we suggested in chapter 1, while such an economy depends upon workers who are capable of updating their knowledge and their competence, it does not require in all major economic sectors a large number of workers with a high level of education. Adaptability is certainly in demand; education, much less so: there is a distinction between the importance of innovatory capacity – as an arm of competition – and the general level of education called for by the knowledge society.

The OECD is sometimes lucid on this question, pointing out that 'discussion of the effects of technology on occupational composition tends to focus too much on the manufacturing sector and the top end of the service sector. These are both sectors exposed to international competition, where qualifications are valued, and where the demand for unqualified workers has fallen. This focus brings with it a tendency to exaggerate the central role of education and qualifications in the future of work'.[47] The organisation recognises that it would be 'tempting' to believe that 'everybody can now participate in the new economy', but feels obliged to temper this optimism: 'there are many jobs located outside the most dynamic and highly qualified sectors. It is reasonable to suppose that there will continue to exist marked differences in the occupational demand of qualifications ... (and) expansion is often accompanied by an increase in the proportion of non-qualified to qualified staff'.[48] Empirical studies confirm this view. British research into work skills, for instance, suggests both that there has been an increase in demand for skills at the higher end of the labour market, and that the number of unskilled jobs (6.9 million, in the British economy in the late 1990s) far exceeds the number of low-skilled workers.[49]

Far from seeing a market-driven rise in general levels of technological knowledge, then, we are witnessing a polarisation.[50] The shortage of qualified labour required to fill a relative handful of specialised jobs, linked to emergent technologies, tends to conceal the existence of a mass of low-qualified, badly paid and unprotected workers who constitute the other side of flexibilisation. The polarisation in educational demand is a reflection in the field of qualifications of a general social process that strategic organisations have some difficulty in presenting in a positive light. 'Not everyone will enter a career in the dynamic sector of the new economy;' recognises the OECD, 'in fact, the majority will not manage it – from which we should conclude that education programmes cannot be designed as if the entire school population were going to reach their higher levels."[51] The problem is resolved by invoking the virtues of precariousness: 'the vast reservoir of "little jobs" offers a perfect medium-term response to those who ask themselves what should be done while they wait for their long-term education and training strategy to bear fruit' (OECD 2001).[52]

It is in this context that the opposition to the Lisbon process takes on a fuller significance. While it focuses centrally on the deregulation of the labour market, and of the provision of services, it has also developed an educational dimension. Demeulemeester and Rochat succinctly summarise a critical perspective on learning in the knowledge economy discourse that is widely shared. The EU's experts, they argue, want to make education and training

> much more responsive to market needs. In this sense, they consider (it) just as a tool in promoting material welfare and competitiveness. In this way, they introduce short-termism and commercial concerns in a world which was initially devised to prepare for the long run adaptiveness of society and individuals, not solely from an economic point of view, but also social, moral and political.[53]

Critiques of this kind counterpose to current policy orthodoxy a tradition of learning that gives more weight than does knowledge-economy discourse to the autonomous role of educational institutions, to the professional judgements of teachers and to a broad conception of non-specialised education, removed from immediate economic concerns – to 'slow', rather than 'fast' knowledge. Though it is often dismissed within policy orthodoxy as archaic, and as bound up with the defence of sectoral interests, this critique homes in on some of the most obvious weak points of knowledge economy discourse, Its emergence suggests that the battle for 'political, intellectual and moral leadership', which Jessop suggested is integral to the knowledge economy project, has not yet concluded.

Notes

1. Anders Hingel, *Education Policies and European Governance: contribution to the interservice groups on European governance* (Brussels: European Commission, 2001).
2. Op.cit. p. 4.
3. Laval and Weber, *Le nouvel ordre éducatif mondial*, p. 113.
4. Hubert Ertl, 'European Union Policies in Education and Training: the Lisbon agenda as a turning point?' *Comparative Education* 42.1 2006 pp. 5–27, p. 12.

5. See the summary in J-L Demeeulemeester and D. Rochat, *The European Policy Regarding Education and Training: a critical assessment*, Skope Research Paper no. 21, Autumn 2001. ESRC funded Centre on Skills, Knowledge and Organisational Performance, Oxford and Warwick Universities.

6. European Commission, Growth, Competitiveness, Employment Luxemburg, 1993; *Teaching and Learning, towards the knowledge society* (Luxemburg: 1995). See the discussion in Fatima Antunes, 'Globalisation and Europification of Education Policies: routes, processes and metamorphoses', *European Educational Research Journal*, 5.1, pp. 38–56, 2006.

7. See the summary provided on the EU Education and Training 2010 website http://ec.europa.eu/education/policies/2010/et_2010_en.html.

8. Roger Dale, 'Globalisation, Knowledge Economy and Comparative Education', *Comparative Education* 41.2, pp. 117–49, 2005.

9. European Council (2000) Conclusions of the European Presidency Council in Lisbon, 23–24 March.

10. Ibid.

11. Ibid.

12. European Commission, *The Concrete Future Objectives of Education Systems* (Brussels: European Commission, 2001).

13. Hingel, *Education Policies and European Governance*, p. 15.

14. Viviane Reding (2003), quoted in Antunes, 'Globalisation and Europification of Education Policies', p. 41.

15. See the discussion in Jacky Brine, 'Lifelong Learning and the Knowledge Economy: those that know and those that do not – the discourse of the European Union', *British Educational Research Journal* 32.5, pp. 647–66, 2006.

16. World Bank, *Education Sector Strategy* (Washington: World Bank 1999) available on the website of the International Labour Organisation http://www.ilo.org/public/english/employment/skills/hrdr/publ/pdf_06.htm.

17. Manuel Castells, *The Information Age: economy, society and culture Volume 3: End of Millennium* (Oxford: Blackwell, 1998) p. 341.

18. Castells, *The Information Age*, p. 147.

19. Bob Jessop, 'Cultural political economy, the knowledge-based economy, and the state', in ed. *The Technological Economy*, D. Slater and A. Barry (London: Routledge, 2005) pp. 144–66.

20. OECD, 'Rethinking Human Capital', *Education Policy Analysis* Paris pp. 123–4, 2002.

21. OECD (Elena Arnal, Wooseok Ok and Raymond Torres) 'Labour Market And Social Policy – Occasional Papers No. 50: knowledge, work organisation and economic growth (Paris: OECD 2001) p. 4.

22. European Round Table (1989) 'Education and Skills in Europe', *Inquiry by the European Round Table Education and Training in Europe* (Brussels: European Round Table of Industrialists).

23. World Bank, 'Constructing Knowledge Societies: new challenges for tertiary education' (Washington: World Bank, 2002) p. 27.

24. Ibid.

25. For an example, Angelos Agalianos, 'Crossing borders: the European dimension in educational and social science research' in *The World Yearbook of Education 2006: Education and Policy* ed. Jenny Ozga (London: RoutledgeFalmer, 2006).

26. International Labour Organisation (1998) *World Employment Report 1998–9: Employability in the Global Economy – How Training Matters* (Geneva: ILO).
27. OECD 2001 Investing in Competencies for All (Communiqué) Meeting of OECD Education Ministers, Paris, 3–4 April.
28. The Kok Report, *Facing the Challenge: the Lisbon strategy for growth and employment. Report from the High-Level Group chaired by Wim Kok* (European Communities: Luxemburg, 2004) p. 8. The report notes that the US accounts for 74% of top 300 IT companies and 46% of top 300 firms ranked by R&D spending.
29. David-Pascal Dion, 'The Lisbon Process: a European odyessey' *European Journal of Education* 40.3 pp. 296–315, 2006.
30. See the discussions in Nico Hirtt, *Education et formation 2010: comment Mme Reding a fait accelerer la cadence* www.ecoledemocratique.org 7 March 2005; Laval and Weber, *Le nouvel ordre éducatif mondial*, pp. 123–6.
31. European Commission, *European Report on Quality of School Education: sixteen quality indicators* (Brussels: May 2000).
32. European Commission, White Paper, *European Governance* 2001 http://europa.eu.int/comm/governance/governance_eu/nat_policies_en.htm.
33. Dale, R. 'Forms of Governance Governmentality and the Eu's Open Method of Coordination' in *Global Governmentality* ed. Wendy Larner and William Walters (London: Routledge, 2004).
34. Roger Dale, 'Globalisation, Knowledge Economy and Comparative Education', *Comparative Education* 41.2 pp. 117–49, 2005.
35. B. Lange and N. Alexiadou, 'New Forms of European Union Governance in the Education Sector – a preliminary analysis of the implementation of the Open Method of Co-ordination (OMC) in the UK'. Paper to the European Conference on Educational Research Geneva, 2006.
36. *Presidency Conclusion*, Lisbon European Council, 23 and 24 March 2000, para. 37.
37. Nafsika Alexiadou, 'Europeanisation and Education Policy' in *World Yearbook of Education 2005: globalisation and nationalism in education*, ed. D. Coulby, C. Jones and E. Zambeta (London: Kogan Page, 2005).
38. European Commission, 'Implementing the "Education and Training 2010" Work Programme: 2005 Progress Report – Spain' (Brussels: 2005); European Commission, 'Implementing the "Education and Training 2010" Work Programme: 2005 Progress Report – Germany' (Brussels: 2005); European Commission 'Implementing the "Education and Training 2010" Work Programme: 2005 Progress Report – France' (Brussels: 2005). By contrast, the UK document reverses the order of connexion: the Lisbon declaration is 'in line with the thrust of our domestic policies'. The Italian report suggests whole-hearted agreement with Lisbon, without pointing to concrete measures that align Italian schooling with EU priorities.
39. Haut Conseil de l'Education, 'Recommandations pour le socle commun' 23 March 2006. http://www.hce.education.fr/.
40. Dale, 2004.
41. ETUC, 'The EU's Lisbon Strategy', www.etuc.org.
42. See the website www.unice.org, in particular the document, *Release Companies' Potential: Lisbon Status* 2004.
43. Fondation Copernic, *Europe: une alternative* (Paris: Syllepse, 2003).

44. Nico Hirtt, *Education et Formation 2010*, www.écoledemocratique.org, 7 March 2005; European Commission, *Education et formation 2010: l'urgence des réformes pour réussir la stratégie de Lisbonne*, 2004.
45. Kok Report, p. 9.
46. John Lichfield, 'TV Offensive fails to halt French drift to No vote', The Independent, 18 May 2005.
47. 'Investing in Competencies for All: Communiqué' Meeting of OECD Education Ministers, Paris, 3–4 April 2001.
48. Ibid.
49. A. Felstead, D. Gallie and F. Green, *Work Skills in Britain 1986–2001* (Nottingham: DfES, 2004).
50. Brown, 'The Opportunity Trap'.
51. OECD, 2001.
52. Ibid.
53. Demeeulemeester and Rochat, *The European Policy regarding Education and Training*, p. 15.

3
System Change: Local Autonomy and the Evaluative State

'Education is not for sale' – the slogan of anti-globalisation protesters everywhere – suggests that what neo-liberalism is fundamentally 'about' is privatisation, and that the school is subject to an inexorable process through which it will pass from public control into the hands of private business. This is not, in fact, happening. Privatisation is certainly a powerful force, whose forms we sketch in our next chapter. It is best understood, however, not as the key that unlocks the ultimate meaning of contemporary education, but as one part of a more general process of transformation, by means of which schooling is remade so as to align it more closely to social change. The 'truth' of the protestors' slogan is that this is a process that is taking place 'under the sign of capital', so that reforms that are motivated in terms of the need for education to respond to new complexities and social diversities, and therefore appear to have a strong element of technical rationality, turn out to be articulated with perspectives in which the relationship of schooling to the interests of business – broadly understood – is dominant.

In this chapter, we will discuss changes in the regulation of education systems. Schooling is regulated by many factors, some of which – especially in quasi-market systems where parental demand and entrepreneurial vigour are important influences – cannot be precisely specified by policy design. Some of these are discussed in a later chapter, where we consider quasi-market dynamics in relation to educational inequality. Our focus here is more on regulation through policy design, and on the intentional efforts of governments to re-regulate schooling, through changes in national legislation and decision making that affect such key elements as the provision and control of resources, the locus of decision making, the influence of different types of educational actor and the specification of objectives and procedures. Arguably, it is in these areas that schooling in Western Europe has most powerfully experienced the impact of a new policy orthodoxy. In exploring them, we aim to highlight not only patterns of convergence and diversity – which have already been very ably covered in other research – but also the articulation of re-regulation with aspects of the neo-liberal programme and the ways in which it encompasses a strategy for moral, intellectual and political leadership that undermines previous projects of educational reform.[1]

The French sociologist Francois Dubet is one of those who think that the old educational system has failed, and that its defenders overlook its failings. Rejecting neo-liberal change, they refuse to come to terms with 'glaring inequalities', middle-class flight into the private sector, 'poor performance' and 'the difficulties the school experiences in educating the neediest pupils'. In these circumstances, Dubet argues, the only way of preserving values of 'equality, freedom, culture and social integration' is to allow individual schools a certain degree of autonomy, so that they can 'adapt to the needs and wishes of their pupils'. From this point of view, public education will only survive if it is decentralised. But decentralisation must be accompanied by regulation, in the form of common examinations and common curricula. 'We know', Dubet concludes, 'that the most equitable and efficient systems are those that combine autonomy for schools with a strong capacity to administer, control and monitor the system from the centre.'[2]

Dubet sketches here the two complementary poles of a current orthodoxy in policy design and offers a positive reading of them: central regulation and local diversity are the basis of a new system in which equity and efficiency go hand in hand. He stands, thus, on the left wing of a policy orthodoxy which embraces governments, social democratic parties, managers of education and the international organisations whose positions we began to sketch in chapter 2. All are agreed that centralisation of strategic decision making at the level of national government should be accompanied by decentralisation of operational power at the level of delivery – since decentralised systems 'are also the most flexible, the quickest to adapt ... and have the greatest propensity to develop new forms of partnership.'[3]

They are agreed, too, on what must link these levels – a system of performance indicators that function as a central mechanism of accountability, of 'management by objectives'. These are the devices which connect 'the strategic plans of the centre (the policy-producing arm of the restructured state) with outcomes of practice at the periphery (individual institutions)'.[4]

In this chapter, we want to explore further this double-headed system of centralisation/decentralisation, in terms of its elaboration by international organisations, its impact on national education policies and politics and the extent to which it has already been implanted in the practice of institutions. The 'new' system has in one sense been in place for some time already. It is nearly 20 years since the OECD first called for a system based on 'greater accountability, greater incentives and the involvement of non-government providers'[5] and more than 10 years since it introduced its study *Governance in Transition* with the claim that

> a new paradigm for public management (NPM) has emerged, aimed at fostering a performance-oriented culture in a less centralised public sector. It is characterized by
> - focus on results, efficiency, effectiveness and quality,
> - decentralised management to increase *operative* autonomy and flexibility,
> - alternatives to public provision,
> - competitive environments, user fees/vouchers (cost recovery) and internal markets,
> - strengthening of *strategic* capacities at the centre,
> - client orientation.[6]

The paradigm is lucid and comprehensive. Its intellectual underpinnings have been clearly and repeatedly stated by the OECD, the World Bank and the many other organisations which define educational purposes in terms of cost-effectiveness and technical efficiency and which see NPM as providing the technologies that can achieve such purposes. NPM is a systemic paradigm. It applies, certainly, to the workings of individual institutions, but also ranges more broadly, and includes both national and international dimensions. In this sense, it includes the OECD's Programme for International Student Assessment (PISA), as well as the EU's OMC. Such programmes, by defining the indicators against which progress should be measured, establish goals for national systems and work towards the creation, in Europe, of a more unified 'educational space', based on the assumption that nation states, provinces, school systems and educational institutions 'share' some concerns and goals, so they can be meaningfully compared.[7]

PISA is especially important in this respect. Since the late 1980s the OECD's central project has been to develop indicators for evaluating education systems and the conceptions of efficiency and quality they contain. The INES project *International Indicators and Evaluation of Education Systems* began in 1988 and from the mid-1990s onwards represented a key-OECD activity.[8] From 1996 *Education at a Glance* was published annually – a collection of statistical data from member countries which were presented in terms of indicators. In parallel with it appeared *Education Policy Analysis* – essays on central questions of education policy. In the mid-1990s, national coordinators, whose task was 'to contribute to the diffusion of an indicator culture within education circles', were appointed.[9] The OECD had used certain types of indicators previously: from the 1960s onwards, it has measured educational progress and human-capital investment in terms of years spent in formal education and level of education completed. But the new evaluation regime was significantly different.

The OECD now assumed that 'the widespread acknowledgement of the benefits of education and other forms of learning should not lead governments and others to invest indiscriminately in human capital. In deploying finite resources, they need to know *which forms of investment produce the best value for money*'.[10] From this point of view the OECD considered its previous indicators too indiscriminate:

> Estimates of the stock of human capital skill base have tended, at best, to be derived using proxies such as level of education completed. When the interest in human capital is extended to include attributes that permit (...) to equip people to become 'lifelong learners', the inadequacy becomes even clearer.[11]

So while not abandoning its benchmarks, the OECD developed alongside them three approaches to improving measurements within the framework of international comparative studies which directly examine the attributes of human capital:

- Student achievement in particular areas of knowledge and competence at different stages of school education (in particular, science, mathematics, literacy);
- Competences of school-aged children that cross the boundaries defined by subject curricula;
- Adult skills and competences relevant to everyday life and work.[12]

In this shift from input to output indicators, the PISA surveys were key. 'By directly testing for knowledge and skills', they enabled governments to 'examine the degree of preparedness of young people for adult life'. At the same time, they tested 'the effectiveness of education systems', against a common, econonomised definition of quality, which swiftly acquired an objective status.[13] Like any institutionalised system of measurement, PISA did not simply describe facts; it created them and gave them significance. It served to re-regulate schooling by specifying with scientific force a set of objectives for the school, around which reform projects could cohere.[14]

Strengthening the national state

Decentralisation develops not *against* the state but *because* of it. The state is both a designer of change – often in partnership with private sector organisations such as the Bertelsmann Foundation in Germany or the Price Waterhouse Coopers consultancy in Britain – and the most significant actor in the new systems which such partnerships bring into being. This double role is necessary both because the social agents pressing for change are usually in political terms rather weak – there has been little popular mobilisation in favour of decentralisation of a neo-liberal kind – and because the mechanisms of the quasi-market in education – greater autonomy of schools as provider units, parental choice and transaction-based funding (i.e. per capita funding) – are insufficiently powerful surrogates for supply and demand in real markets to drive the reforms which governments want. They have to be supplemented by forms of state regulation that go beyond the construction of the conditions of the market itself to more interventionist policies. In this area, government strategies have been supplied by the repertoire of the NPM. They entail both the creation of new central powers – to allocate funds, set targets, define curricula and pedagogy, closely direct teacher training, audit and inspect performance – and the invention of national regulatory agencies at a distance from government but serving government strategy.

England provides the richest example of this many-sided centralisation. In political terms, its most striking feature is the 're-agenting' of education, so that the social actors characteristic of an earlier period (local authorities, teacher trade unions) play a greatly diminished role. In contrast with the period of social democratic reform, the development of policy through a process of encounter between different social interests has become less important than its elaboration through networks of operationally powerful but not strongly autonomous agencies, local and national, whose origins and points of reference lie in the priorities of national government. Such agencies – whose work is complemented by that of the private interests we discuss in the following chapter – have various functions. Firstly, they standardise provision – the national curriculum of 1988 was the first step in this process. Secondly, they develop a set of performance indicators in the form of measurable and comparable data, generated primarily by scores in national tests and examinations. Thirdly, they feed data to schools, so that their performance can be compared to other schools and under-performance can be identified and acted upon. (English data systems are now sophisticated enough to allow comparisons between schools with similar socio-economic populations.) Finally, a school system focused on 'quality' requires a set of rewards (such as extra funding) and government-generated sanctions – legislation proposed by the Blair government in 2005 gives inspectors the power to close failing schools or to dismiss their managements.[15] To carry out such tasks, New Labour retained the agencies of Conservative centralisation and added others of its own making. Permanent agencies such as the school inspection organisation Ofsted, the Training and Development Agency (for teachers and other school staff), the Standards and Effectiveness Unit at the Department for Education and Skills and the Qualifications and Curriculum Authority are complemented by major conjunctural initiatives – notably the Literacy and Numeracy Strategies – which are nationally directed and locally pervasive.[16] The Specialist Schools and Academy Trust, at one point a mere relic from Conservative times, has grown into a powerful body that sets much of the agenda for the government's programme to establish 'independent state schools'. Together, these agencies link the micro-world of classroom interactions to macro-level objectives of standards and achievement and in so doing create new roles for old 'partners' – not least for teachers. Not the least of their effects is to 'sterilise' school systems, so that they are less likely to generate alternative models of education.

The English system has been emulated only in part. In the case of Italy, for instance, governments have tried to use the law-making powers of the state to break up existing configurations of educational influence, and have to this extent intensified processes of centralisation. Institutional novelties like the Italian National Institute for the Evaluation of the School System (Invalsi), are also a feature of an emerging educational order. Before Invalsi, there was no national system for evaluating the work of schools. But as one employers' federation notes, such initiatives tend to be isolated, so that 'really effective and regular evaluation of school and student performance does not seem to be widespread in European countries, even if each country is seriously working on the issue'.[17] Likewise, the Deutsche Bank complains that right across Europe 'there are big shortfalls in the monitoring of schools' performances'. The Bank's solution involves an increase in central power: performance standards should be set at federal level and assessed by universal and compulsory tests. Moving in this direction, the Federal Government broke new ground in 2002, by declaring educational policy to be a 'national task': leaving policy in the hands of *Länder* had created significant performance gaps between pupils from different regions. The following year, the *Länder* Education ministers agreed upon national competence-based standards against which students would be assessed. In this way, with increasing speed, and constant reference to international comparisons, the German educational state is being remade, with government working to set up a regulatory framework and to enable autonomous developments in cities and regions. All the same, the achievement of a dense network of state-empowered agencies working to evaluate and control educational processes remains, for the moment, an English phenomenon.

Decentralisation: new and old

This manifest strengthening of state powers coexists with repeated critiques on the part of business organisations, of what the Deutsche Bank calls the 'dominant position of the state'. The target here, of course, is the 'old' state of an earlier period, in which what neo-liberalism calls 'producer interests' had achieved some influence. Enumerating the consequences of the old state's monopoly for German education, the Bank complains that 'there is only limited competition in relation to performance'; this 'leaves hardly any room for a qualitative differentiation within the service' at the same time as it produces 'a reduced ability to perform on the part of pupils'.[18] Its solution is a system that is decentralised, differentiated, competitive and open to private providers. Such a system will guarantee higher levels of quality.

The system is, of course, based on principles different from those that motivated earlier types of decentralisation. Decentralisation has not always been articulated with a neo-liberal programme. In France, the 1980s movement from a strongly centralised state to more decentralised forms of regulation shows this very clearly. Acknowledging the nineteenth century – and indeed pre-revolutionary – antecedents of the 'educator state', Demailly and her colleagues stress that it reached its fullest extent in the mid-twentieth century. It was the result of a 'vast movement of rationalisation undertaken by the Fifth Republic' – a movement that transformed and expanded secondary education in particular, on the basis of a plan that asserted national need and was implemented through technocratic mechanisms. The system established in this period still has considerable force: it is at national level that the greater part of the education budget is controlled and that regulations for budgetary distribution are drawn up, procedures for the overall management of the teaching force established, curriculum and pedagogy designed and inspection and evaluation organised.[19] But, as Charlot noted, this system of planning had in practice been overtaken by local realities: in system-management terms, the centre lacked the capacity to control an ever more complex set of local developments.[20] The French state turned, therefore, to measures that denationalised some functions of the state, without, however, ditching the ideology of the republican school; if anything, *l'égalité des chances* was more central a principle in the 1980s than in earlier times.[21]

The devolution of central powers took several forms. *Déconcertation* meant that the centre shared some of its management responsibilities with regional bodies; *décentralisation* entailed the creation of independent decision-making centres at local level: communes became responsible for aspects of primary schooling, departments for the *collèges* and regions for the *lycées*. Alongside these developments emerged a third type of decentralisation, associated with the project of *Zones d'éducation prioritaires*. The ZEPs, located in 'disadvantaged' areas, were seen by policymakers as marking a break from republican centralism and a turn towards mobilising local capacities against school failure. They led to the emergence of distinct and various municipal education spaces, very heterogenous in terms of their objectives, but more or less unified around the theme of 'putting the child at the centre of the education system' that had been endorsed by 1989 legislation. In these spaces, educators in some cases saw themselves less as auxiliaries of the central state, than as advocates of alternative policy models.[22]

It is therefore possible to speak of a decentralisation whose antecedents pre-date neo-liberalism and are in part connected to an egalitarian project. But this does not mean that there are no later links to more market-centred models of reform. 'It is possible to observe a tension', write Duru-Bellat and van Zanten, between on the one hand a 'redistributive logic oriented towards the reduction of inequalities via forms of action that are better targeted, closer to their intended beneficiaries and more co-ordinated between the various providers'; and on the other, a 'logic of neo-liberal laisser-faire ... even though this does not declare itself as such'.[23] Thus, despite the endurance of the *carte scolaire* as a means of regulating and restricting school choice, researchers have noted the same phenomenon of competition between schools for certain kinds of pupils (and between parents for certain kinds of schools) that have emerged in other countries. The devotion of school resources to marketing has become commonplace, as have decisions by principals to maintain the attractiveness of the school to middle-class parents through grouping the 'best' pupils in elite classes.[24] This drift at the level of the locality has been reflected in political discourse: both Nicolas Sarkozy and Ségolène Royal, presidential candidates of the left and the right in 2007, called for an end to the *carte scolaire*.

A similar shift from local experiment to state-promoted laisser-faire can be detected, though on a smaller scale, in Italy. Monosta writes, in relation to the 1970s, of 'a significant movement for democratisation of school management [that] grew up during the early 1970s', involving elected boards of management which included representatives of head teachers, teachers, parents and, from upper secondary schools, even pupils.[25] Their powers were limited, however, and the funds at their disposal very small. Even so, the contrast between the principles of 1974 and the ideas of the school autonomy set out in later policy are plain: notions of equality and democratisation have been replaced by a discourse of quality and autonomy.

The Bassanini law of 1997 instituted a principle of autonomy, applicable to all educational institutions, which were enjoined to adapt their provision in response to local need – a principle which was in 2001 written into the Italian constitution and acclaimed by international opinion. Through autonomy – as the OECD's review of Italian education argued – attention could shift from laws that defined inputs (class size, pupil hours etc.) to a focus on learning outcomes and their national standardisation.[26] In the same period, the centre-left government introduced parity between private schools and public schools. Letizia Moratti could thus claim in several senses that her 2003 legislation was not a new Berlusconian adventure but an expression of a policy continuity which sympathetic academic commentators saw – potentially, and grandly – as a means of freeing civil society from the suffocating grip of the centralised state.[27] However, Moratti's programme accentuated the articulation between decentralising measures and a broader neo-liberal programme. It reduced the duration of schooling, subsidised private education – threatening increased competition between public and private sectors – and proposed measures whose outcome would be a reduction in teachers' jobs and an increase in their workload. 'Choice', 'quality' and 'autonomy' were inscribed not in a paradigm based on the associative ideals of a pluralist civil society, but in one that promised marketisation and an empty purse.

Always keeping in mind the great political transformation that decentralisation represents, it is to the detail of its processes that we now turn.

Forms of decentralisation

Education has followed in the tracks of uneven economic development and (in several cases) the regionalised reshaping of the nation-state. The former has often been a 'spontaneous' development: the concentration of private education in London or Madrid is a consequence both of the contemporary distribution of wealth and of the survival of traditional, elitist institutions. The latter is in some cases (Spain and more recently Britain and Italy) a product of struggles around issues of devolution and autonomy – in Spain the pressure of the Autonomous Communities has led to a 'practically total decentralisation' in respect of many aspects of administration:[28] final power over the schools is in the hands of the Councils of Education of the Autonomous Communities, which apply and adapt central legislation to their own territories. In Germany regionalisation is rooted in history and was confirmed in the post-war settlement; in France it is a relatively recent project of the central state. But whatever its provenance, regionalisation is now intertwined with processes central to NPM: the emergence of new, private providers; networking between public and private sectors; and the devolution of some decision-making responsibility to a subsidiary level.

Regionalisation is thought by policymakers to entail several advantages. As Charlot notes, the French modernisation projects of the 1980s and 1990s aimed to 'increase the spaces of responsibility at every level of the system, giving to the various decision makers the possibility of implementing real choices in the framework of broad national objectives' – though these choices were related to the building and management of schools, rather than the areas of curriculum and assessment, where the Ministry of Education retains control.[29] The regionalisation installed by the Moratti reforms is meant to have similar effects, calling into being a class of regional educational leaders at the same time as it promotes large-scale private involvement in vocational education.[30] In Spain, the regional autonomy enshrined in the 1978 constitution served to deflect political struggles away from a national focus, at the same time as it nurtured significant differences between rich and poor regions, in terms of the provision and quality of services and the pay and working conditions of teachers. Attac-France predicts similar consequences: the decentralisation of vocational education, announced in 2003 by the Raffarin government, for instance, amounts to the 'liquidation' of the laws and regulations which hold in place a unified system of national provision and the handing over of educational power to local, market-driven influences.[31] Critics of the Moratti legislation assume a similar development in Italy, especially given the influence of the Lega Nord, which openly pushes for a redistribution of resources in the direction of the more dynamic regions of Italy.

From one point of view, this unevenness is rational: where there is a demand for education, spending can rise; poor regions, lacking effective demand for high levels of schooling and vocational training, will find themselves 'naturally' held in check. But from another perspective, uneven development is a problem for national states. Regional problems of underfunding can bring governments into conflict with strong local movements of protest – as Claude Allègre found in Le Gard in 2000 – and in the process regional cases can come to be seen as symptoms of a national problem.[32] Alternatively, as in Germany, conflicts between centre and region can have long-term strategic effects. There are significant and enduring differences between *Länder*, in terms of educational organisation, ethos and performance: in the 1970s the *Länder* controlled by the right acted as a brake on the equal opportunity policies of the SPD. After 2000, regions such as Bavaria, Baden-Württemberg and Hesse accepted the theses of international policy orthodoxy, and pressed for *Länder* to be given complete authority to set education budgets and manage provision. Claiming that PISA results demonstrated the efficiency of systems like Bavaria's, and contrasting the performance of the CDP heartlands with the Federal average, they resisted government attempts to federalise policymaking, at the same time as they pressed for changes in the federal-level system of resource redistribution towards poorer *Länder*. In this latter sense, regionalisation contributed to a substantial legitimation crisis for a federal state which could guarantee neither a certain equalisation of educational resources, nor a cohesive response to new policy problems.

Decentralisation at the school level

Regionalisation is in some cases connected to the decentralisation project, but – as the English experience shows – it is not essential to its implementation. More generally significant is a shift in the governance from centre – or regional centre – to school. As with regionalisation, there are differences between the various national projects of school-level decentralisation – with England devolving more powers of financial action than other countries – but in many other respects differences now seem to relate more to the pace of implementation rather than its basic character. The Thélot Report claimed, 'The scale on which the mobilisation of [reforming] skills and energies can best be mobilised is that of the individual institution'.[33] This proposition meets with assent across Europe, and across much of the political spectrum: decentralisation is seen as democratic, empowering and efficient, allowing for 'the adjustment of the school curricula to the actual needs of the community'.[34] 'We desire greater autonomy for schools,' states the programme of the German Greens: 'higher quality, diversity and autonomy, and competition over the best school for children, all require being able to choose'.[35] In the same vein, the British Conservative Party commits itself to 'devolving budgets to schools wherever possible and practicable, such that schools are trusted with the greatest available sums to allocate under their own budget headings'.[36] In Italy it has become the task of individual institutions to concretise the 'offer' made by the education system, in the form of localised plans that emphasise the personalisation of the curriculum.[37]

As the Greens recognise, decentralisation may be presented as a democratising reform, but it is also one which is in most cases connected to marketisation. It usually involves the creation or extension of market or quasi-market relations, in at least three senses. Firstly, there is the quasi-market of supply and demand in relation to school admissions and 'parental choice' – a strand we explore further in chapter 5. Secondly, decentralisation gives rise to market relationships between schools and external suppliers, through which schools purchase from private companies or state agencies a range of goods and services, from building maintenance to the provision of training and support for teachers. Finally there are the market disciplines connected to these factors – pressures to hold down costs, to establish and market a public image, to raise new income and to manage staff in line with these priorities. Through its responses to these incitements and constraints, the decentralised school becomes an institution of a new type, with an ethos and a set of purposes markedly different from its predecessors.

To capture what is involved in the gradual and complex process of decentralisation, we will look at two national cases, the first is that of Germany – a decentralisation which is still in important respects 'to come'; the second is England, where nearly 20 years of government-driven change has implanted a well-developed form of decentralisation that has become the norm throughout the state system of schooling.

Germany: change through pilot projects

McKinsey consultant Jürgen Kluge advises German educationalists:

> To begin the necessary turnaround, we must place all the elements without exception on the test-bench and start to modernise our educational system with a whole ensemble of measures designed to act together. ... We must free schools from their bureaucratic embrace and give them freedom of action. In return we should demand quality and accountability. This has a variety of consequences for their internal life, ranging from financial independence via personnel policy to a differentiation in the service offered and different ways of structuring lessons. We need independent schools and independent pupils.[38]

In calling for 'modernisation', Kluge is of course pushing at an open door; and his attack on 'bureaucracy' hits only at a system which is entering a self-willed process of late modernisation.

Since the mid-1990s, the individual school and its capacities to improve standards has become the central focus of school research in Germany and the main question in public debate has been how to break the shackles of the bureaucratically governed school administration and set free innovation and creativity in a new 'institutional setting'. A decisive role in initiating and organising public discussion was played by the Bertelsmann Foundation and Reinhard Mohn, owner of the publishing and information technology corporation that is the foundation's funder. Mohn, together with Volkswagen and Deutsche Bank representatives, economists and educationists, was a prominent member of an Education Commission ('Future of Education – School of the Future') set up by the SPD in North Rhine-Westphalia in the early 1990s.[39] Their report, published in 1995, is a crucial text. It contains all the main features of the new institutional setting – semi-autonomous schools, competition, evaluation, competencies and key qualifications, modular structures, tighter connection of schools and the economy – but promotes them not as a single synchronised solution but as an incremental strategy: ideological cohesiveness is accompanied by tactical caution.

The main instrument of incremental change is the pilot project – an instrument which allows for the careful development of the necessary organisational inputs as well as for the acculturation of staff. Time, incrementalism and experiment are all thus important to a strategy that gains in conflict management and legitimation, what it lacks in terms of decisiveness. In the mid-1990s, some social democratic state governments, for instance in Hamburg, Bremen, Hesse and North Rhine-Westphalia, introduced elements of a decentralised and target/output-based steering strategy in education administration. In the context of a general discourse of autonomy and responsibilisation – *Eigenverantwortung* – these administrations brought about reforms that were in substance small, but in terms of their significance as historical markers, much greater. Head teachers' powers were strengthened, and heads enjoyed autonomous control over a small percentage of the overall budget – a budget that had previously been controlled in classic bureaucratised style on the basis of the regulations of the state finance system – the *Kameralistik*. A host of projects fostering decentralised development were introduced in North Rhine-Westphalia, the most heavily populated of the *Länder and* a traditional SPD stronghold. In Hesse, the SPD/Green coalition government introduced in the early 1990s some measures of decentralisation. School Councils were established, through which parents, teachers and students were given some control over pedagogical and organisational questions; in some parts of the Land, management of buildings and maintenance passed to local authorities. Shortly before its election defeat in 1999, the coalition moved up a gear, committing itself to the formal introduction of *Neue Verwaltungssteuerung* – New Public Management. Again, this was in the form of a pilot project, limited to one district – with the intention that by 2008, with the full support of the coalition's CDU successor, it should become state-wide. Entitled 'Steering by Objectives', the project involved the contractualisation of relationships between individual schools and the Land authority, through the specification of financial outputs which the schools committed themselves to achieve. Over the same period, North Rhine-Westphalia piloted the recommendations of a succession of projects instigated by the Bertelsmann-NRW report of 1997, Schule & Co. Through 'self-steering' and quality assurance – by 2006 over 1200 schools were using self-evaluation instruments designed by Bertelsmann[40] – projects such as the Land's NRW Schule 21 intended to manage resources effectively and improve the output measures of schools. They created a framework in which it would be possible to hire personnel on conditions which the school management thinks are best for the school, and in which decisions on organisation at school and classroom levels could be taken at institutional level. Likewise, the SPD–PDS coalition in Berlin set up in 2003–4 the 'Autonomous Schools Model project' – another pilot – that aimed to 'change educational governance by setting standard targets and controlling costs'.[41]

What had begun at project and experimental level, heavily propelled by the Bertelsmann foundation, after 2002 shifted towards the level of *Länder*-wide policy. Adhering to international policy paradigms in its support for semi-autonomous schools, competition, evaluation, competencies and key qualifications, modular structures and the closer connecting of schools to the economy, it emphasised rationalisation, efficiency and privatisation within the structures of a system based on strict social selectivity. Thus the viewpoint of the 1970s – to leave the system more or less as it was – was replicated in a new form of 'modest modernisation'.

These extensive pilots are signs of a powerful consensus among policymakers: Christian Democrats, Greens, Social Democrats and the Party of Democratic Socialism are all committed, alongside the most influential business groups, to changes that are not in formal terms constitutional but that involve significant *de facto* shifts away from elected administrations (local, regional and national) towards unaccountable but financially autonomous school managements. Ingrid Lohmann notes that when the public purse is declared empty, the pressure on schools to secure their position by participating in such change is increased, and that the rhetoric of partnership and civil society that accompanies it obscures the fact that in practice it is only some sorts of partner, and some sectors of civil society, that are encouraged to have an influence.[42]

England

In 2000, the employers' federations of seven European countries published a report that summarised their agenda for school systems in Europe, making use of all the familiar terms of NPM discourse in its call for a programme that included 'national standards of achievement and independent evaluation', 'competition between schools to raise standards', 'autonomy for schools', reform of the management of staff and teaching methods' and 'the quality control of teaching and learning'.[43] Surveying the state of progress towards these desiderata, the employers concluded that of all countries, it was England that was performing best.

This was a verdict that would have surprised those critics whose accounts of the structural problems of English education had dominated the 1980s.[44] How had an apparently inert system come to experience such a broad and dynamic programme of change? Part of the answer lies in the intensity with which educational failure was perceived: critique, initially from the right, and subsequently from within the Labour Party, contributed to the crisis of the reforming bloc.[45] (In West Germany, by contrast, the success of the post-war settlement, in terms of economic growth and stability of employment and welfare erected social and cultural barriers to neo-liberal change.) Translating crisis to political capital, Thatcher's government was able to defeat teacher trade unionism, deprive local authorities of their educational powers and introduce a wide-ranging programme of change. Nowhere else was centralisation/decentralisation so openly pursued as a confrontational political strategy; nowhere was it presented so strongly as a central part of the response to a century of decline.

The actions of the central state apart, confrontation is most obvious in the management régimes of the decentralised school. Policy has sought to develop – in spite of difficulties in the recruitment and retention of heads, especially in the primary sector – a strong management cadre. Head teachers now possesses management functions previously located higher up the state education hierarchy: they are responsible for managing the workforce, for 'product' innovation and for navigating successfully the complex environment of the marketplace and government imperatives, and their powers in these respects go further than those established in other countries. Since the LOCE of 1995, head teachers in Spain are no longer elected by school-workers, and their powers have increased. Likewise in Italy, where Maccarini comments on the post-2003 status of school principals that they have become the 'pivots of reform' and networkers *par excellence*:

> One might almost say that the essence of school autonomy rests on the new responsibilities of the director, which from now on will include managing the institution, representing it legally, organising its efficiency, co-ordinating the management of human, material and financial resources, maintaining relations with trade unions, working in partnership with other organisations.[46]

But these are still lesser powers than those possessed by English heads, who in association with their governing bodies have powers to determine teacher numbers, and to make spending decisions. They also have available a range of measures for the control and direction of a workforce deprived of national negotiating rights, dispossessed by law (The Teachers' Pay and Conditions Act of 1987) of the capacity to refuse managerial directive and subject to salary-related 'performance management' of their work.

Head teachers in England are thus the interface between particular forms of centralisation and decentralisation, the decisive link between government policy and its implementation by teachers. They themselves have to be motivated, and provided with a technology and a value-system for use in the management of their workforce, in the context of a system of government-driven targets, rewards and sanctions. Since the authoritarian managerialism that was essential to the task of replacing the old school regime has had negative effects on teachers' morale and commitment, the agencies of government have made a new turn. There is an emphasis on securing the willing cooperation of school staff, with head teachers being encouraged to create an 'open cooperative culture', in which teachers are made to feel involved in the 'visions, strategies and plans' of the school, and to feel responsible for 'customer satisfaction'.[47] As Hatcher notes, this turn to 'total quality management' encompasses rather than rejects a focus on performance indicators such as pupil test scores; it is a discourse appropriate to a period in which the problem for reform is less the overt resistance of teachers than a certain withholding on their part of consent.

In matters of budgetary control, entrepreneurial initiative, differential (bid-based) funding and devolved managerial authority, England – as the employers note – leads the field. Government would like this autonomy to develop further. Successful schools will gain 'earned autonomy', and with it the freedom to vary the frameworks that regulate the national curriculum and the pay and conditions of teachers.[48] They could also take on a more active economic role. The 2002 Education Act empowers school-governing bodies to form, become a member of or invest in companies to purchase or provide services and facilities to schools and communities. In this way, schools might become commercial entities, selling goods and services in an emergent market. Schools, in this context, are not restricted to being the objects of intervention by private companies. At least in terms of policy's intentions, they become themselves an entrepreneurial force, operating in the admissions market and seeking business subsidy and tie-ins. ('You must never turn down opportunities to get money' said the head of a primary school in Surrey which had just sold to a local estate agent the right to be hyperlinked to the school's website'[49]). Decentralisation in the English context is an ethical revolution too.

Notes

1. See the work of the project, 'Regulation and Inequalities in European School Systems', to be published as C. Maroy et al., *Ecole, régulation et marché. Une analyse de six espaces scolaires locaux en Europe*, (Paris: Presses Universitaires de France, 2007, coll. Education et sociétés).

2. Francois Dubet, 'The French Education System: institutional transformation or neo-liberal shift?' *Newsletter of the Institutional Institute for Educational Planning* (Paris: IIEP-UNESCO April–June 2004) pp. 12–13.

3. European Commission, *Teaching and Learning: towards the learning society*, White Paper on Education and Training (Brussels: European Commission, 1995) quoted in Nico Hirtt, 'Three Axes of School Marchandisation,' *European Educational Research Journal* 3.92 2004, pp. 442–53.

4. M. Henry et al., *The OECD, Globalisation and Education Policy* (Oxford: Pergamon, 2001) p. 34.

5. OECD, *Structural Adjustment and Economic Performance* (Paris: OECD, 1987) p. 45.

6. OECD, *Governance in Transition: public management reforms in OECD countries* (Paris: OECD, 1995) p. 8.

7. Alexiadou (2005) in Coulby et al.

8. Henry et al., *The OECD, Globalisation and Education Policy.*

9. OECD/Centre for Educational Research and Innovation (CERI), quoted in Henry et al., *The OECD, Globalisation and Education Policy* p. 89.

10. 'OECD (1998) Human Capital Investment: an international comparison' Paris, OECD, p. 53.

11. OECD, *Measuring Student Knowledge and Skills: a new framework for assessment* (Paris: OECD, 1999), p. 11.

12. OECD, human capital investment: an international comparison (Paris: OECD, 1998) pp. 83–4.

13. OECD, 1999, p. 11.

14. This is not to deny that in some circumstances, PISA findings could be used to serve more critical ends. In Belgium, the Appel pour une école démocratique employed PISA data to expose the shortcomings of policy for the education of migrant children. See Nico Hirtt, *PISA 2003 et les résultats des élèves issus de l'immigration en Belgique* www.ecoledemocratique.org, June 2006.

15. 'Inspectors get power to shut down schools', Times Educational Supplement 13th May 2005 p. 13.

16. See K. Jones, 'An old future; a new past: Labour remakes the English school' in R. Johnson and D. Steinberg, *Blairism and the War of Persuasion.*

17. Danish Employers' Federation www.da.dk/bilag/bildungsbroscheuere.engl.pdf.

18. Deutsche (2003) *Mehr Wachstum fur Deutschland.*

19. Lise Demailly et al., 'Analyse de l'évolution des modes de regulation institutionalisée dans les systeme éducatif francais'. Paper prepared for the research project, *Changes in regulation modes and social production of inequalities in education systems: a European comparison* March 2002, http://www.girsef.ucl.ac.be/France2.pdf.

20. Bernard Charlot, 'La territorialisation des politiques educatives: une politique nationale', in B. Charlot, B., (ed), *L'école et le territoire* (Paris: Armand Colin, 1994) p. 36.

21. *Le Monde* notes that the expression *égalité des chances* was used for the first time by Jean-Pierre Chevenement, education minister, in 1986. *Egalité des chances, une expression, un principe et une loi.* 1 December 2006.

22. Demailly et al., pp. 22–4. Marie Duru-Bellat and Agnes van Zanten, *Sociologie de l'école* (Paris: Armand Colin, 2006) pp. 89–90.

23. Duru-Bellat and van Zanten, *Sociologie de l'école*, p. 90.

24. Ibid.
25. Monasta, *Education in a Single Europe*, p. 242.
26. OECD, *Reviews of National Policies for Education: Italy* (Paris: OCED, 1998).
27. Andrea Maccarini, 'La réforme de l'éducation en Italie: un exemple de gouvernance?', *Education et Sociétés* 14.2, 167–188, 2004.
28. Pauli Davila Balsera, 'The Educational System and National Identities: the case of Spain in the twentieth century', *History of Education*, 34.1, pp. 23–40, p. 37, 2005.
29. Charlot, 'La territorialisation des politiques educatives', p. 3.
30. Gennaro Capasso, 'Scuola Devoluta: regionalizzazione, territorialità' Giornale di Cobas-Scuola March–April 2005, p. 4. Despite the 2006 change of government in Italy, and despite the failure of devolution/regionalisation proposals to pass the test of a national referendum, it seems likely that the 'rational core' of the Moratti legislation – which, as Maccarini comments, is supported by the entire political class – will be retained and even raised to a new level. Luigi Berlinguer, architect of centre-left reform in the late 1990s, commented, 'The management of all schools, not only the technical schools [i.e. the Moratti proposal] is to be transferred to the regions. This will be difficult, delicate and unpopular with teachers as well as presenting a risk for the historical lack of equilibrium between the Italian regions. However, it is absolutely necessary and must be resolutely carried out.' *Italia Oggi* 20th June 2006.
31. Attac-France, 'Décentralisation solidaire ou marchande' (Attac: Montreuil-sous-Bois Mai, 2004).
32. Gilbert Estève 'Flashback on a 45 Day Campaign: the teachers' strike in the south of France' *Education and Social Justice*, 2.3, pp. 51–5, 2000.
33. Quoted in Nathalie Duceux, 'Du rapport Thélot à la loi Fillon', *Critique Communiste* , p. 12, 2004.
34. UNESCO/World Education Forum (2000) *Country Reports: Italy*, p. 3.
35. Party Program and Principles: *The Future is Green: Alliance 90/The Greens* p. 55 http://archiv.gruene-partei.de/dokumente/grundsatzprogramm-english.pdf.
36. Conservative Policy Unit, *No Child Left Behind* (London: Conservative Party, 2002) p. 5.
37. Maccarini, 'La réforme de l'éducation en Italie'.
38. Reference to follow.
39. Zukunft der Bildung – Schule der Zukunft: Denkschrift der Kommission Zukunft der Bildung – Schule der Zukunft Luchterhand-Verlag, 1995.
40. Ingrid Lohmann, 'Jedes Schule ein kleines Unternehmen', *Freitag* 4 August 2006, www.freitag.de.
41. http://www.senbjs.berlin.de/bildung/schulreform/thema_schulreform.asp.
42. Lohmann, 'Jedes Schule ein kleines Unternehmen'.
43. CBI, *In Search of Quality in Schools: the employers' perspective* (London: CBI, 2000).
44. From a long list Corelli Barnett, *The Audit of War* (London: Macmillan, 1986) stands out.
45. Ken Jones, *Right Turn: the Conservative revolution in education* (London: Hutchinson, 1989).
46. Maccarini, 'La réforme de l'éducation en Italie', p. 180.
47. Richard Hatcher, 'The Distribution of Leadership and Power in Schools', *British Journal of Sociology of Education*, 26.2 2005, 253–67.
48. DfES, *Investment for Reform*, chap. 5 (London: DfES, 2002).
49. *Times Educational Supplement*, 17 October 2003.

4
Privatisation: From the Margins to the Centre

Among the regulatory forces discussed in the previous chapter, one – privatisation – stands out, because it has a double function. Privatisation is in part, and importantly, about the introduction to the governance of education of new interests and perspectives. But it needs also be discussed directly in economic terms – for education is one of the sectors newly identified by capital as an important source of value. We have suggested already that the extent and shape of privatisation are matters of important and unresolved debate. In this chapter, we attempt to sketch privatisation's forms and trajectories. Once again, these are more visible in England than elsewhere; and while we do not believe that England represents a future to which other countries are, as it were, naturally and heliotropically turning, England certainly provides both a repertoire of policy change and a demonstration of how the intensification of private-sector activity depends upon legal, political and cultural changes that the government has done much to initiate and that are the outcomes of sharp contestation.

A new market for capital

In no country has the expansion of education under state control led to the abolition of private education. Even at the high point of post-war reform, private sector institutions remained significant in several ways – as elite bastions, as continuing forms of religious influence, as signifiers of political freedom and in some cases as relatively cheap alternatives to state provision. These forms of private provision have been in several respects important to the continuing reproduction of social inequalities – the English public schools and religious education in Spain are cases in point. Alongside them, private extra-institutional activities such as home tutoring have never ceased to be significant, while state education also provided profitable opportunities for private capital in many fields, from construction to publishing.

The privatisation that is now on the agenda of global agencies and European governments is in part occurring through a deepening and extension of these activities – the conversion of home tutoring from a sector based on part-time self-employment to one involving public companies is a one case in point; large-scale capital investment in private schooling is another. But present expansion amounts to more than a quantitative increase in old forms of private sector education and is better seen as part of a much bigger upheaval. In David Harvey's words, neo-liberal strategies involve a process in which problems of capital over-accumulation and unprofitability are resolved through the opening of 'new territories' to capitalist development – a process in which 'state power' is a major player.[1] The privatisations that swept through Britain in the 1980s and countries such as France and Italy in the following decade were the first stage in such a process, in which state industries from electricity to tobacco were alienated to the private sector. From the late 1990s, a second wave of privatisation has occurred, in which education has a significant part. It is one of Harvey's 'new territories', in which potentially profitable sectors are alienated from the public domain to the private, and investment opportunities are created in emerging areas of activity.

The action of governments is essential to this colonisation of public territory and to the subsidising and protection of nascent enterprise that accompany it. Thus the Confederation of British Industry compliments government on legislation that has 'created the conditions within which an initial market could be established that actively encouraged new entrants'.[2] Giovanni Cimbalo writes of similar developments in Italy where, 'in the present state of the "education market" ... there are no profit margins which do not derive directly from state assistance and public funding'.[3] Others offer empirical support for this claim: in Lombardy, for instance, the burgeoning private sector (businesses, religious organisations and some trade unions) controls almost the whole of the vocational education sector, but can only do so on the basis of massive subsidy from the regional government and the European Social Fund.[4] In addition to market-making of this sort, privatisation requires a labour of legitimisation: if education is to become a site for the accumulation of capital, then both government and business interests need to ensure that this is regarded by their populations as both normal and advantageous. So when Blair speaks of the advantages of private sector involvement, he refers not only to a 'financial endowment' but to the sector's 'vision' and 'commitment', qualities that he implies are not possessed by the public sector.[5]

For the analysis of privatising processes, then, understanding of state involvement is essential. 'State' is of course a term with an international dimension. As we have suggested in chapter 2, the privatisation of public services is an agenda promulgated by the supranational organisations that seek to shape the global economy. Thus for the World Bank 'although the state still has a central role in ensuring the provision of basic services – education, health, infrastructure – it is not obvious that the state must be the only provider, or a provider at all.'[6] For the Centre for Educational Research and Innovation (CERI), the end of the era of public provision is also the end of national systems of education. CERI, the education arm of the OECD, talks of the coming permeability of national educational borders, envisaging the 'substantial involvement of trans-national as well as national companies in schools'.[7] The General Agreement on Trade and Services (GATS) – established under the auspices of the WTO in 1994 and continuously renegotiated since then – provides the potential legal framework for such liberalisation, since it would remove any internal government restrictions on the provision of public services, including education.[8]

But there are unresolved difficulties here for national governments. On the one hand, especially for countries such as Britain, the United States and Australia, where edubusiness is strong and has international ambitions, the prising open of national boundaries has clear advantages. On the other, giving up control over systems which for more than a century have been centrally important in shaping collective identities is not something that can be lightly done: 'schools are institutions of the state,' read the Prussian Land Law of 1794, and such concerns with education as a means of state-building cannot easily be set aside.[9] The dilemmas consequent upon such traditions, alongside the strong political opposition that GATS has stimulated, explains the inconclusive nature of GATS discussions. In 2000, Pascal Lamy, then EC Trade Commissioner, was insisting that liberalisation was a two-way street: 'if we want to improve our own access to foreign markets then we can't keep our protected sectors out of the sunlight...'. But by 2003, Lamy was less bullish: the EC would not further commit Europe's education sectors to the free market rules of GATS.[10] Thus, the creation of a global framework within which the liberalisation of education systems would become virtually compulsory for national governments has yet to come about and to that extent the fears of the anti-globalisation movement have not been realised. For all that, privatisation has taken off, with extensive international ambitions but practical parameters that are at present national: it is driven by the policy options and capacity for action of particular national governments; it is therefore unevenly developed, and the domains of the companies that drive it are for the moment mostly located within national frontiers.

Forms of privatisation

In this chapter, we focus on five forms of privatisation. The first is outsourcing – the alienation of public educational provision and the accompanying development of private companies, providing educational goods and services for a profit. The second is aspects of commercialisation– the entry of private companies into public educational space through advertising, sponsorship and other activities aimed at the direct selling of products or the promotion of pro-business ideas to pupils and to their parents. The third is supplementary education – the provision of education goods and services outside the state system but based on demand generated by it, as students/families seek positional advantage within a competitive education system – for example, private tutors for examinations and software for home learning. The fourth is the impact of 'new' privatisation on older forms of private provision and the final is the wider economising processes through which business interests impose themselves on schools.

Outsourcing

We begin with the outsourcing of state education, focusing on England, where it is most strongly developed. The process began in the 1980s, when the Conservatives deregulated the provision of school meals and transport, opening the way for local authorities to contract the work to private companies. After Labour's election victory in 1997, outsourcing developed rapidly right across the public sector and now affects every part of the education system, as an integral part of the modernising project. Modernisation in its English form includes such features as curriculum standardisation, management training, performance management of teachers, extensive inspection of schools, assessment systems, target-setting and monitoring of student performance. In each of these instances, government has turned as a matter of course to the private sector, arguing in the process that the sector is both cost-effective and dynamic, and is uniquely capable of modernising change. 'For most of the twentieth century,' wrote Blair's education advisor in 2001, 'the drive for educational progress came from the public sector'. Now, though, it is the 'growing and vibrant private sector' that possesses ... the energy, knowledge, imagination, skill and investment ... to meet the immense challenge of educational reform'.[11] As a result of government support – which has increased to the point where the share of 2004–6 school expenditure involving the private sector amounted to between one-fifth and one-quarter – a range of private enterprise activities has developed.[12] One of the consequences of the attrition of Local authorities has been the emergence of a layer of petty entrepreneurs – self-employed consultants, often ex-heads and ex-LEA advisers, working for LEAs, schools, government agencies and private companies, often on a succession of short-term contracts. It is estimated that there are at least 8,000 education consultants in the private sector, including 5,600 free-lance inspectors on Ofsted's books. In 2003, £400 million were spent on private sector consultancy – the equivalent of £15,700 for every school, including nursery and private schools, in England.[13] Alongside this layer (and gradually supplanting it) have emerged a number of big- and medium-sized education businesses. Some of these, especially the medium-size companies (such as Nord Anglia, 2004 turnover £50 million) confine themselves mainly to education. Others, such as SERCO, a British-based spin-off of the American RCA, generate massive business – SERCO's 2003 turnover was £1.6 billion, 73% of it generated within Britain – and operate across a range of sectors, from education to 'defence', transport to catering. All emphasise that they are companies of a new kind, sensitive to the needs and ethos of the public sector. Thus the Tribal Group, established in 1999, according to its website is 'the second fastest growing company floated on the Stock Exchange between 1998 and 2002', stresses that 'many of our directors and con-sultants have public sector backgrounds and strongly identify with the aims and objectives of our client organisations'.[14]

But whatever the rhetoric of Downing Street advisors and the compa-nies themselves, it is less the creativity and sympathetic qualities of the private sector than the cost reductions it can achieve that make it attrac-tive to the government. In the case of school meals, privatisation has reduced costs by holding down both wages and nutritional levels – the latter, a problem belatedly recognised by government in 2006, when it took action to raise them. In other cases, the private sector has been able through the technology-based standardisation of its products to achieve efficiencies and economies of scale. The use of ICT is central here. In the field of assessment, for instance, the multinational publishing company Pearson Longman has bought a share of Edexcel, one of the main institutions responsible for public examinations. Their new company, London Examinations, set up in 2005, promised a 'technology-based approach to marking and processing examinations'.[15] Initiatives of these sorts are most profitable, of course, in the context of the standardisation of teaching and learning systems. Standardisation has offered business opportunities to companies like Sam Learning, a privately owned business which claims a client base of 800,000 students in British secondary schools, and which has developed learning systems that use ICT to track student achievement and offer 'personalised' learning packages.

The private sector offers advantages beside those of cost. Outsourcing works on the basis of contract; contracts allow government to specify objectives in concrete and narrow terms, which private companies can closely follow. Such arrangements minimise the 'noise' – the tendency to adapt and deflect government initiative – that has occurred when the implementation of reforms has been left to public sector professionals. One study of the private sector involvement in the performance management of teachers makes this point very well, albeit in relation to local authorities rather than to the internal functioning of the school. Mahony and her colleagues are told by one of their interviewees that

> The DfEE could not have implemented the policy without the private sector providing a regional infrastructure. ... They didn't want to manage it centrally. They didn't trust LEAs to deliver it. ... And, doing it through contractors is effectively doing the thing directly.[16]

Similar examples can be found in other fields – from Capita's role in the training of teachers in the teaching of literacy and numeracy – a five-year contract worth £177 million – to the private sector's operational responsibility for school inspections. In cases like these, privatisation is best understood not so much as a private sector intrusion into the state that weakens its capacities, but as a regulatory strategy on the part of government that removes agentive power from social interests that are seen as lacking the capability and the will to implement modernisation, and concentrates it at the service of a central power. In return for their role in this centralising process, private sector companies enjoy a close relationship with government agencies, and can rely on 'soft' contracts, often on an extensive national scale. Hence the sector's expansion. In the words of the British company Capital Strategies, 'there is currently a keen appetite in the private equity community for public sector professional services companies, reflecting ... the excellent growth fundamentals ... generally enjoyed by these markets'.[17] And as the Tribal Group puts it, 'the substantial investment in and modernisation of public services presents a window of opportunity' through which private companies can shape 'the future of public service delivery.'[18]

The largest project involving the private sector is the Private Finance Initiative (PFI). Building and renovation used to be funded by grants from government to LEAs and by LEA borrowing. Under the PFI, by contrast, LEAs enter into a contract with a private sector consortium to design, build, finance and operate school buildings, and to provide other services such as cleaning, catering and ground maintenance. The consortium is paid back by the LEA over a period of time, generally 25–30 years. During this period the school premises are owned, managed and operated by the company,[19] rather than the local authority or the school governors. By September 2005, there were over 200 PFI schools projects in England, which were worth £1.6 billion. They have provided above-average profits in spite of some well-publicised failures, notably that of the construction company Jarvis. According to a report in *The Guardian*, 'Construction companies engaged in the private finance initiative expect to make between 3 and 10 times as much money as they do on traditional contracts'.[20] Profit margins range from 7.5% to 15%, and from 10% to 20% for equity holders in the consortium company. The UK construction industry grew by over 8% in 2003 while in Germany and France the sector slumped by 2.5% and 0.7% respectively, according to a report by the European Construction Industry federation, which identified PFI as the main reason for the strong UK performance. The *Financial Times* confirmed that PFI is becoming an attractive option for investors – after the financial risks associated with the construction phase of projects, they offer the prospect of a guaranteed long-term profit.[21] Not surprisingly, PFI contracts have become tradable commodities. The trade union Unison reports that a number of merchant banks have establishment investment funds specifically geared to the takeover of PFI projects.[22]. Through such takeover, control over school facilities can thus pass from one company to another without reference to the public interest. PFI consortia are emphatic that trading of this kind is a purely private matter: 'these are not public assets but private sector concessions,' the chief executive of one PFI consortium has argued – 'so during the period of the concession the private sector effectively owns the school'.[23]

It is perhaps at this point that the tensions between government policy and private interest are likely to emerge. But at present there is no foreseeable end to the enthusiasm of the Labour government for the private sector. Edubusiness is seen as a growing part of the services sector, and an area in which the state should come to the assistance of the private sector in promoting the accumulation of private capital. Since 1997, government, working with the lobbying organisation the 'Liberalisation of Trade in Services Committee', has fostered the development of British edubusiness as a major player in the global services economy, fostering the growth of firms that have become 'leaders in the field, having helped transform privatisation from an academic concept into practical policy capable of application throughout the world'.[24] SERCO is thus able to argue that 'our strength in the UK education market provides a very strong platform for participating in education development on an international basis'.[25] Most recently, the employers' organisation the Confederation of British Industry, has urged government to outsource more state education provision, so that 'the UK does not lose its position as a leading player internationally'.[26]

Commercialisation

Alongside privatisation – and often in advance of it – the school is increasingly becoming a commercial as well as an educational space. Again, this is a development not only tolerated but encouraged by governments. The DfES in England has an 'education-business' website, which lists the benefit to large companies of involvement in schools: they can 'acquire better market knowledge, tap into local creativity to develop new products and gain new and more loyal customers'.[27] More guardedly, the Jospin government of the late 1990s promulgated a 'code of good practice' permitting commercial advertising and sponsorship if it presented 'a pedagogic interest'. Likewise since 1997, many German states – Berlin, Sachsen-Anhalt, Bremen and North Rhine-Westphalia among them – have made legislative changes so as to allow billboards to be put up in schools. The European Commission, meanwhile, published in 1998 a report *Marketing and the School*, which criticised abuses but also approved the 'added value' of advertising in opening up the school to the wider world (Laval, p. 164).[28]

In these increasingly favourable circumstances, commercialisation takes three main forms. The first and most widespread is the direct sale of products – fizzy drinks, crisps etc – to pupils, usually through vending machines. The financial value of such sales to schools is considerable – the British teachers' union, NUT, estimated that it could amount in a large school to £50,000 in a year. For many schools this was an inducement that over-rode nutritional conceptions.[29] The second form is 'cause-related marketing' – schemes which provide educational benefits in return for purchases (e.g. vouchers and tokens with products which can be exchanged for books and computers). Advertisers use these schemes to reach not just pupils but also their parents, aligning family budgets with commercially promoted educational benefits. The biggest British supermarket company, Tesco, launched a voucher-based 'Computers for Schools' scheme, in which vouchers gained by shopping at Tesco could be accumulated and exchanged for school IT equipment. The rate of exchange was not generous. The consumer magazine *Which?* estimated that people would need to buy nearly £45,000 worth of shopping for one scanner, which the store itself sold for £80. Similarly, a school participating in the 'Cadbury Get Active' campaign would need to encourage children to spend more than £2,000 on chocolate and consume nearly 1.25 million calories to win the volleyball posts and net offered through the scheme.

In addition to stimulating the sales of particular products, the commercial sponsorship of school materials and activities has a more general intended effect on pupils, parents and teachers.[30] It educates children and young people in consumerism and in doing so presents a partial view of the world: Laval analyses a teaching pack produced by Renault; it contains a film about the history of the company which excludes the voices of Renault workers and is silent on the company's collaboration with the Nazis. Sponsorship also has a powerful effect on the culture of teachers and school management: it promotes the idea that education and business are in harmony, aligns schools with commercial agenda and promotes an entrepreneurial ethos as schools are driven for financial reasons to seek sponsorship. As one head teacher commanded his pupils, in response to a campaign by the Pepsico-owned Walker's Crisps that offered books in exchange for empty crisp packets: 'Get munching!'

The third form of commercialisation – the sponsorship of educational resources – deepens these tendencies towards the integration of the work of the school and the strategies of business. In some cases such sponsorship is designed to promote purchases by children of a particular product. In other cases, these business strategies are on a grand scale. In 2003, Microsoft reached an agreement with the French government to update, for free, the software systems of primary schools, collèges and lycées. The agreement, which also included arrangements for the training of staff and the licensing of Word and Windows, was transparently an attempt to make Microsoft the official IT language of the French school system, at the expense of freely provided alternative systems such as Linux.

At other points, the intended commercial benefit is more indirect: to promote a point of view and climate of opinion favourable to an often controversial product – Shell has a long history of sponsoring curriculum material on the environment – or to help transform education into a more business-friendly milieu. This was the purpose of what has been so far the most contested episode of commercialisation. Crédit Industriel et Commercial, one of the largest French banks, organised for several years a role-play game – 'Masters of the Economy' – that involved some 30,000 students in simulated stock-market trading. Teachers in England – where key materials related to the teaching of citizenship are sponsored by Barclays Bank – would have accepted such an initiative as normal. In France, it remained problematic. Supported by Attac-France, Gilbert Molinier, a teacher at the Lycée Auguste Blanqui, in Seine-St-Denis, argued that the bank's invitation to schools was unlawful and took legal action against the school's principal. In 2004, the tribunal examining the case found that the invitation issued to the school was impermissible under French law – which forbids initiatives of a commercial character within the school.[31] When Molinier turned to the courts, he was appealing to a model of education, and of its separation from immediate economic interests, that continues to hinder a remaking of French schooling along standard 'anglo-saxon' lines.

Supplementary education

Even more widespread than commercialisation is the direct funding of education provision by families at point of use through the payment of fees, rather than funding provision through the general tax system so that it is free at point of use. The example which has attracted most attention in this respect is the move by several European governments to introduce fees for university tuition – an initiative fought hard, though so far unsuccessfully, by students in Britain and Germany between 2003 and 2006. Less controversial is the pervasive practice of schools asking for donations, often on a regular basis, from parents, to cover various costs or pay for additional resources and activities. Although a principle of schooling in France is that it is 'gratuit' as well as secular, in practice every French school relies on discretionary regular donations from parents, the *coopérative scolaire* – the inadequate level of state funding accounting for the importance of parental donations. In addition, parents pay for supplementary provision. In the state-subsidised private schools of Spain – the 'centros concertados', which in theory provide an education free at the point of use – there exist numerous demands (uniforms, reinforcement classes, extra-curricular activities) all of which involve extra costs. Parents' willingness to pay such costs acts in practice as a filtering mechanism to determine entry to the school – Bernal notes, in the case of Zaragoza, that this is an effective method of excluding children from Gypsy families.[32]

Parents also invest enormously in private tuition and educational materials, especially software for home learning and textbooks and workbooks for practice in answering exam questions. These materials, distributed as much through supermarkets as through traditional bookshops, are driven by and geared to improving performance within the state system, in particular to improving test and examination scores. Such investment, evidence of a commercialised and utilitarian 'learning society,' is spread across social classes. More elaborate educational purchases, however, are the prerogative of middle-class parents. Even here there are some exceptions: in England, supplementary classes run by community organisations for African-Caribbean children attempt to compensate for relatively low levels of achievement by them in the state school system. But across Europe, the growth of private home tutoring, provided for profit by individuals and increasingly by companies, speaks of a middle-class attempt to maintain and improve positional advantage in the education system and acts as a powerful reinforcer of social inequality. In Italy the number of students attending private ' exam factories' to obtain their diplomas has risen.The Moratti reform enormously facilitated this process through a revision of exam procedures. In London, according to research conducted among final-year primary schoolchildren, home tutoring has become the norm for middle-class students, and is leading to rapid further increases in educational and social segregation.[33]

Striking evidence of the increasing educational and economic importance of tutoring is provided by the growth of the France-based company Acadomia. Acadomia, founded in 1993, has 54 (franchised) branches in France, alongside others in Spain, Germany and Italy. According to Thierry Brulavoine, in 2005 it had 15,000 tutors, 50,000 pupils on its books and a 2001 turnover of €22 million.[34] Acadomia is significant not only because of its size and rate of growth, but because of the organisational model it represents – a reliance on precarious labour, on favourable government treatment through the tax system, on extensive national advertising, on a skeletal infrastructure, on a growing set of customer needs and, not least, on partnership arrangements with a number of other corporations. Arrangements with insurance companies offer parents teaching from Acadomia when their child is ill and absent from school. Through an arrangement with the electrical chain store Darty, Acadomia will assist parents with computer installation. A deal with Vivendi allows teachers to buy educational materials at a reduced price, and similar deals with other companies permit free access to educational websites. All in all, Acadomia suggests something of the possible future of private education, a formidable interlinked culture of extra-institutional learning.

Private schools

In each of our countries, the private sector forms a significant part of the education system. The EU statistical agency, Eurydice, surveyed in 2000 the extent of private provision – around 30% in Spain, 20% in France, 7% in Britain and Germany and 6% in Italy.[35] As we indicated in chapter 1, much of this provision is tied to long-established interests, both religious and secular-elitist. Over the last 15 years, however, shifts in policy and new social demands have nearly everywhere led to a strengthening of the private sector, and in some cases to the emergence of new kinds of private schools, strongly orientated towards the for-profit supply of education. The perceived crisis of public education is an important factor in this shift: private education, whether in low-cost church schools, or in secular establishments, is seen by many parents as an alternative to state provision.

In France, the Mitterrand government of the early 1980s failed in its efforts to bring to an end the dual system of state and private (subsidised) schools inherited from the beginning of the Gaullist era. As a result, there remains in place a private system, which – at one point or other in their careers – involves one-third of the school-student population. The subsidised school now constitutes not so much a religious haven as a model of institutional autonomy which neo-liberals seek to emulate, restoring respectability and attractiveness to ideas which defenders of the republican school see as a return to the anti-statism and anti-centralism of the early nineteenth century.[36]

In Italy too, conflicts that have their origins in earlier periods have developed – under the sign of neo-liberalism – in new directions. As we sketched in chapter 3, in 2000, the Italian parliament at the behest of the d'Alema government approved a law that allowed private schools equal status with the public sector. The legislation provided the occasion for contest between the proponents of the *Scuola della Repubblica* (who defended broadly universalistic arguments) and a wide range of Catholic, privatising and modernising forces who advanced a programme of choice and diversity, supposedly in line with contemporary demands and lifestyles, which required a break with the 'uniformity' of the education system underwritten by the constitution. Thus, while the law was seen by its many critics as part of a slow shuffle towards privatisation, it also presented a different model of inclusion, of the role of education in the national culture, and of Italian identity. As in France, the unravelling of the school of the republic was connected to the political and cultural issues that lay at the heart of the post-war polity.

In 2002, in defiance of the constitutional ban on the public funding of private education, Berlusconi's government took d'Alema one step further and initiated a national fund aimed at subsidising enrolment in private institutions. Subsequently eight Italian regions – including the biggest, Lombardy – introduced various forms of educational voucher, reimbursing parents for the tuition fees they paid to private schools. Though presented as an extension of choice, the vouchers were in reality not much more than 'a disguised transfer' of public funds to private schools, with many institutions raising the level of their fees to benefit from the new arrangements.[37] Analysts of the changes anticipate a slight rise in private sector enrolments, but no significant alteration in the sector's status as a means of providing for the 'rich and lazy', dealing with students who are 'in trouble with their educational career' and generally offering an education 'of a lower quality than public schools'.[38] If the government intended its policies to transform private provision and to encourage the emergence of new kinds of provider, it has not so far succeeded.

In Spain the church-controlled private sector is stronger, and its contribution to the creation of the school system based on principles of autonomy correspondingly greater. Until the end of the 1960s, the Catholic Church exercised an almost absolute monopoly in secondary education. The 1970s saw an expansion of public education, to the point where it surpassed the Church sector in size. Rather than seeking to establish a universal public system of schooling, however, the PSOE government of the early 1980s made a strategic decision to compromise with the Church. The LODE legislation of 1985 endorsed both the regionalisation of education, and the presence of a strong and subsidised private, religious sector. The subsidies came to be called 'concertaciones' (agreements). This was a change in more than name: the subsidy recognised the subsidiary role of the private system, while the agreement was a modality of private control of the public provision of school places. Autonomy and public–private 'partnership' were established as central principles of a system that was informally differentiated on grounds of social class. In contrast to Italy, the subsidised schools took on a central importance as a means of social selection. Pupils with lower prospects came to be concentrated in the public schools, especially as attendance at a subsidised school came to be seen as essential to educational advance. In Madrid, between 1999 and 2002, the six points by which the private sector was ahead of the public in the size of its student population had become a difference of more than 25 points (63% to 37% public), an increase which, if not generalisable throughout the Spanish state, at least indicated with some starkness a growing tendency.[39] The Zapatero government elected in 2004 provided no more than a footnote to this history, reversing efforts to place religion at the centre of the curriculum, but allowing the extension of subsidies to non-compulsory education: the LOE of 2006 gave the *concertadas* equality of status with the public sector, complete financing for non-compulsory provision and a greater funding increase than the public schools.[40]

In Northern Europe, the links between private education and religious institutions are certainly not insignificant: the Labour government's post-2002 programme to establish City Academies – state-funded but privately managed schools – depended heavily on the educational entrepreneurialism of religious organisations and individual believers. But in general, the expansionary dynamic of private education has other sources. In West Germany, the post-war state was committed to the support of private education, and offered various kinds of subsidy to parents and to schools – tax allowances, transport costs, even some support for capital expenditure. The political weight of the private sector, however, was not substantial: it was justified as an approved 'alternative' to public education, rather than a privileged enclave. This situation is now changing. According to the Eurydice survey, 1% of primary pupils and between 7 and 10% of gymnasium pupils were in private institutions. While many of these are managed by religious organisations or trusts, an increasing number are owned by private, for-profit companies, such as the for-profit Phorms company, which in 2006 established the first in a small chain of primary schools and whose chief executive told *Deutsche Welle* that 'education is a product that people are willing to pay for.' Certainly, while the expenditure of the German state on education is falling, private expenditure on education is growing – thanks in part to the imposition of university tuition fees, but thanks also to spending on private schooling.[41] Since reunification, private schools in Germany have grown rapidly in number – by 30% since 1995 – with much of the increase occurring in the *Länder* of the east.[42] With this involvement, and in the context of the 'PISA shock' experienced by the public system, the private sector is becoming more central to policy debate, though without the controversies that have attended change in Italy. In the process, public opinion is 'softened': the normative force of the idea of education as a public good becomes diminished.

In Britain, elite private schools have long supplied business, the law, cultural institutions and politics with personnel and a defining ethos: there can be no questioning of their centrality. The elite schools do not for the most part operate as profit-making businesses; the service they provide to capital is of other kinds. Nevertheless, the growth of private enterprise in education has had some effect on this sector, too. The leader here is the private equity group Englefield, which established through its subsidiary 'Cognita' is claimed to be the largest chain of private schools in Britain. Englefield's mission is to 'focus on situations where the changing environment creates strongly supportive macroeconomic and/or sectoral forces' and it believes that in the provision of private education it has found such forces.[43] By 2005, the company, headed by the former chief inspector of schools Chris Woodhead, had come to control, through a process of takeover, some 20 private schools, in the belief that there exists a market for relatively low-cost private education, among parents for whom 'choice' has become a necessity, but entry to elite schools an impossibility. Cognita is not alone in this belief. The Dubai-based Global Education Management Systems (GEMS) announced in 2005 that it intended to combine the establishment of low-cost private education with involvement in government initiatives where a private sector partner is sought. GEMS accordingly invited onto its board of directors a number of former high-ranking state functionaries.[44]

The privatisation of influence

Writing about the European Constitution in the aftermath of the French and Dutch referenda of 2005, Alain Supiot cites the pledge made by the rejected treaty to 'promote a skilled, trained and adaptable workforce and labour markets responsive to economic change'. He comments that in thus attempting to 'adapt the workforce to the requirements of the market', the treaty had effectively 'reversed the priorities established by the international community as it emerged from World War II, when the idea was that the economy and the world of finance should service and not dominate humanity'.[45] Supiot may be overstating the international community's intentions in this latter respect, but when he identifies a transformation in the discursive and institutional frameworks that address the relationship between the economic and the social, he is on solid ground. In education such a transformation has not only been effected at the level of government policy; it also involves the growth of a public–private educational complex, in which the private sector occupies the roles of both think-tank and operational partner to a public education policy which, in some cases, no longer remembers what it was like to work without it.

Adapting the workforce to market requirements entails developing forms of influence over and intervention in the school system, and these forms need to be distinguished from the strictly economic aspect of privatisation. This influence is exercised in order to create a workforce capable of contributing to the profitability of the economy in general, or specific sectors of it, or even of specific employers. As the European Commission put it:

> There is a convergence between the member States on the necessity of a much greater involvement of the private sector in the systems of education and/or vocational training and in the formulation of policies of education and training in order to take account of the needs of the market and of local circumstances, for example in the form of the encouragement of collaboration between companies and the education and training system and the integration of lifelong learning by companies in their strategic plans.[46]

The terms in which this policy shift is motivated are discussed in chapter 8. Here we want only to focus on some of national forms which the private–public complex takes.

The difference between countries in this respect remain striking – though nowhere has the appetite of business for educational change been sated. The Italian employers' federation, the Confindustria, was a signatory in 2002 to a memorandum of understanding with the Ministry of Education which underlined its central role in the operationalising of educational reform, through pilot projects – particularly in vocational education – and the training of teachers. Nevertheless, it is plain from the statements of its leaders that it regards educational reform in Italy as having reached only the early stages of a pro-enterprise turn.[47] Likewise in France in 2005, despite more than a decade of attempted change, the new leader of the employers' federation, MEDEF, still found it necessary to insist that his 'first focus' would be on the education system to improve the country's 'bad economic culture'.[48] In England, the capacities of business for intervention and influence are more developed. This is not only a matter of leverage gained through recent participation in privatisation, but a process with deeper roots. Employers dominate the Learning and Skills Councils which control the post-16 vocational sector. They will also have a central role in the 'work-related learning' which will be a feature of the 14–16 curriculum. As a government policy document of 2005 put it, 'we intend to put employers in the driving seat, so that they will have a key role in determining what the "lines of learning" should be and in deciding in detail what the Diplomas should contain'.[49]

It is in England, too, that the government has introduced a policy which goes further than any other Western European country in establishing a formalised relationship between representatives of business interests and secondary schools – the sponsorship of schools by companies and business entrepreneurs. Sponsorship has two functions: to encourage an entrepreneurial spirit among school management, and to tie schools more closely to the world of business. The creation of a sponsorship culture has been a long business, and is still unfinished. It began in the 1980s, with the Conservatives' programme of City Technology Colleges. Having lapsed for much of the 1990s, it was revived and then extended by the Labour government. In 2002, Labour announced plans for the construction of 200 'academies' by 2010. Academies are new state secondary schools in socially disadvantaged areas, funded directly by government and set up under private school legislation so that they fall outside the legislative and curricular framework which governs other state-maintained schools. The government intended academies to be sponsored by businesses, business entrepreneurs, churches or voluntary bodies. Sponsors would appoint a majority of the school governing body, meaning that they would control the school, including the appointment of the head teacher and the employment and promotion of teachers; ownership of the land and buildings of the existing state school would also be transferred to the governors. 'I realised,' one observer commented 'just what immense power a sponsor has, simply by contributing £2 million out of £30 million. For £2 million, small change for some very wealthy individuals, the sponsor was effectively buying the school'.[50] It was this sort of power that allowed creationist car-dealer Sir Peter Vardy to write anti-Darwinian perspectives into the science curriculum of the City Academy he sponsored in northeast England and that also enabled the 'Bexley Business Academy' to set up its own mini stock exchange and trading floor.

Sponsorship thus involves the introduction of new social actors to the educational scene – a process that has been fraught with difficulty. It is one thing to abandon the principle of publicly funded and publicly controlled schooling; it is quite another to assemble the forces that can reconstruct it along privatised lines. Major financial and industrial companies tend to seek to influence education more through national and regional pressure than through hands-on involvement. The only major social force immediately willing to commit itself to sponsoring large numbers of schools was the Church of England, which in the late 1990s took a decision to expand its presence in secondary education. Since there are obvious limits to Church participation, Labour, in its search for further sponsors, ventured initially into a kind of capitalist *demi-monde* populated by *parvenu* businessmen who are seeking cheap ways to achieve a new level of social and political status. The results of this exploration were predictable: it emerged in 2006 that Labour was offering ennoblement and a seat in the House of Lords to those willing to sponsor an Academy.

By 2007, however, the academies programme had taken a new turn. An important influence here was the government's 'Building Schools for the Future' (BSF) project, the vehicle for the material rebuilding of almost the entire English school system, designed with a heavy emphasis on private sector involvement.[51] Since, the government made clear that BSF funding would only be available to authorities that involved themselves in the Academies project, LEAs were in effect driven – in some cases willingly – towards academies, and towards the private sector. Major local authorities such as Manchester and Birmingham decided to adopt a policy of public–private partnership; in this way, they increased their influence beyond the minimal level envisaged in the government's initial 2002 programme, and at the same time promised to reconstruct large sections of the local school system on a basis of private involvement in educational governance, and acceptance by schools and authorities of local labour market needs. Agreements made between the authorities and significant public and private sector business interests aimed to establish citywide schemes of vocationally orientated education, based on the academy principle. In Manchester, for instance, the local authority developed an education plan that identified employment specialisms and lined up businesses to back them; with the local authority underwriting the scheme, businesses ran no risk. New schools to be built under the plan included the 'East Manchester Academy' specialising in construction and the built environment and sponsored by Bovis Lend Lease and Laing O'Rourke, the 'Manchester Health Academy', sponsored by NHS trusts, and the 'Manchester Airport Academy', specialising in business and enterprise – and sponsored by Manchester Airport.[52] In this way, the government's vision of an education based to a significant extent on public–private partnership began to become organic to local systems.

Limits to privatisation

It is clear, then, that along a number of axes, processes of privatisation are expanding and accelerating. Even so, despite all the new institutional settings, business opportunities and pathways of influence that now lie open to educational capitalism, its representatives remain discontented. French and Italian business leaders speak darkly of 'corporatist' opposition; diagnoses of German economic decline never fail to mention the contribution of expensive and ineffective schooling to that process. In England, the failure to advance privatisation further and faster has been irksome to neo-liberals. *The Economist* (3 May 2003) concluded in 2003 that 'the record of privatisation in education is mixed.' Private firms lack experience and competence; the public sector remains rule-bound in its understanding of educational practice. Similar issues were the subject of a critical report, 'The Business of Education Improvement', published in 2005 by the Confederation of British Industry (CBI), in which the CBI discussed in passing the embedded difficulties faced by edubusiness, difficulties that are both 'cultural' and 'political':

> The government's early contribution was significant and innovative. It created the conditions within which an initial market could be established that actively encouraged new entrants into the market. But, despite the initial success of the policy, the market in major LEA outsourcing has failed to move beyond early interventions. The government's belief that voluntary partnerships would emerge over time has proven to be misguided. The failure to develop the market beyond the initial intervention process stemmed, in part, from the apparent stigma associated with public-private partnerships (PPPs). Also significant was an underestimation of the cultural and political resistance from local authorities to a change in their role from direct providers to commissioners of services.[53]

It is plain from this that business interests think both that privatisation can be developed much further, and that there remain (even in England) cultural and political obstacles to privatising processes that cannot easily be worn away – though the Manchester initiative is a significant indicator of a change in direction. Certainly, the Labour Government wishes to push further ahead. In 2006, notwithstanding the scandals associated with its Academies project, it introduced legislation to reconstruct the entire education system of England around the principle of school sponsorship: schools would be encouraged to become 'trusts', in which charities, churches and businesses would all be invited to participate. The state's role would be that of funder and regulator; management would pass into other hands and the scope for for-profit activities related to education would be enlarged.

Does this mean, though, that we are approaching the point of the 'privatisation of everything'? Here there are reasons to be cautious. The Business Advisory Committee to the OECD produced a paper for the 2004 OECD Meeting of Education Ministers, in which both the necessities and limits of privatisation were clearly stated:

> In our view, Government has the primary responsibility for initial education. Employers and companies contribute by working with Government and educational institutions to provide clear goals for education according to the needs of the market.[54]

From this perspective, post-14 education is certainly viewed as a field of opportunity. Likewise, business influence upon the school curriculum is seen as imperative. But compulsory schooling is still seen as an area where the state has primary responsibility. Governments, so far as we can tell, concur. Schools have complex and long-term functions – for social inclusion, for the reproduction of national identities – that governments are not willing to give up, especially in a period where they see 'civilisational' conflict as a major problem. Privatisation strategies have not yet offered government a means of addressing such issues. Nor are governments at present willing to face the political controversies attendant upon large-scale privatisation. Privatisation is a powerful, ever-extending force which, left unresisted, will reshape the contours of European education. That is enough reason to take it seriously. Its ultimate horizons are less easy to discern.

Notes

1. Harvey, *A Brief History of Neoliberalism*, p. 145.
2. CBI, *The Business of Education Improvement* (London: CBI, 2005) p. 6.
3. Giovanni Cimbalo, 'Le regioni alla ricerca di una identità inesistente ... La strategia legislativa delle Regioni per la gestione differenziata del sistema scolastico', G. Giappichelli, editore, Torino: 2003, p. 8.
4. See Stefano Iucci (2003) 'La Sperimentazione della Moratti: un bilancio negativo (e costoso)' www.rassegna.it/2003/speciali/scuola/moratti2.htm.
5. Tony Blair, quoted in the *Times Educational Supplement*, 2 April 2004.
6. World Bank 1997, quoted in Dexter Whitfield, *Public Services or Corporate Welfare: the nation state in the global economy* (London: Pluto Press, 2001) p. 20.

7. CERI/OECD, *Knowledge Management for the Learning Society* (Paris: OECD, 2000) p. 56.
8. Antoni Verger Planells, 'GATS, Privatisation and Education: when education becomes a marketable commodity', paper prepared for International Higher Education and Research Conference (Melbourne: 2005).
9. See Lutz R. Reuter, 'Privatization of Education: the case of Germany', *Education And The Law*, 14.1–2, 91–8, 2002.
10. Richard Hatcher, 'Changing the school system in England: business agendas and New Labour's policies', paper presented at the COFIR 'Formazione "glocale": un' altra educazione e imPossible?' Arezzo, March 2003.
11. M. Barber, 'High expectations and standards for all, no matter what: creating a world class education service in England' in *Taking education really seriously: Four years' hard labour*, ed. M. Fielding, (London: Routledge, 2001) pp. 17–41, p. 39.
12. Estimated on the basis of the CBI's figures. CBI, *The Business of Education Improvement*, p. 10.
13. *Times Educational Supplement*, 14 May 2004.
14. www.tribal.group.co.uk.
15. www.edexcel.org.uk; www.samlearningco.uk/aboutus/corporate.html.
16. Pat Mahony, Ian Menter and Ian Hextall, 'Building Dams in Jordan: Assessing Teachers in England: a case study in Edu-business' *Globalisation, Societies and Education* 2.3, 277–96, 2004.
17. Capital Strategies, p. 3.
18. www.tribal.co.uk.
19. Unison, *PFI – against the public interest: why a licence to print money can also be a disaster* (London: Unison, 2005).
20. *The Guardian*, 5 September 2003.
21. *Financial Times*, 24 April 2004.
22. Unison, *PFI*.
23. Ibid.
24. International Financial Services, *Privatisation: UK expertise for international markets* (London: 2003) p. 13; Unison, *A web of private interest: how the big five accountancy firms influence and profit from privatisation policy* (London: 2002).
25. Qualifications and Assessment Authority, QAA News 6 September 2000 (London: QAA, 2000).
26. Confederation of British Industry, *The Business of Education Improvement* (London: CBI, 2005).
27. Department for Education and Skills, Education-Business www.website. http://www.dfes.gov.uk/ebnet/business/.
28. Christian Laval, *L'école n'est past une entreprise* (Paris: La Découverte, 2004).
29. The market for junk food has been thrown into difficulty by a 2006 turn in government policy, which banned, from 2007, the selling of low-nutritional items from school vending machines, and introduced new nutritional standards for school meals. According to *The Guardian* 'Pay more or we quit, canteen operators to tell schools' 18th September 2006, 'Catering executives have told the Guardian that unless they receive adequate compensation for abandoning junk food, they will quit schools where they cannot make a decent return.

30. Laval, *L'école n'est past une entreprise.*

31. See the report, 'Une victoire contre la marchandisation de l'école' on the website www.attac.fr (6 October 2004).

32. J-L Bernal, 'Parental choice, social class and market forces', p. 784.

33. Diane Reay and Helen Lucey, 'The Limits of "Choice": children and inner city schooling', *Sociology* 37, 121–42, 2003.

34. Thierry Brulavoine, 'L'Acodomia aide l'état' www.ecoledemocratique June 2005.

35. Eurydice, 'Private Education in the European Union: organisation, administration and public authorities' role', *Eurydice* December 2000 www.eurydice.org.

36. Lelièvre, 'The French Model of the Educator State'.

37. Giorgio Brunello and Daniele Checchi, *School Vouchers, Italian Style* (Bonn: Institute for the Study of Labour, 2005) p. 7.

38. Ibid., p. 7.

39. See the discussion in issue no. 3, *Crisis* published by the Colectivo Baltasar Gracian in June 2003. www.colectivobgracian.com/revista.

40. STES-i, 'Reports from National Education Networks: Spain' in *Bulletin on Educational Systems in Europe* prepared for European Educational Network of the European Social Network, Athens 2006.

41. Klaus Klemm citing data from the Statistischen Bundesamt, *Frankfurter Rundschau* 9 May 2006.

42. Anonymous, 'Berlin School Wants to Profit from Education', *Deutsche Welle* 13 October 2006 www.dw-world.de.

43. See the website www.englefieldcapital.com.

44. Times Educational Supplement, 25 March 2005, 'Rise of the Empire of Sunny'.

45. Alain Supiot, 'Refeudalising Europe', *London Review of Books* pp. 18–21, p. 18, 2005.

46. European Commission, White Paper, *Growth, Competitiveness, Employment,* Brussels, quoted in Laval, *L'école n'est past une entreprise*, p. 23.

47. See the article by Confindustria vice-president Silvio Fortuna, *Università: Una riforma per l'eccellenza*, 'Il Sole-24 Ore' di Sabato, 14 Febbraio 2004, p. 22.

48. The Economist, 30 June 2005, 'Looking for Love: who can restore the reputation of business in France?'

49. DfES, *14–19 Education and Skills* (London: The Stationery Office, 2005) p. 45.

50. Peter Hyman, *1 out of 10: from Downing Street vision to classroom reality* (London: Vintage Books, 2005).

51. Local BSF projects have to be run by a Local Education Partnership, which builds and operates the new and refurbished schools. The LEP is a joint venture company controlled by the private contractors, who have 80% representation on its board, with the local authority having 10%.

52. Andrew Adonis and Richard Leese, 'A New Blueprint', *The Guardian* 9 January 2007.

53. CBI, *The Business of Education Improvement*, 2005, p. 6.

54. Business Advisory Committee to the OECD (2004) *Briefing paper for the 2004 Meeting of Education Ministers*, Dublin.

5
Inequality Remade

Expectations and eventualities

The politics of educational equality has experienced over the past 70 years several transformations. 'L'accès des universités à l'élite d'intelligence et non plus à l'élite de la fortune' demanded the far left of the French workers' movement in 1940.[1] This encounter of trotskyism and meritocracy, surprising to our eyes, typified a wider understanding. 'In the not so distant past,' suggests a recent UNICEF report, 'it was possible to believe that the provision of free compulsory education through secondary school and the opening up of higher education to all on the basis of merit, would carry nations far down the road towards equality of opportunity'.[2]

To a certain extent, the meritocratic dream has been realised. 'The (post-war) rise in the level of education among British, French, German, Italian and Spanish populations is a continual process which forms part of the economic and social history of these developed countries,' wrote Béduwé and Planas in 2003.[3] In the process, and partly as a result of the occupational changes to which educational expansion has been linked, gendered inequalities – in attainment at least – have diminished. Across Europe, girls' educational performance has improved, equalling and then overtaking boys after decades of inferiority. But, as Colin Crouch, points out, movement along the axis of gender serves also to highlight the obduracy of class inequalities. 'Once families decide that they will apply their stock of cultural capital to help their daughters as much as their sons, there is nothing in social theory to suggest that they will not be able to succeed.'[4] But no similar process – and certainly no reliance on meritocratic principles – strongly mitigated the effects of social class. Sociological research of the 1990s, looking back at the post-war period, no matter the society whose experience it explored, arrived repeatedly at the same conclusion: despite a massive expansion in access to primary and lower secondary education, 'expansion of education does not consistently reduce the association between the social origin of students and their educational attainment'.[5] Crouch, summarising Blossfeld and Shavit (1993), described the post-war history of equality in these terms:

> (There was) certainly an enormous expansion of education, with compulsory secondary education becoming virtually universal ... Inequalities in opportunity at this first transition point virtually disappeared. However, at the later transition points, into advanced secondary education and into higher education, a lack of expansion of supply concomitant with the new large numbers coming through from universal secondary education led to new bottlenecks. Almost everywhere this produced a reassertion of social selection based on parental advantage ... In most countries, children from lower social backgrounds did not experience an increase in their educational opportunities until higher groups had fully satisfied ... their demand for it.[6]

The entry of the mass of the population into higher levels of education was thus a by-product of the middle-classes' capacity to saturate a given level of the system: only when this had occurred, could the system expand further, to involve the 'less privileged classes'.[7] The role of reform was not 'to revolutionise the distribution of schooling between strata but rather to enable education expansion while maintaining the relative shares (of the classes)'.[8] For this situation, the French researcher Pierre Merle has coined the term 'démocratisation ségrégative': educational expansion has allowed students from working-class backgrounds the opportunity of a longer, better education, at the same time as the school continues to secure the reproduction of established privilege.[9] Although there exists no large-scale, systematic comparative research into the questions of access, attainment, social class and type of schooling which might allow Merle's hypothesis to be generally validated,[10] there is all the same a great deal of partial evidence from all our countries to suggest that what Merle has identified in France is the common pattern of contemporary education systems. From a point of view concerned with what is new about education systems operating under neo-liberal influence, these results pose some further questions. If, in relation to social inequality, education systems share a common pattern, is this effect intensified or diminished by recent changes in social and/or policy contexts? And – if such an effect exists – are the mechanisms through which it is produced different from those of the past?

Access and attainment

In broad terms, attainment at all levels of primary and secondary education in Western Europe continue to rise: there are plateaus and 'dips' – at baccalauréat level in France, for instance, or at age 11 in England – but the general tendency is clear, and does not seem to have been disturbed by recent policy. Nevertheless, for how long such a rise can continue, given the existence of large 'excluded' populations, is an open question.[11] Certainly, the attempt by states to meet post-Lisbon targets of increasing attainment at upper-secondary level have been problematic.

In terms of access, the picture is also – up to a point – positive. In their 2005 survey of intergenerational mobility in Northern Europe and North America, Blanden, Gregg and Machin note that

> the staying on rate [in upper secondary education] increased from 1974 to the late 1990s for both income groups [the richest 20% and the poorest 20%] ... The speed of the increase has varied substantially for young people in different periods. It is clear that between 1974 and 1976 ... staying on rates for children from the richest backgrounds were rising faster; this led to an increase in educational inequality. From 1986 to the late 1990s, the staying on rate of those from the poorest backgrounds was rising more quickly, leading to a reversal in the extent of educational inequality. Over the 1990s, young people from poorer backgrounds have clearly taken up the opportunity to stay on in post-compulsory education, as never before.[12]

However, this encouraging picture was complicated in several ways. In Britain, for instance, the relationship between family income and the level of educational attainment reached by students grew stronger for the cohort born in 1970 than it had been for the cohort of 1958: additional opportunities to stay in education both at age 16 and 18 were taken up mainly by those from better-off backgrounds. Students born in the late 1970s and 1980s (most of whose education was gained in Conservative times) experienced a narrowing of the class-based gap in post-16 education, but a widening in the inequality of access to higher education. As the performance at certain levels of higher social groups reached saturation point, and as the performance of students from less advantaged backgrounds continued to rise, so there was a narrowing of the attainment gap – but inequality then migrated, as it were, to a higher level of the system.

A similar, if not identical, pattern of social differentiation obtains at other levels of education. The DfES notes that between 1998 and 2004 in terms of attainment at the average level of performance (level 4) for 11 year olds, 'the most rapid improvement was seen in the most deprived schools'. However, at higher levels of performance, the situation was reversed: here, at level 5, the rate of improvement was higher and faster in the most advantaged schools.[13] Moreover, in 16+ examinations, while there has been a certain narrowing of a social class-based attainment gap, the differences still remain very wide. When the Office of National Statistics noted that in 2002 three-quarters of pupils from a higher professional background achieved good GCSEs, compared with just a third of those with parents involved in routine work, it confirmed just such a pattern – and registered, not for the first time, the disappointment of earlier expectations.[14] In France, the same kinds of process are at work. The proportion of the age cohort gaining a baccalauréat has steadily risen – from 26% in 1981, to 43.5% in 1990 and 62% in 2004. But success remains strongly linked to social background – 90% of the children of executives and teachers reached baccalauréat level, but only 51% of the children of manual workers.[15]

Class as destiny?

On the basis of these relentless sociological studies, a report by UNICEF's Innocenti Research Centre was able to declare in 2002 that 'across the industrialised world, a family's social, cultural and economic status tends to act as a rifle barrel setting an educational trajectory from which it is difficult for a child to escape'.[16] But the mixed terms of this metaphor suggest an area of uncertainty: the trajectory is under some conditions and to some extent escapable. It is important to explore this area of uncertainty, for not to do so is to be led towards a perspective from which there is no difference between the educational régimes established under the pressure of post-war movements of reform, and those which rest upon exceptionally strong structures of differentiation.

As Schnepf remarks, though the effects of social class on educational attainment are pervasive, some school systems do more to mitigate inequality than others. Similarly, the relationship between school performance and home background 'does not follow any immutable law but varies considerably from country to country.'[17] We can explore this variation by looking at policy extremes – at negative cases, where the absence of reform has produced effects of marked inequality and low attainment, and at positive instances, in which reform has led to unusually homogenous patterns of schooling, and to a lessening of inequality.

Among negative cases, Germany stands out. Following reunification, the East German model of the unitary secondary school, the *allgemeinbildende polytechnische Oberschule* was abandoned, leaving the tripartite model of the West securely in place. The sorting of children into different school tracks happens at a notably early age, around 10. The sorting process is based on a formal recommendation made by the primary school that is itself strongly conditioned by class-related perceptions of student ability – Schnepf refers to a study of Hamburg demonstrating that 'children from less educated families had to show higher ability than their peers in order to be recommended for a gymnasium'.[18] In addition, parental intervention can be decisive – Schnepf notes that 'better-educated parents can be expected to push for recommendations over school tracks to be put aside, whereas lesser-educated parents sometimes do the opposite'. Conversely, Flitner suggests that 10% of parents – mostly from the working class – turn down a place at Gymnasium, 'wanting not to expose their child to educational pressure'.[19]

The outcome of orientation is that the son of a middle- to upper-social class family is three times more likely to attend a Gymnasium than that of the son of a skilled worker; and once locked in to the tripartite Gymnasium-Realschule-Hauptschule system few children change their type of school, even though analysis of students' performance in international tests suggests that a large number of them have been allocated to a school of the 'wrong' type.[20] In turn, the students' institutional location determines their occupational future: the importance of particular qualifications in the German labour market means that the track a child ends up in has a particularly strong impact on later life, and Schnepf notes a striking 'school effect' on wage levels – the wages of people who have been to a Gymnasium are 63% higher on average than those of people who had attended a Hauptschule.

Thus the German case, in which patterns of attainment and access are significantly different from those of France and Britain, provides the strongest plank in the argument of those who have tracked comparative patterns of schooling and equality and have concluded that 'social inequality in achievement among students tends to be more marked in countries with strong (educational) segregation'.[21] The finding is borne out by other experiences. In Italy, the proportion of the population (25–34) that has attained at least upper-secondary education is strikingly low – 57% against a 2002 OECD average of 74% – and levels of social mobility are also low.[22] These patterns correlate with an education system in which differentiation is accomplished less formally than in Germany, but is effective nonetheless. Recent research confirms earlier work in showing a continuing and stable influence of social origins on upper-secondary access and outcomes in terms of graduation from upper secondary, except for limited equalisation of agricultural classes; Shavit and Westerbeek identify the key moment as the transition from *scuola media* to the *liceo* or to technical/vocational education; at this point, track selection seems to depend upon the wishes of students and parents, but in reality choice is shaped by teachers' evaluation of students and their corresponding recommendation, affected by the same perspectives that are at work in Germany.[23] The result is a system that 'lets the student population sort itself, on the basis of individuals' financial and cultural background', with an apparent openness disguising strong processes of social selection (Bertola & Checchi 2001:1). Choice of upper-secondary school – the choice between liceo, technical education and the course of a shorter length provided by the vocational school – is more strongly correlated with parents' level of education than in most other OECD countries, and thus at higher levels of the system, class-based inequalities of participation are very evident – less than 10% of the children of fathers whose maximum level of education was the *scuola media* achieve a university degree.[24] The implementation of the Moratti reforms, despite their rhetoric of 'flexible pathways' between academic and vocational education, would accentuate this tendency; with vocational education under the control of regional authorities while the licei remained within the national system, the reforms would block those means of connecting vocational education to the possibilities of higher education which had been opened by sanctioned experimentation and informal practice under the old system.[25]

Against the record of Germany and Italy, other experiences can be set. Looking at the post-war Swedish experience of diminishing educational inequality, Shavit and Blossfeld attribute it to an 'equalisation of living conditions ... probably the major reason for the declining association between social origins and educational opportunity'.[26] Alongside this kind of 'social effect' on inequality can be set more direct 'educational effects'. A comparison of England and Scotland provides a good example of the intertwining of the two. The social relations of the two countries are very similar, as are the labour markets that students enter. But in some respects, their educational systems – which are separately governed – diverge. In England, the project of comprehensive reform was effectively suspended in the 1980s, uncompleted; after 1988, a process of marketisation began, so that England combined strong residues of traditional forms of student selection in some regions with new forms of selection in others, at the same time as economic change was producing new patterns of social division. In Scottish secondary schools, by contrast, comprehensive reform was accomplished by the early 1980s and the principles of 'diversity and choice' that underpinned the marketisation of English education were not applied north of the border. Researchers have tracked the divergent consequences of the English and Scottish paths. Lindsay Paterson has noted a decline in patterns of social segregation in Scottish schools, despite the effects of poverty, unemployment and a measure of parental choice, and recent research has suggested that Scotland has the least socially segregated school system in Europe.[27] Linda Croxford and David Raffe, on the basis of data from the whole period between 1984 and 2002, concluded that the attainment of working-class students was higher in Scotland than in England, and that at age 16 'over time social class differences in (educational) attainment have narrowed in Scotland, but there is no evidence of any similar change in any of the English regions'.[28] Tentatively, Croxford attributed this pattern of educational divergence to a particular cause: alongside possibly more powerful effects, the market régime may have been the mechanism by which the middle class in England maintained its relative advantage and resisted the Scottish trend towards narrowing inequalities.[29]

The case of Scotland/England is thus a kind of natural experiment – producing complex and sometimes cryptic data – through which can be understood the achievements of reform and the impasses created by elements of early selection and social polarisation. In this sense, it provides a means to appreciate a more general, European process. Post-war policies expanded public education and allowed access to previously excluded groups. They raised levels of attainment, and in some cases lessened attainment-related inequalities too. Even in cases where their achievements seem limited, it can be argued – as do Shavit and Westerbeek in relation to Italy – that they held back the development of extremes of polarisation: without the *scuola media* the fruits of educational expansion would have fallen still more copiously to the privileged. But it is difficult to see how such processes can continue without substantial redistributive social change to support them, and without further attention to those 'deep' elements in the grammar of schooling through which inequality is reproduced. It is precisely these problems that current policy orthodoxy places beyond limits. Instead, it fosters a hybrid system, in which – in social situations characterised by sharp polarisation – the historic failings of the school in relation to equality of opportunity are maintained, while newer elements of market relations and government regulation reinforce selection mechanisms and stimulate competition for positional advantage. In the following section we explore relations between marketisation, social segregation and the polarities of educational attainment. We do so with particular reference to urban education, often in the past the site of egalitarian innovation, where shifts in this network of relations appear in their clearest form.

Pursuing advantage

The project of educational equality has been undermined first of all by the social polarisation that has accompanied neo-liberalism. The proportion of poor people in Britain, for instance, doubled to almost 20% between 1980 and 1999; these households contain a third of all children of school age. In France, inequalities in income distribution once again began to grow from the mid-1980s onwards: incomes from profits rose, while unemployment and job insecurity increased, with predictable social consequences, that are especially evident in urban contexts. Boltanski and Chiapello speak in this context of 'ghettoisation, the de facto creation of extra-legal zones ... the development of violence among increasingly young children, the problem of integrating populations of immigrant origin'. More concretely, a primary head teacher in Aulnay, on the northern fringes of Paris, speaks – in the wake of the 2005 riots – of a situation in which deindustrialisation means that 'all those who can, have left ... There remain ... the rest. Those who have replaced the former inhabitants have sunk into social decline. A spiral of isolation, of withdrawal, of failure is in place. A working-class suburb has been transformed into a ghetto.'[30] In Italy, Ginsborg tells a similar story of the urban periphery, which has experienced a poverty that is 'spatial and social', as well as economic.[31] Spain, with its historically high levels of unemployment, and Germany, where Schroeder's Harz IV programme threatened to unravel post-war systems of social protection are no exception to a general, polarising tendency.

But the pressures of neo-liberalism are not only felt by the most excluded groups. They create also a crisis in the reproduction of middle-class opportunity. For the expanded professional groups and middle-classes of post-war Europe, sharper economic competition means that there are few guarantees that their children 'will maintain, let alone surpass, the social position of their parents'.[32] Striving to preserve positional advantage in relation to the rest of the middle class, and haunted by proliferating experiences and images of urban insecurity, these groups are much less likely now to accept the structures of opportunity offered by the relatively universalistic school systems of earlier decades. The accelerating quasi-marketisation of schooling – the tendency towards inter-institutional competition in choice-shaped systems – especially in the cities of Europe, connects to their fears and aspirations. The rules of engagement permitted by the educational market provide the urban middle classes with a more reliable way to preserve their advantages than the rules of engagement associated with earlier school regimes such as selection – whose reintroduction as an explicit principle would be fraught with difficulty – or the pre-market comprehensive system.

Urban education is thus shaped by two broad forces. On the one hand, a process of social polarisation that creates a large peripheral class; on the other, a middle-class pursuit of new strategies of educational advantage. Uneasily positioned among these tendencies are a variety of class fractions. The public school system is a site for the display of tensions within and between such groups: between, for instance, members of the less stable fractions of the working class and immigrant groups on the one side, and members from the more stable fractions of the working class and from the lower-middle classes on the other side.[33] The whole ensemble is sometimes shaped by organised collective action – through parents' associations, through coalitions opposing disadvantage or through action by educational unions 'that are often the last and only trace of the workers' movement in the urban peripheries'[34] – but more fundamentally its workings are determined by the millions of micro-decisions made within individual families, the outcomes of which give the school system its distinctive new institutional pattern.

The pattern has two main elements. The first is a tiered school system – a status hierarchy of schools which to a large extent maps on to class differences. The second is a system of within-school differentiation that privileges some social groups at the expense of others. Neither is a completely new feature of public schooling, but both are exacerbated by the effects of educational markets: English researchers, for instance, have found that 'parental choice', a key feature of markets, was potentially most damaging to the 'average inner city school likely to lose children from higher socio-economic families to other comprehensives and to local grammar schools'[35] – effects which we will trace by summarising research conducted in the four cities of London, Paris, Berlin and Zaragoza.

London is the most divided region of Britain, with by far the highest proportion of people on low income as well as the highest proportion on high income. It has the largest proportion of students attending private schools, and has a state sector that is institutionally diverse and socially segregated. (According to the official who was supposed to bring some coherence to this diversity, there are more than 200 different admissions criteria in existence: with 33 boroughs, churches and lots of individual schools all having different policies.[36]) In this complex and divided system, two interdependent processes are at work, facilitating the strategic withdrawal of the middle classes, and the effective exclusion of the poorest.[37] High-income families tend to avoid state secondary schools in many inner London boroughs precisely because many of the pupils in such schools are from families who would be classified as being among the excluded at the bottom. In some cases, this involves opting into the private sector, but even where better off families continue to use state schools at secondary level they often employ other mechanisms of 'exclusion at the top', such as moving house into the catchment areas of what they perceive to be the best state schools, which consequently become 'colonized' by the middle class. In extreme cases, whole boroughs come to be regarded as unsafe for middle-class children. The falling quality of public services in large swathes of the inner cities is thus itself partly an outcome of the withdrawal of support for them by growing numbers of relatively advantaged people. This process of social closure begins early; Ball's interviews with middle-class parents in Inner London elicited a consistent strategy on the part of parents. 'There were loads of children there,' said one mother of a disadvantaged primary school, '[who] had special needs and they have lots of children who are refugees who really didn't speak English, and I just thought, it's not appropriate for a bright little girl who, you know, is going to need quite a lot of stimulation'.[38]

Middle-class parental demand, and the Labour government's responsiveness to it in the form of national regulation, also shapes the internal organisation of schools. 'I liked the fact,' said another of Ball's interviewees, 'that they catered specifically for children's abilities in subjects that I think are difficult to teach in a mixed-ability group ... It was one of the points we thought were positive.' Since 1997, government has shared this evaluation. The government's White Paper *Excellence in Schools* asserted that mixed ability teaching had failed and advocated increased selection in the form of ability setting, accelerated learning groups, provision for 'gifted and talented' pupils and the establishment of work-based tracks at age 14. 'A major focus of reform initiatives has been to endorse differentiation by ability as an essential feature of good practice' and this has legitimated the tendency of teachers to adapt their teaching to their perceptions of the child and to provide those deemed to be of lower ability with a less demanding curriculum.[39] The resulting prioritisation of the interests of the higher performing and better off is unsupported by research evidence about the beneficial effects of 'setting', but its impact on social differentiation within comprehensive schools has been well documented. A case study of two London secondary schools demonstrated what the researchers called a process of 'educational triage'. In order to gain a high place in local league tables of examination performance, the schools focused their resources on students capable of gaining 'A-C' grades at GCSE (16+) level; other students were neglected, in ways that highlighted, particularly, class and ethnic divisions within the schools.[40] More generally, the pressures of competition in an educational quasi-market not only encourage the system as a whole to become more 'middle-class friendly", but also promote within schools 'an ethos and hidden curriculum that reward the social and cultural capitals that middle-class students are more likely to possess'.

Researchers in France make a similar point. Despite the letter of the law – the Haby legislation of 1975 that officially ended streaming – schools have continued to 'obey the logic of social distinction' through such means as the creation of subject-based option groups that act as a magnet for middle-class parents.[41] Schools have taken advantage of their 'margin of autonomy to boost their image and attract students of a higher social status, rather than develop initiatives in favour of the learning and integration of all pupils and in particular those most disadvantaged educationally and socially'.[42] Given such possibilities, parents scramble to evade by various means the restrictions of the *carte scolaire*, which assigns students to particular schools: 40% of Parisian parents manage to achieve *dérogation* from the school to which their children have been allocated.[43] At the same time, 'competition, fragmentation and erosion of democratic control' restrict 'the system's capacity for collective action to promote equality.'[44] Experience in the ZEPs tends to confirm such an analysis. Even in the difficult conditions of the 1990s, there was a strand of practice in the ZEPs which aimed to construct a 'school of the people':

A school where children of the popular classes can succeed. Its first priority is the ... quality of its pedagogic provision ... Its second priority is

> social and ethnic mixing ... breaking up the special streams of classes
> for students in great difficulty, voluntary and collective action
> against *dérogation* and the formation of ghetto schools.[45]

But it is precisely this collective effort that is called into question by
a process of change which threatens to convert the ZEP programme into
'a means of managing social inequality', on a par with a general pattern
of polarisation. In their account of contemporary Bordeaux, Felouzis
and Perroton note the impact of *dérogation* on the *collèges* of the city:
schools that should have accepted 25% of students from a migrant
background take 50%. Those who escape, or wish to escape, express a
fear of permanent social exclusion; those who remain fiercely question
the purpose of schooling.[46] Conversely, there are the developments
tracked, for instance, by van Zanten in 2002. In the major cities there is
'a process of locational concentration in a limited number of residential
areas' among whose benefits to bourgeois groups is 'easy access to the
most prestigious public and private schools'.[47] Van Zanten charts in this
context the results of parental strategies and sympathetic local government policies in one Parisian suburb where:

> the municipality has profited from decentralization laws to develop
> an exceptionally explicit policy of attracting middle-class and upper
> middle-class families through residential projects elaborated in rela-
> tion with property developers.

In the primary sector (controlled by the municipality), most of the
schools have been 'enlarged and embellished' to suit the aspirations of
such families. In the *collèges* – under the control of the *département* – a
more fraught situation exists. Those parents who have failed in the
fierce competition for places in the most prestigious schools constitute
an active force in the schools of 'average reputation', exerting 'individual pressure on teachers and collective pressure on head teachers and
the administration'.[48] As in London, the 'best' public schools are led to
develop further practices of selection, the provision of special subjects
and internal tracking, that deviate from official norms, but are tolerated
by the local education authorities as the best means of competing with
a strong local private sector. The result is a class-driven diversification
between and within institutions that is unevenly and gradually changing the face of French schooling.

Spain, the OECD notes, views 'comprehensiveness and inclusiveness
as attributes of compulsory schooling'. Public schools are governed by a

principle of equity, with selection on the basis of race, religion, 'or any other condition' being in breach of the Spanish constitution.[49] Nevertheless, like Italy, the country has low levels of participation in upper secondary education: only 57% of students continue beyond 16, a long way short of the EU's 2010 target of 85%, with those from 'a low socio-economic background' particularly unlikely to participate.[50] The reasons for this discrepancy between principle and practice are in important part social: *bachillerato* success and university entry, for instance, are heavily weighted regionally, in favour of the richer areas. But as in France, social difference passes through and is reinforced by, unequal educational processes. The Spanish school system, with its strong and subsidised private sector, provides favourable conditions for polarisation. Only 63% of Spanish schools providing compulsory education are in the public sector; 3% belong to 'business groups or private corporations with links to the new private universities and with certain influential groups in the Catholic Church'; and the remaining 34% are – as we saw in chapter 4 – privately managed institutions, which in return for comprehensive state subsidy, agree to fulfil the criteria of inclusivesness set out by the 1985 LODE legislation.[51] In practice, these institutions, the *centros concertados*, break this agreement. This is particularly clear in relation to migrant communities; in 2004–5, there were more than 400,000 school students from migrant families, but only 18% of them attended a subsidised school.[52] The *centros concertados* also find means of excluding other groups of pupils: nominally 'free of charge' they interpret this term 'fuzzily':

> Since the extra academic or additional services such as lunch and other items (dress, school material, books, travel or sport additional activities, etc.) have increased in recent years, even though they are not supposed to be obligatory.[53]

In his study of the Aragonese capital, Zaragoza, José Luis Bernal maps the local level workings of this divided system, in which schools of formal similar status admit students from very different populations. Tracking the relationship between school choice, institutional characteristics and social class, Bernal highlights similar tensions between and within classes to those discussed by researchers in England and France. Zaragoza, like other Spanish cities, has a differentiated school system, in which alongside the public school exist both subsidised and non-subsidised private schools. These institutional differences map onto class divisions. Movement of students across the city is commonplace, so that socio-cultural rather than geographic space is a determinant.

'Most middle-class children are distributed among middle-class public and private schools, leaving the rest of the public schools to the working class and the underprivileged.'[54] Within the public school sector, there is a clear divide between schools that cater to a stable, largely indigenous working-class population, and those that 'have a high proportion of families that belong to the underprivileged segment', which Bernal describes as containing 'gypsies, emigrants and other socially isolated groups'. This pattern of distribution, he remarks, is becoming fixed.

Berlin's secondary school system is in class terms less exclusive than that of Germany as a whole: proportionately, there are more Gymnasium places, and the chances of students from working-class backgrounds attending them are higher. In Berlin, also, questions of parental choice of secondary school are less central. In practice, the orientation process that occurs at the end of primary schooling links social and academic selection, and as a consequence middle-class parents do not need to 'shop around' for the best schools and their children do not generally need to travel to a school outside their immediate residential area.[55] Choice of primary school, especially in areas which are socially and ethnically mixed, is more delicate, since choice is not a right that is formally recognised in Berlin. For this reason, there has been a certain turn on the part of parents to the presentation of false addresses, to demands for 'derogation', and in general a willingness to consider means by which in special circumstances their child can change school. These circumstances tend, according to Flitner, to be racialised ones. Her (admittedly small) sample of middle-class parents accepted a certain measure of ethnic diversity as normal, but if the measure was exceeded, they sought to move their child from one primary school to another. (More than 50% of pupils in the primary schools of areas such as Kreuzberg, Tiergarten and Wedding are from migrant families, and the explanation for this includes not only residential segregation but parental decision.) Choice of Gymnasium, too, tends to be racialised: 75% of Gymnasium students in Berlin go to school within their own local area – but this falls to 54% in the ethnically mixed area of Schöneberg, As for ethnic minority students, the proportion of Gymnasium students from non-German-speaking families is 2.8%;[56] but in the prosperous white district of Zehlendorf, the figure is nearer 70%.

The racialisation of inequality

Most of the research discussed above suggests that residential segregation and parental choices contribute to considerable differences in the ethnic composition of schools, and that this generally works to the disadvantage of ethnic minority students. Other research adds to the picture, showing that – especially but not only in the least egalitarian systems – racial inequality in attainment is exceptionally strong. Analysing PISA data, for instance, Schnepf arrived at findings that confirmed Flitner's comments about the salience of 'race' – in Germany students from a migrant background scored three times as badly as native population, much worse than similar groups elsewhere in Europe.[57] But Germany is more an extreme than an exceptional case. In England, not all ethnic minority students experience comparative failure – children from Indian families, for instance, perform well. But where race and (lower) social class intersect it is a different story: the ethnic minorities with proportionately large numbers in lower social groups have the lowest educational attainment. In 2004, the percentage of black Caribbean pupils getting five or more grades A* to C at GCSE and equivalent was 36% compared to 52% of white children and the gap between the performance of black children and those of their peers, in terms of performance at GCSE, widened between 1991 and 2001.[58] Lower levels of performance are often accompanied by strong elements of segregation. Because the French government does not collect educational statistics that would allow a correlation between educational experience and what in Britain would be called 'ethnic origin', it is difficult to construct a national picture. But local studies are clear: Felouzis and Perroton speak of an 'apartheid scolaire' operating in Bordeaux, and accounts of the northern suburbs of Paris tell a similar story.[59] The phrase seems aptly to describe parts of London: in the East End of the city, white parents fleeing Bangladeshis have 'taken over' four church secondary schools in which Bangladeshis make up only 3% of the pupils, while they form 90% of pupils in the next-door secular schools.[60] Similarly, though less dramatically, in Bordeaux, scarcely a city of migrants, 40% of students from a North African, black African or Turkish background are concentrated in 10% of the *collèges*. These schools take in students from the most disadvantaged milieux, or those who are repeating a year, so that the education of ethnic minority students takes place in difficult conditions.[61]

But racial disadvantage is not the automatic product of social inequality. It stems also from systematic processes of discrimination that operate within schools. 'Ce sont surtout les Maghrebins qui seront orientés dans cette voie', commented one Parisian teenager when the de Villepin government introduced plans for vocational tracking at 14, her comment suggesting much about the collusion of schooling in the production of inequality that researchers also identify.[62] A recent report on England identifies similar issues. Black boys were three times as likely to be excluded from school as their white counterparts. Black school students in

London claimed that low teacher expectations played a major part in the underachievement of Afro-Caribbean children, and complained of inadequate levels of positive teacher attention, unfair behaviour-management practices, being watched with suspicion in break times, being subject to negative stereotyping and simply being disliked on account of being black.[63] The account of educational triage presented by Gillborn and Youdell suggests comparable conclusions: there exists a 'rationing of education' which leaves black children (and poor white children) concentrated at the bottom of tiered class groups in the key subjects of Maths and English. Such processes are among the hidden hands that transform micro-level experience into macro-level inequality.[64]

The redress of inequality?

According to Wolfgang Streeck, Director of the Max Planck Institute, we have reached the end of an era of redistribution: 'redistributive social policies are increasingly perceived by Europe's political classes as excessively expensive.' In their place, 'the emphasis of the political discourse is shifting towards *investment* in the ability of individuals and communities to survive in intensified international competition' and 'redress of inequality ... is sought through broad and equitable investment in productive capacities, especially in the 'human capital' of individuals ... whose optimal development ... becomes a public concern.'[65]

With the first part of Streeck's analysis one can concur: in education, as elsewhere, the impetus to redressing inequality through state action has weakened. But his optimistic reading of current trends is hard to credit; there is little in current education policy to suggest that investment in human capital is seriously intended as a means of reducing inequality – as opposed to raising attainment or achieving a measure of social inclusion. In their review of what PISA data tells us about those features of schooling conducive to inequality, Duru-Bellat and Suchaut write that

> any restriction on enrolment or early setting aside of certain students, any grouping by distinct level or streaming ... and all phenomena of segregation between schools ... tend to increase social inequality in performance without improving average level or even elite level.[66]

Yet these findings, which are consistent with the major discoveries of sociological research throughout the post-war period, do not find an echo in policy, which, as we suggest in our next chapter, is informed by, and elaborates, a quite different set of values and purposes.

Notes

1. La Vérité, no. 2, 15 September 1940. Reprinted in facsimile (Paris: Etudes et Documentation Internationales, 1978).
2. Unicef Innocenti Report Card, *A League Table of Educational Disadvantage in Rich Nations* UNICEF (Florence: Innocenti Research Centre, 2002) p. 22 (henceforth 'Innocenti').
3. Catherine Béduwé and Jordi Planas, *Educational expansion and the Labour Market* (Luxemburg: Cedefop, 2003) p. 136.
4. Crouch, *Social Change in Western Europe*, p. 242.
5. Yossi Shavit and Hans-Peter Blossfeld, *Persistent Inequality: changing educational attainment in thirteen countries* (Boulder: Westview Press 1993) p. 20.
6. Crouch, *Social Change in Western Europe*, p. 239.
7. Yossi Shavit and Karin Westerbeek, 'Educational Stratification in Italy: reforms, expansion and equality of opportunity' *European Sociological Review* 14.91, 33–47, p. 34, 1998.
8. Ibid., p. 45.
9. Pierre Merle, 'Le concept de démocratisation de l'institution scolaire: une typologie et sa mise à l'épreuve' *Population* 55.1, 15–50, 2000.
10. Marie Duru-Bellat and Annick Kieffer, 'Inequalities in Educational Opportunities in France: educational expansion, democratisation or shifting barriers?', *Journal of Education Policy* 15.3, 333–52, 2000.
11. Béduwé and Planas, *Educational expansion and the Labour Market*, chap. 4.
12. Jo Blanden, Paul Gregg and Stephen Machin, *Intergenerational Mobility in Europe and North America* (Centre for Economic Performance: London School of Economics, 2005) pp. 10–11.
13. 'Has the social class gap narrowed in primary schools? A background note to accompany the talk by Rt Hon Ruth Kelly, Secretary of State for Education and Skills: Education and Social Progress' 26 July 2005 (London: DfES, 2005) http://www.dfes.gov.uk/rsgateway/DB/STA/t000597/IPPR_Speech.pdf.
14. Penny Babb, *A Summary of 'Focus on Social Inequalities* (London: Office for National Statistics, 2005) p. 10.
15. Duru-Bellat and van Zanten, *Sociologie de l'école*, p. 46.
16. Innocenti, p. 21.
17. Innocenti, p. 3.
18. R.H. Lehmann, R. Peek and R. Gänsfuß, *Aspekte der Lernausgangslage und der Lernentwicklung von Schülerinnen und Schülem, die im Schuljahr 1996–7 eine füunfte Klase an Hamburger Schülen besuchten* available from http://www.hamburger-bildungsserver.de/lau/lau5/.
19. Elisabeth Flitner, 'Conditions culturelles et politiques du choix de l'école à Berlin', *Education et Sociétés* 14.2, 33–49, p. 37, 2004.
20. S. Schnepf, *A Sorting Hat that Fails? The Transition from primary to secondary School in Germany'*, Innocenti Working Paper 92, UNICEF (Florence: Innocenti Research Centre, 2002).
21. Marie Duru-Bellat and Bruno Suchaut, 'Organisation and context, Efficiency and Equity of Educational Systems: what PISA tells us', *European Educational Research Journal* 4.3, pp. 181–94, p. 189, 2005.
22. Daniele Checchi, *The Italian Educational System: family background and social stratification*, Working Paper presented to the ISAE conference 'On Monitoring Italy' January 2003.

23. Gabriele Ballarino and Daniele Checchi, *Sistema scolastico e disuguaglianza sociale* (Bologna: Il Mulino, 2006); Shavit and Westerbeek, 'Educational Stratification in Italy'.
24. Ballarino and Checchi, *Sistema scolastico e disuguaglianza sociale; Se la scuola non ci rende uguali* La Repubblica 28 November 2006.
25. John Polesel, 'Reform and Reaction: creating new education and training structures in Italy', *Comparative Education* 42.4 549–62, 2006.
26. Blossfeld and Shavit, *Persistent Inequality*, p. 19.
27. Lindsay Paterson, *Scottish Education in the Twentieth Century* (Edinburgh: Edinburgh University Press, 2003) p. 140; S. Jenkins, J. Micklewright and S. Schnepf, *Social Segregation in Secondary Schools: how does England compare with other countries?* (University of Essex: Institute for Social and Economic Research, January 2006).
28. 'The relative position of working-class pupils improved in Scotland over the period 1984–99, while it deteriorated in England. This narrowing class gap occurred within the comprehensive sector as well as across the whole education system. By the late 1990s, the gap in attainment between working-class and professional/managerial-class pupils was substantially narrower in Scotland than in England or Wales.' Linda Croxford and David Raffe, 'Secondary school organisation in England, Scotland and Wales since the 1980s', Discussion Paper for Seminar on *Policy Learning in 14–19 Education*. Joint seminar of *Education and Youth Transitions Project* and *Nuffield Review*, 15 March 2005. The paper focuses on differences in attainment at 16. The picture after 16 is different: as Paterson has written in *Scottish Education in the Twentieth Century* (p. 193) that the 'democratisation of secondary schools was not followed by a coherent and relevant democratisation of the universities and colleges', and the outcomes of the 'Education and Youth Transitions' likewise highlight this difference; above 16, class-related inequalities of attainment have increased in Scotland, while diminishing in England. See Centre for Educational Sociology, *Social-Class Inequalities in Education in England and Scotland*, Special CES Briefing no. 40 (Edinburgh: CES, May 2006).
29. Linda Croxford and David Raffe, 'Education Markets and Social Class Inequality: a comparison of trends in England, Scotland and Wales' (Edinburgh: Education and Youth Transitions Project, October 2005).
30. Jean Dugas, 'Les "3000" à Aulnay', *L'Ecole Emancipée* 90.4, 13, December 2005.
31. Luc Boltanski and Eve Chiapello, *The New Spirit of Capitalism* (London: Verso 2006) p. xxxix; P. Ginsborg, *Italy and Its Discontents* (London: Allen Lane, 2001) p. 61.
32. Brown, 'The Opportunity Trap', p. 152.
33. Van Zanten, 'Educational change and new cleavages', 2002 and 'New Modes of Reproducing Social Inequality in Education', 2005.
34. Dugas, 'Les "3000" à Aulnay'.
35. E. Parsons, B. Chalkley and A. Jones 'School Catchments and Pupil Movements: a case study in parental choice' Educational Studies 26.1 March 2000, pp. 33–48, p. 47.
36. N. Pyke, 'Bring Back Banding' (interview with Tim Brighouse) *The Guardian*, 8 January 2004.

37. Michael Young, 'Some Reflections on the concepts of social exclusion and social inclusion: beyond the third way' in *Tackling Disaffection and Social Exclusion*, ed. A. Hayton (London: Kogan Page, 1999).

38. Stephen J. Ball, *The More Things Change ... Educational Research, Social Class and interlocking inequalities* (London: Institute of Education, Professorial Lecture, 2003) p. 15.

39. Susan Hart et al., *Learning without Limits* (Buckingham: Open University Press, 2004) p. 10.

40. David Gillborn and Deborah Youdell, *Rationing Education: policy, practice, reform and equity* (Buckingham: Open University Press, 2000).

41. Duru-Bellat and van Zanten, *Sociologie de l'école*, p. 44.

42. Demailly et al., 'Analyse de l'évolution des modes de regulation', p. 44.

43. J-M. Drevon, 'Banlieues: il y a le feu!' *L'Ecole Emancipée*, pp. 10–11, December 2005, p. 11.

44. Ibid.

45. Gerard Chauveau, 'Les Rencontres de Observatoire des Zones Prioritaires', no. 40 avril 2003 – summarised in *L'Ecole Emancipée*, Jan/Fev, pp. 13–14, 2006.

46. Georges Felouzis and Joelle Perroton, 'Un New Deal pour l'école', *Le Monde Diplomatique* décembre 2005, pp. 14–15.

47. Agnès van Zanten, 'New Modes of Reproducing Social Inequality in Education: the changing role of parents, teachers, schools and educational policies', *European Educational Research Journal* 4.3 155–69, 2005.

48. Van Zanten, 'New Modes of Reproducing Social Inequality in Education', p. 300, 2002.

49. Liliana Jacott and Antonio Maldonaldo Rico, 'The Centros Concertados in Spain, parental demand and implications for equity', *European Journal of Education* 41.1, 97–111, p. 97, 2006.

50. OECD (R. Teese et al.) *Equity in Education – Thematic Review, Spain country note* (Paris: OECD, 2006) p. 35.

51. Jacott and Maldonaldo Rico, 'The Centros Concertados in Spain, parental demand and implications for equity', p. 100.

52. Ibid.

53. Jacott and Maldonaldo Rico, 'The Centros Concertados in Spain, parental demand and implications for equity', p. 101.

54. J.-L. Bernal, 'Parental Choice, Social Class and Market Forces: the consequences of privatisation of public services in education', *Journal of Education Policy* 20.6, pp. 779–92, 2005.

55. Elisabeth Flitner, 'Conditions culturelles et politiques du choix de l'école à Berlin', pp. 33–49.

56. European Coalition of Cities Against Racism, *Study on Measures Taken by Municipalities for Further Action to Challenge Racism through Education* (Graz: ECCAR Occasional Papers, 2005) www.etc-graz.at

57. Schnepf, *A Sorting Hat that Fails?*, p. 17.

58. Salah Mamon, *Race and Class*, p. 86.

59. See the supplement to *L'Ecole Emancipée*, December 2005.

60. Polly Toynbee, 'Religious schools are indoctrinating and divisive. The people don't want them. So why are MPs backing them?' *The Guardian*, Friday, April 14, 2006.

61. Felouzis and Perroton, 'Un New Deal pour l'école'.
62. Flora Yanga interviewed by Régis Boselli, 'Contre Feux', *L'Ecole Emancipée*, pp. 18–19, p. 19, December 2005.
63. Brian Richardson (ed.) *Tell it Like it is: how our schools fail black children* (Stoke-on-Trent: Trentham Books, 2005).
64. S.J. Ball, C. Marques–Cardoso, D. Reay, M. Thrupp 'Changes in Regulation Modes and Social Reproduction of Inequalities in Education Systems: Education Policy in England – Changing Modes of Regulation, 1945–2001, p. 18, www.girset.ucl.ac.be(2002).
65. Streeck (1999) quoted in Nafsika Alexiadou, 'Social Exclusion and Educational Opportunity: the case of British education policies within a European Context' *Globalisation, Societies and Education*, 3.1, pp. 101–25, p. 110, 2005.
66. Duru-Bellat and Suchaut, 'Organisation and context', p. 189.

6
Teaching and Learning – The Terms of Modernisation

In the previous three chapters, we have shown how policy orthodoxy has attempted to transform the institutional design of educational systems. In this chapter we again find a detailed policy template – consisting of new approaches to curricula, pedagogies, assessment, in-school selection and academic/vocational pathways. Its impact is considerable. At first sight, this impact is surprising. Of course, education's relation to the labour market has always been central to its purposes. But equally, ever since the establishment of national systems of education, curriculum and pedagogy have been deeply implicated in the reproduction of national identities, while schooling's function in transmitting the more general cultures associated with humanist traditions has also been important.[1] That these positions, along with the progressivism that was a significant feature of the post-war period, should be so clearly sidelined, says much for the political weight and effectiveness of the strongly economised discourse that has become the vulgate of European policy for teaching and learning.

To understand the significance of new programmes for curriculum and pedagogy, we need to grasp not only the problems they seek to address, but also the conflicts out of which they emerge. We can understand the conflicts in terms of three broad tendencies that have shaped teaching and learning in the expanded education systems of post-war Europe: 'traditional humanism', 'progressive education' and 'modernisation' – we should perhaps say 'new' modernisation to distinguish the modernisation programmes of contemporary governments from similarly named projects of an earlier period. The categories do not account for all classroom practice – in particular they shed little light on the low-level uncertificated programmes of basic skills and acculturation which dominated mass education until the 1960s and are still in some sectors powerful today. Nevertheless it is in terms of these tendencies that we can best understand the shaping of policy, the inspirations of educational movements and the defining of the terms of educational conflict – both in the period between 1960 and the 1980s, and now, in neo-liberal times.

A restricted humanism

Before the 1960s, if the mass of school-age children were educated at all, it was in the belief that only a few were capable of benefiting from education's higher levels. Those who defended selective systems sought legitimation by appealing to time-honoured knowledge traditions. The administrators who developed post-war schooling in England, for instance, often cited Plato's *Republic*, and with the divisions of humanity established there. 'You are all of you in this land brothers,' Socrates wants to tell the citizens of his imagined society. 'But when God fashioned you, he added gold in the composition of those who are qualified to be Rulers; he put silver in the Auxiliaries, and iron and bronze in farmers and the rest'.[2] The *Gymnasium* teachers who in the 1960s argued against educational reform put things in similar terms. The varieties of school in the German system 'corresponded to different kinds of life experience ... to the manifold conditions and forms of the spirit ... and to different tasks and interests'.[3] To break with these fundamental characteristics of humanity would be to relinquish the heritage of civilisation. As the American poet (and English conservative) T.S. Eliot explained in 1949, the 'headlong rush to educate everybody' entailed 'lowering our standards' and 'abandoning the study of those subjects by which the essentials of our culture are transmitted; destroying our ancient edifices ...'.[4] Or, in the more succinct phrase of another literary conservative, 'more will mean worse'.[5]

In these ways, a conception of learning which emphasised the all-round development of the individual and the necessity of linking personal formation to the cultural achievements of 'humanity', became tied to the defence of socially selective education. From this perspective – in which the role of the school was to enable access to traditional disciplinary knowledge for those able to benefit it – it was difficult to think about curriculum change, so that it was still possible in 2006 to describe the curriculum of upper secondary education in Italy as 'designed for the most privileged social groups and experienced users of education',[6] and that of Spain as equally problematic:

> The academic conservatism of secondary teacher education – knowledge-centred, context-insensitive, teacher-centred – favours classroom practice which is equally conservative. The teacher has been

trained in his or her undergraduate years to focus on concepts, principles, theory and rules, and to study in a relatively unsupervised and independent fashion. The emphasis on abstract and private learning enters classrooms which today accommodate the whole of the age-group. Moreover, the high level of social selection which operates through this system of cultural transmission ensures that most students in compulsory secondary education will be taught by men and women with limited understanding of student home background and culture.[7]

There was much more to humanism than this: as we shall see, its links to elitism were not unbreakable and its attachment to disciplinary knowledge offered at later moments a perspective from which to criticise economistic reform. But for much of the post-war period it was deployed as part of a conservative discourse that warned against the effects of educational expansion and curricular change. In the process, its critical dimension was muted: as Vertecchi points out, Italian schooling in the post-war period was shaped by an idealist culture which tended – in the manner of Gentile – to encourage obedience and tradition rather than critique.[8] In this sense, he argues, the legacy of fascism endured.

Progressive education

We use 'progressive education', not to designate a theoretical position, nor a coherent body of practice, but rather a loose collection of economic and social assumptions, philosophies, classroom practices, political alliances and strategies and professional orientations which together formed the dominant educational ideological complex of the mid-century. Given some rough unity by principles of child-centred learning and cultural relevance, progressivism in this broad sense was constituted as an antidote both to the traditional humanism of academic education, and to the narrow curriculum and harsh pedagogic régimes of mass schooling. It was an international movement. Drawing, often eclectically, from a variety of intellectual backgrounds – from Montessori to Freire, Froebel to Vygotsky – it spoke of reshaping the content of education, and of a new relationship between teachers, students and communities. It presented itself as the matrix of curricular and pedagogic reforms, which – driven by the decentralised initiative of educational professionals – could engage with the mass of students and resolve the problems of an educational expansion that was taking place unaccompanied by any systematic programme of curriculum change. On this basis for a short period it gained the acceptance of governments that sought to match education to what were perceived as new social and economic needs, and which lacked the capacity to generate responses of any other kind.

The literature critical of progressive education, both as classroom practice and educational philosophy, is abundant. There were many on the left who argued that its account of child development was 'biological', that its understanding of learning offered insufficient space to systematic instruction and that its grasp of learning's social determinants was uncertain.[9] Other critics represented it not as a movement of educational radicalism, but a variant of an 'elementary school' tradition that was more concerned to manage deprived children than to enable access to traditions of disciplinary knowledge, and was in many cases the result of teachers' capitulation to a powerful network of influence and patronage rather than the product of deep conviction.[10] For the right progressivism was destructive of traditional disciplinary knowledge – a view that was also more widely shared[11] – and an underminer of cultural tradition. For critical sociology, progressive rhetoric concealed low expectations, socially conditioned, of working-class children; or was based on an invisible pedagogy that reflected the cultures of middle-class families and disadvantaged other children.[12]

For us, many of these criticisms are telling – although it should be said that they were not the exclusive preserve of the cultural right or of academic sociology but were debated quite widely in the progressive movement itself. However, we are not concerned so much here to defend the detail of any particular version of progressivism as to suggest its social dimensions and political effect. An important part of its inspiration came from the social movements of the late 1960s, and their challenge to a society that stunted individual potential and created profound social inequalities. For many teachers and students, educational critique and progressivist practice were parts of a wider movement, whose aims went beyond classroom reform to include social and cultural transformation of many kinds – in the family as much as in the workplace. Curricular and pedagogic initiative arose from this more general turbulence, and in this sense progressivism – even in its milder forms – was politically troubling.

England

In England, the 1960s and 1970s were the high period of comprehensive reform, which saw the partial integration of mass and academic education. Primary schools lost their function of preparing children for the '11+' exam that determined secondary school entry, and were thus unusually open to reform. In this context, progressive discourse saturated the reports of government on educational change and deeply affected the training of teachers. For a period, there was embedded in policy orthodoxy a view of learning which elevated 'finding out' above 'being told', and in doing so rejected previously dominant educational philosophies in favour of a naturalist theory of education which had its roots in romanticism. 'The child,' argued the influential Plowden Report on Primary Education, 'is the agent of his own learning'; children learned through 'individual discovery, first-hand experience and opportunity for creative work'.[13] The curriculum should be thought of in terms of activity and experience rather than 'knowledge to be acquired and stored' and the school's role was to 'devise the right environment for children' in which they could 'be themselves and develop at the pace appropriate to them.'[14]

Plowden principles influenced the working practices of many primary schools, though these were never the majority. It also established itself at secondary level, particularly in urban areas. Here its attractiveness as a radical orientation towards student experience outweighed its theoretical deficiencies, while its tendency to view the child as an asocial individual became, as it were, spontaneously modified in the encounter of teachers with youth cultures. The official curriculum, one critic wrote in 1975, had rendered education 'primarily a medium of economic exchange' and 'emptied it of its potential as a means of self-realisation'.[15] Child-centredness from this perspective entailed a focus on dimensions of working-class experience that the official curriculum neglected. The East London teacher Chris Searle – suspended for a period for publishing his students' writing – advocated 'a new methodology and classroom consciousness of working-class students themselves using their own local resources, perceiving their own neighbourhood, families, history and themselves – in short their class – as relevant and proper material to form a basis of knowledge and identity'.[16] From this position – that the histories and cultures of hitherto unrecognised groups should be central to the curriculum – it was a short step to other forms of action. In one characteristic leaflet, the London Association for the Teaching of English (LATE) called for links between teachers and social movements outside the school, since classroom change 'was brought about first by the voice of black pupils and the black community' and 'second by (the fight against) overt racism on the streets.'[17]

Germany

In the same period, a revival of the *Reformpedagogik* traditions of the 1920s mingled with the ideas of Freire and Freinet to affect elementary education in some West German *Länder* – most notably Hesse. The new curricula – the *Rahmenrichtlinien* – of the late 1960s integrated play into the learning process, tended to prioritise *freies Schreiben* and creativity above grammar and correct spelling and sought to value children's interpretations of texts and ways of solving mathematical problems; they related the pace of learning to the development of the individual child, and set aside time for children to pursue self-chosen tasks. They also gave a new importance to the pedagogic work of the teacher, of whom they made challenging demands: in place of the uniform textbook, learning materials were diversified and often teacher (and parent) made; curricular innovation, in relation to sex education, or to the social consequences of science, demanded new pedagogic capacities. The teacher's role in the assessment of pupils also changed, at least in the early years of the elementary school. In most *Länder,* the traditional *Kopfnoten* which provided headings for the end-of-year report – *Fleiß, Aufmerksamkeit, Ornung* and *Betragen* – were regarded as above challenge, as compelling summarisations of the purposes of schooling.[18] In progressive *Länder* they were abandoned, along with the numerical marking system which had summarised children's development in the starkest of forms. Instead, teachers wrote evaluative and developmental comments: the function of the school in relation to assessment had not changed, but under progressive influence its form was modified.

Italy

In Italian primary education, progressive education found space in which to develop. In 1976, the authors of *Red Bologna* argued that in that city at least, the elementary *doposcuola* – the non-compulsory afternoon hours of schooling, run by the muncipality – had become a site of collective creative work. Here, the standard methods of progressivism – the extended inter-disciplinary project, collaborative and mixed-ability learning – were deployed in ways that came to influence the mainstream of state schooling.[19] The reforms of 1974 (the *decreti delegati*) gave these approaches further impetus, in elementary schools and in the *scuola media*. Democratising management, increasing community involvement and licensing research and innovation on the part of teachers, they sustained an intense period of change: 'our school was rich in projects, enthusiasms, hopes', wrote teachers at a school in

Piedmont; 'the rigid separation of boys and girls came to an end, the girls no longer wore their black smocks.'[20]

But these approaches were not dominant, and the contrast between statements of intent and actual practice was striking. (Monasta compares an official pledge to 'remove the social and economic obstacles which limit the freedom and equality of citizens and prevent the full development of human beings and their full participation in the political, economic and social management of the country' with a failure to take infrastructural and teacher training measures that might realise such an objective.[21]) Still less were such measures implemented in upper secondary education. In Italy, more than anywhere else in the 1960s and 1970s, the upper secondary school, the *liceo*, was the site of prolonged and serious social confrontation. The occupation of schools by students, repression by state authorities and – later – violent conflict between left-wing and fascist students marked a period of Italian education in which – as the autonomist Paulo Virno put it, 'two opposing powers confronted one another', neither able to attain a decisive influence.[22] The demands of students were radical – 'the control and eventual elimination of marks and failures, and therefore the abolition of selection in school ... setting of the curriculum from below'[23] – but their impact on the pedagogy and curriculum of the *liceo* was not strong. School-student numbers increased, the population of universities grew, but no social force, central or local, had the capacity to promote widespread qualitative change in educational process. Secondary education remained strongly disciplinary and essentially based on knowledge transmission – the generation of 1968 itself had a fundamental attachment to classical humanism and disciplinary knowledge. As Giorgio Porrotto – advocate of a business-driven project of modernisation – noted in 2003, 'the question of pedagogy does not really exist in Italy ... Where it does exist it deals with infants and totally ignores secondary education'.[24]

France

In France and in Spain, the impact of progressivism was significant but delayed. In France, the continuing centralisation of educational initiative had for a long period acted against the possibility of local-level reform. The Haby directive of 1975, which prohibited streaming within the *collège unique*, promoted no new forms of pedagogy that might enable teachers to respond to different classroom situations. It was not until 1979 that schools were empowered to utilise 10% of their teaching time on self-determined *Projet d'Activités Educatives* (PAE). At this point, as in England, government initiative provided a framework for local intervention on the part of teachers who had for several years already been involved both in both trade-union militancy and pedagogic experiment. As in other countries, their work insisted on the collective dimension of learning, the cultural affiliations of the school and the self-activity of students as producers of meaning. The influence of French variants of progressive education, notably the Freinet movement, was strong:

> We secured a lot of funding for the PAEs. It allowed us to produce newspapers, to write and perform plays or to make films for European educational networks. For several years we organised an event in the town, an entire day when the whole school was outdoors, with students and teachers all together ... And there were also the collège fêtes, where the whole *quartier* turned up, and where we had to manage it all through a mixture of dialogue and firmness.[25]

Subsequently, under the Mitterrand government, progressivism enjoyed a time in the sun. The Legrand Report of 1982 allowed institutional autonomy for the *collèges* in relation to teaching methods, and endorsed particular progressivist themes – notably interdisciplinary study and a degree of personal tutoring.[26] Official rhetoric, as in England, placed 'the child' at the centre of education – an important feature of the 1989 legislation mentioned in chapter 3. In some respects, however, this was a controversial emphasis, whose departure from knowledge traditions that were focused on subject mastery, across a range of disciplines, was problematic as much to sections of the left as to the right. Writing in the early 1970s, Basil Bernstein distinguished between 'English' and 'European' versions of educational knowledge. In (pre-reform) England, knowledge was framed in such a way that the boundaries between school and 'commonsense' knowledge were relatively weak. Teacher discretion over content and pedagogy was considerable and pupils had 'many options within the pedagogical relationship'. European traditions of school knowledge, by contrast, emphasised the inculcation of formal, disciplinary knowledge, across a range of subjects. Even after the formidable attacks mounted by Bourdieu and Passeron against the indifference to social and cultural difference embodied in these traditions, and the symbolic violence attendant upon their transmission to students from outside the dominant cultural groups, 'classical' forms of knowledge provided a deep-rooted reference point for those who distrusted new projects of reform.[27]

Spain

There were similar complex tensions in Spain, where the impact of progressivism on state schooling was delayed by the endurance of the Franco régime. Francoism in education meant a model of vertical control – homogenous and closely defined curricula for the whole of the Spanish state, into which teachers had little input. Even so, there had developed by the mid-1970s, illegally and outside the régime's control, an *Alternativa,* in which anti-authoritarian and Marxist ideas intermingled and which linked pedagogical initiative to the demand for a secular and democratic system of public schooling. With the success of the PSOE in the 1982 election, these movements were integrated into governmental projects, and orientated towards a long process of curricular and pedagogic reform. Initially, the process relied heavily on the capacity of teachers; it was assumed that 'real change in the quality of education requires the adoption and putting into practice of processes of experimentation and collaboration among teachers'.[28] The educational model emerging from these efforts was both rich and unclear. It brought together, in Sacristán's words:

> The principles of progressive pedagogy from Europe and America, of activist pedagogy and more specifically the popular school of Freinet, the Italian co-operative movements; it borrowed Dewey's approach to learning, the anti-authoritarianism of 1968 French pedagogy, ingredients of Romantic pedagogy which favoured new humanist relations in teaching, of Piagetianism, aspiration to interdisciplinarity and complementarity in intellectual formation and a certain militancy against hegemonic textbooks. It stressed the importance of incorporating popular culture, of artistic expression through diverse media, a formative model of student assessment, introduction of new technologies, excursions into the outside world to study social, geographical and cultural realities ... establishing connections between intellectual and physical development, stimulating the participation of students and the take-up of action research.[29]

The LOGSE legislation of 1990 – which established a common curriculum up to the age of 16 – was both the culmination of progressivist influence and its undoing. Sociological critique had already focused on the effects of progressivism's hostility to disciplinary knowledge: it had created a classroom in which the grammar of learning was obscure, and in which the students most likely to be successful were those whose cultural backgrounds corresponded to models of learning implicit in progressive pedagogy – the middle class.[30] LOGSE, extrapolating the pedagogic principles of primary education to the entire system, did not address these criticisms. It privileged a pedagogy based on constructivist theories and standardised a model of the curriculum in which content and knowledge were relativised and lost importance in relation to a new stress on 'process', on abilities or skills and on 'education in values'. At the same time, according to many critics, LOGSE's indifference to disciplinary knowledge meant that it instigated what was at some levels of schooling a lowering of standards. The level of linguistic, mathematical or scientific knowledge at the end of the 16+ ESO (compulsory secondary) cycle was no higher than what was demanded at the end of the old primary (General Basic Education) at 14 years.[31] To these fundamental problems, which deprived the LOGSE reforms of the support of important sections of teachers, were added others. LOGSE was born out of a culture of sponsored experiment. But the experiments were not evaluated, and they were extended without any adequate attempt to retrain teachers or provide schools with resources; and as Spain entered neo-liberal times, problems of underfunding and of a weakness of pedagogical culture in schools grew in severity. A sympathetic critique of the attempt to embed some progressive principles in such a system concluded that material constraints rendered it implausible:

> Programmes of the public schools tend to put greater emphasis on transversal matters which are not easy to evaluate in terms of academic outcomes, such as peace education, multiculturalism and citizenship, sensitivity to local context, and inclusive education. The problem is that these curricula and programmes are offered in public schools with scarce financial funding without increasing the human resources.[32]

Or as, Gramsci put it, the problem of educational reform is not just programmatic but 'human' – here, of the dispositions of teachers and 'the entire social complex which they express'.[33]

Progressivism lost

'We can afford free men,' wrote one English progressive in 1968, 'and we need them'.[34] But this way of coupling educational change to economic necessity was increasingly rejected by the international policy orthodoxy that by the late 1970s had begun to develop another sort of educational programme, less reliant on the uncoordinated and disputatious initiative of educationalists. The shift away from educational practices influenced by progressivism has been prolonged and complicated; it remains unfinished. Its pace and extent have varied from country to country, depending in part on the political strength and social implantation of the forces which have opposed it. But amid these complexities and strong patterns of variation, three factors stand out, as determinants of the fate of the progressive project. The first is what might be called its impossibility. Progressivism sought to produce 'free men' in an increasingly unfree and unequal society. This did not mean that it was from the beginning doomed, or foolish. But like any social movement or reforming force, its achievements, in the absence of more general social transformation, were limited, provisional and liable to reversal and collapse. It relied upon a continual investment of energies which generational ageing and two decades of neo-liberal austerity and attrition made it hard to sustain. The situation is well expressed by the French activist already quoted above. Asked whether all the great 'moments pédagogiques' are located in the past, he replied

> Yes, things have changed. The investment (of energy) is no longer the same. In the end you get discouraged by a succession of policies that aim at the dismantling of public services, at the worsening of conditions of work, the increasing demands that are made of teachers, outside the hours of teaching, the absence of consultation ... Beyond that, to involve yourself in pedagogic experiment is to expose yourself, and the constant attempts (of management) to repress trade union activity have discouraged that sort of risk-taking. That doesn't mean that there are no longer any initiatives, but all the same they haven't occurred on anything like the scale of previous years. We reject the neo-liberal reforms which seek to turn us away from interdisciplinarity, but these reforms are not the reason why we have stopped being involved in interdisciplinary work.[35]

The second factor affecting the trajectory of progressive education has been the capacity of its opponents to discredit it. The process of discrediting involved a great deal of demagogy, which blamed progressivism for general social ills it realistically could not have addressed. But there was a core of rationality to the criticism: when the Haut Conseil d'Education talked in 2006 of the '150,000 who leave school each year without a qualification' or when the Basic Skills Unit in Britain claimed in 1999 that 20% of the adult population was 'functionally illiterate', real educational problems were being signalled, which required the sort of balance sheet of post-war reform that progressivism never seriously undertook.[36] Conservative rhetoric could fill the resulting absence, counterposing the supposed academic strengths and social cohesiveness of traditionalism to the debilities of progressive practice. Important here was the effect of Thatcherism, which linked discursive criticism to successful confrontation with teacher unions, and with legislation that laid the basis for a new educational order.

It is the varying but increasing capacity of governments to develop such an order that constitutes the third element in the decline of the progressive educational bloc. The mid-century expansion of schooling took place, to some extent, outside the control of governments – teachers' influence on curriculum and pedagogy was strong; the everyday pressures of new student populations on teaching styles and school régimes was considerable. Thatcherism demonstrated that the teaching force could be tamed, through the defeat of its trade union capabilities and the curtailing of its classroom autonomy. This was a massive negative achievement. The next step was to develop and embed a new set of norms and regulatory practices that could re-orientate the work of the school. Here the resources provided by 'modernisation' have been essential.

Modernisation

Modernisation draws from overlapping repertoires, devised primarily by the OECD and the EU, by lobbying organisations such as the European Round Table and by national governments. Its reference points, outlined in chapter 2, are those summarised by the European Commission:

> The European Union has set itself the strategic target of becoming the most competitive economy in the world, capable of sustainable growth, with more, higher quality jobs and greater social cohesion. Achieving this goal requires an overall strategy aimed at preparing the development of the knowledge-based economy and a strategy designed to modernise the European social model by investing in people and by combating social exclusion ... The information explosion demands fundamental rethinking of traditional conceptions of knowledge, its 'transmission', 'delivery' by teachers and acquisition by students. It raises questions about the assessment and learning of knowledge and the more demanding resources of skills, attitudes and motivations to learn. It questions curriculum content and the prioritisation and compartmentalisation of 'subjects'.[37]

This vision of comprehensive transformation involves overturning the established frameworks of curriculum, pedagogy and assessment in the name of quality and innovation, realising modernising purposes that are both economic and social. But it cannot be understood in its own terms. *Pace* its inclusive rhetoric of change, the new kind of modernisation is profoundly dichotomised, and in consequence its notions of quality are from the beginning ambivalent. As we have seen, in 1996, the Reiffers Report castigated to the Commission the reforms of an earlier period for their attempts to introduce egalitarianism to societies which could never be other than stratified;' within an overall policy of expansion, it accordingly insisted on a principle of distinction. Models of academic education could not productively be applied to the education of the mass of the population. This did not mean a return to the curricula of the past, but it did require that any redesign should have in mind a double prioritisation – of the education of elites, and of the most disadvantaged and socially difficult.

In the curricular designs of member states, this approach has been replicated – albeit that the resources devoted to the elite are somewhat greater than those enjoyed by the less successful groups.[38] We suggested in the previous chapter that governments presided for many years over arrangements in which a pattern of apparently common schooling of 5–6 to 16-year olds masked intricate arrangements through which social differentiation was translated into educational distinction. But such arrangements did not work perfectly. One of the problems was the process of 'academic drift' which occurred within common systems that lacked the capacity to establish strong forms of distinction between different groups of students; it was not with unalloyed pleasure that policymakers observed the increasing number of students taking the *bac général* in France in the early 1990s, nor the rapid rise in the student population of Italian universities.[39] At the same time, there was plainly a problem with the disengagement of the least successful students from the entire certification process; while elite groups, unhappy with qualifications systems that had become massified, demanded forms of certification that identified the best-performing students. (In England, this latter demand led to the creation of an A* grade in 16+ exams, distinguished from a mere 'A' grade, and marking out the *crème de la crème.*)

In response to such difficulties, governments are attempting to establish mechanisms to differentiate between students at an earlier point in their school careers, claiming that in this way they will re-engage with the most disaffected, meet the needs of middle sectors seeking relatively high levels of competence and satisfy also the demands of more powerful groups.[40] It is on this basis that we should understand a number of national policy shifts. Inscribed in LOGSE was the principle of dignifying 'vocational education' and directing towards it a large part of the less successful population of state school students, while the majority of pupils in the private sector were turned towards a *bachillerato* which, according to the OECD in 2006, overemphasised 'cultural conservation' and failed to provide 'strands that would open it up to a wider range of students'.[41] In England, the Blair government insisted, as we have seen, that schools abandon mixed-ability teaching, and brought forward to 14 the age at which students could be placed on a vocational track – its 2006 legislation required that students 'choose' at 14 between academic and vocational study.[42] The separation of academic and vocational tracks envisaged by the Moratti legislation and the Thélot Report was based on similar principles. In the same frame belongs Thélot's preference for a programme of basic skills, rather than expanded participation in *baccalauréats*, as the unifying element of schooling; as its critics point out, although most of the age group stays in education until the age of 18, the laws inspired by Thélot limit the common horizon of education at best best 16.[43] In Germany, placing the moment of differentiation at 14–15 has different implications – the proposal is advanced as a means of overcoming the 'rigid' distinctions that are presently made at the end of primary schooling.[44] Overall, the European pattern of differentiation, in which 14–15 has become the age at which educational destinies are settled, suggests that while there is a strong secular trend towards mass participation in certificated education, this movement is heavily qualified by processes of rationing and curricular segregation.

The attempt to settle educational destinies at 14–15 is accompanied by a new emphasis in 5–14 education on the acquisition of 'basic skills' and of 'quality' in the delivery of them. This says much about the acceleration of governments towards a policy orthodoxy in which 'all' students – save those significant numbers schooled in the private sector, and those state school students identified as 'gifted and talented' or as possessing 'special needs' – will experience a common and narrowly defined core, whose effectiveness will be measured by international comparisons.[45] It is in England that the project is most advanced: primary schooling is dominated by the 'National Strategies' for Literacy and Numeracy which – according to Blair's advisors – should occupy more than 50% of the school timetable.[46] These detailed and prescriptive strategies are claimed by the Blair government as its greatest educational success, responsible for increasing the success rate of 11-year olds in national tests; a 'National Literacy Framework' extends the approach to the first three years of secondary schooling.

The English example is emulated elsewhere, though without as yet reproducing the directedness in small things which is the distinctive feature of Anglo-schooling. In France, government reports recommend a common basis ('socle') of essential skills: 'reading, writing, competence in spoken language, familiarity with mathematical operations, the ability to use a computer, (knowledge of) English as a tool for international communications, knowing how to live together as members of the same society'.[47] Primarily, critics allege, for presentational purposes, this essentially economistic approach has grafted on to it a strand of education in 'humanist culture, whose place in a discourse of competences is problematic'.[48] Moratti's intention of bringing to an end the *tempo pieno* of Italian primary education is predicted to have a similar effect: the reduced hours of learning will squeeze out subjects such as music from the common curriculum, leaving them to be taken as options. Likewise in Germany, where the disappearance from Hesse in the 1980s of the *Rahmenrichtlinien* of an earlier period has led to a narrowing of the curriculum, in which reading, writing and arithmetic occupy a central place. These long years of basic-skills acquisition will be subject to strong regulation in the form of national systems for the testing of students, with learning processes evaluated on the basis of reference points external to the school and with systemic effectiveness measured by international comparisons of student achievement. The performance of English children is measured at 5, 7, 11 and 14; in Germany, all 16 states have introduced *Vergleichs* – or *Parallelarbeiten* – systems, where schools set tests during the school year that are marked on the basis of common criteria; even in Hesse, numerical marks have replaced teacher evaluations in the end-of-year assessment of children in years 1 and 2 of the elementary school. By these means, some education administrations are trying to achieve what could be called a national, or at least a core, curriculum. There are counteracting tendencies, however; some *Länder* wish to replace a system of federal affiliations with one in which education is completely in the hands of *Länder*: autonomous schools would then respond to the light touch of individual *Länder*, with minimal federal involvement, and in the context provided by international or EU systems of performance indicators.

Personal, responsible, creative

The ability of schools to inculcate basic skills, and to demonstrate rising levels of attainment, is seen as central by policy, and contributes in important ways to the legitimisation of government policies. But policy design is also based on other principles. It claims to be developing forms of education that enable individuals, each at their own level, to respond to the challenges of a risk society in which successful employment depends upon constant adaptation to new labour-market situations. A spokesperson for the French employers' federation, MEDEF, identifies the issue in these terms:

> The essential recommendation that I would offer is to make the individual responsible for their own courses of study ... There is no longer a role for education in setting normative frameworks; the role of the collectivity is to make possible the maintaining of individual competences ... Thus the logic of *précarisation* is no longer connected with fear or insecurity; although an individual may experience a period of non-employment, so long as he remains 'competent' he can redirect himself towards another job.[49]

The relationship between the highly normative emphasis on basic skills and the insistence that the education of the future must be based upon the individualised acquisition of competences is not without its tensions. They are kept in balance in a number of ways, in which neo-liberal emphases are articulate with others that have a different, even a progressive, lineage. In England, for instance, the ministries of culture and of education fund projects designed to promote 'creativity' in schools. The initiative is justified in terms of the qualities of initiative, creativity and teamworking that are supposedly required by post-fordist economies. More generally, the tensions are managed through strategies in which the requirements of the new social order are translated into the language of personal development. Among such strategies is responsibilisation – what Gewirtz calls 'the process of inculcating a culture of self-discipline or self-surveillance among welfare subjects', through techniques that include portfolio assessment, homework policies, learning contracts and home-school agreements.[50] The responsibilisation of individuals requires the personalisation of the curriculum, a process in which traditional subject boundaries – so MEDEF and the EU expect – will dissolve. Personalisation - *Individualisierung von Lernprozessen, personnalisation des parcours* – has nothing in common, British ministers insist, with the child-centredness of an earlier era. Whereas the ideal of progressive education was a notion of individual development and self-realisation combined to greater or lesser extent with an idea of collective emancipation, personalisation operates with more explicit norms; it is an attempt to identify the individual learning strategies that are most effective in reaching an externally given and predefined outcome. It does not involve a curriculum claiming to respond primarily to students' interests, nor a pedagogy that encourages children to 'be themselves'. On the contrary, it is based on offering support to individual students in order that they may reach defined targets. The support includes the use of ICT (computers) and of 'learning mentors', not necessarily qualified teachers, to work with students in small groups. Above all, it means 'curriculum choice', particularly during the 14–19 stage, when academic and vocational pathways become available.[51] At this point it becomes difficult to distinguish personalised learning from a form of selection, and the appeal to individual need folds into the reproduction of social divisions.

Obstacles

Announcing a programme of modernisation is one thing, implementing it quite another; governments here face a number of obstacles – each more structural than contingent – that arise from the limited capacities of states and the continuing strengths of opposition as well as the contradictions between what states intend and what market-influenced systems let them do. 'As if anything could be restructured in Italy,' wrote Leonardo Sciascia. The jibe, directed originally against the demand of those who kidnapped Aldo Moro for a 'restructuring of Italian prisons', applies just as much to the Berlusconi/Moratti reforms.[52] A supporter of the general line of reforms, Maccarini, noted in 2004 that much of their promise was yet to be realised. The offer of a personalised curriculum – and of school curriculum programmes that respond to the school's unique environment – has foundered: 'uniformity has persisted'.[53] Berlusconi may have made the three 'I's of *informatica, inglese* and *impresa* the cornerstones of a rhetoric of modernisation, but several embedded factors work against him. Humanist cultures are still dominant in secondary education, and provide intellectual resources for a critique of international economism;[54] primary teachers are still conscious of past achievements; the 'softening up' of teachers under Thatcherism, which prepared the way for New Labour's pedagogic régime, has not been replicated. In any case, the long history of underinvestment in Italian education leaves it ill-equipped to deliver credible universal programmes of English land ICT, while business involvement is more likely to fragment the provision of vocational education than to improve it.[55] The position of other states is a little better.

It is difficult to make conclusive statements on the state of curriculum reform in the 16, still relatively diverse, *Länder* of Germany. In general, what has taken place is a reduction to eight years of secondary education and the introduction of a centrally set test (*Landesabitur* or *Zentralabitur*) at the end of the secondary cycle where it had not been common. In this context, between 2004–6, some revisions of the curriculum took place in order to structure the last two years in accordance with the requirements of the *Abitur*. But as regards the 'requirements of the economy' (*Anforderungen der Wirtschaft*) it is unclear what kind of translation of policy discourse into educational practice could occur, beyond the normal rhetoric of the employers' association and the largely consensual emphasis on the three 'Rs'. Nor does Spain represent an unequivocal advance towards modernisation. In the mid-1990s, many commentators were sceptical about the Spanish project of 'profound curricular reform' at a time of 'severe budgetary restrictions'; such problems continue to undermine the public system, have resulted in the growth of sharp regional inequalities and fuelled the growth of the private sector.[56] In France, discussion of curricular reform takes place amid controversy over long-term repercussions of cuts in teacher numbers, and is still shaped by powerful curricular traditions at odds with the precepts of new modernisation.

So England appears to be something of an exception in this context. Unlike France or Italy, Blair's government can claim it 'owns' the curriculum and pedagogy of schools; the battles against professional influence and political radicalism have been won, whatever vestigial attachments to progressivism teachers may retain; New Labour has created a strong educational state that works to highly specified targets, is closely managed, and – compared to the 1990s at least – well-financed. If the neo-liberal claim of installing a 'quality' system of mass education is anywhere being realised, then it must be in England. But in fact the problems of the English classroom remain considerable, and judged in terms of Labour's wish to create a 'world-class' education system, its reform has been far from successful. This English impasse reveals much about the meanings of 'quality' as it is deployed in neo-liberal discourse. The Blair government regards the National Strategies for Literacy and Numeracy as its most strikingly successful achievements; it thinks them responsible for a rise in the level of performance of 11-year olds in national tests between 1998 and 2003 (a rise which has since levelled off). Academic researchers tend to argue the contrary, concluding that 'there is little evidence that (the NNS) has been an "undisputed success"', and that in the case of both strategies 'traditional patterns of teaching have not been dramatically transformed'. On the contrary, 'far from encouraging and extending pupil contributions to promote higher levels of interaction and cognitive engagement,' most of the (teachers') questions were of a low cognitive level designed to funnel pupils' responses towards a required answer'.[57] These specific, classroom-focused criticisms are amplified by wider studies: large-scale projects of standards-focused reform, employing a uniform pedagogy and curriculum content across schools of widely different class and ethnic composition, have not resulted in continuous improvement over a medium-term period, even where that improvement is measured in terms of standardised tests; they have not reduced socially based inequalities of achievement and have in some cases increased them, at the same time as they have narrowed curricula and induced stress among students and teachers.[58] The capacity of systems like the English to bring about enduring qualitative change is thus questionable on several grounds.

These problems lead to the equivocal heart of neo-liberalism's programme of modernisation, and link the English experience more closely to that of other countries more closely than it first appears. Marketed as what its exponents like to call a 'step-change' in educational quality, it in fact proposes a dismantling of the curricula and pedagogies which sustained the uneven advances of the post-war decades, in favour of a model whose most notable features are sharp social segregation, strong managerial direction and an emaciation of teaching and learning. Quite contrary to neo-liberalism's self-presentation, the model is widely perceived by both traditional humanism and progressivism as the contemporary face of educational regression. Humanism objects to its emphasis on 'the basics' and its preference for defining educational outcomes in terms of marketable skills rather than disciplinary knowledge. Progressivism is appalled both at its curricular impoverishment and at its profoundly undialogic model of learning, in which negotiation with the experiences and capacities of learners finds little place. There is, of course, implicit in these judgements a certain unjustifiable nostalgia – traditional humanism left most students confined within a curriculum framework even narrower than that currently proposed; in the period of the *grands moments pédagogiques* of progressivism the initiatives of teachers, students and parents could not cancel out an overall pattern of inertia and inequality. But this should not reduce the force of their critiques. They express a sense of degeneration that is at present one of the main resources that neo-liberalism's opponents possess. Among sections of teachers in England and Spain, there is deep dissent from the principles of neo-liberal pedagogy and curricula. In Germany, both reform pedagogy and *Bildung* offer potential vantage points for criticism. For French opponents of Luc Ferry and François Fillon, their reforms amount to a trivialisation of the republican project, in which curricula will be emaciated and the inculcation of the values of citizenship reduced to the management of behaviour. For Italian protesters, the Moratti reforms threaten to 'impoverish culture and learning' and replace well-founded knowledge traditions with a new and under-funded competence-based curriculum.[59] The difficulty, as always, is to translate these growing critical perceptions to a persuasive and popular alternative.

Notes

1. Robin Alexander, *Culture and Pedagogy* (Oxford: Blackwell, 2001).
2. Jenny Ozga and Sharon Gewirtz, 'Sex, Lies and Audiotape: interviewing the education policy élite', in *Researching Education Policy: ethical and methodological issues*, ed. D. Halpin and B. Troyna (Lewes: Falmer Press, 1994).
3. Philogenverband Nordrhein-Westphalen, *Leitsätze für eine organische Ausgestaltung des gegenwärtigen Schulwesens* (Düsseldorf: Schwann, 1964) quoted in S. Robinsohn, and J. Kuhlmann, 'Two Decades of Non-reform in West German education' (1967) reprinted in D. Phillips, (ed.) *Education in Germany: tradition and reform in historical context'* (London: Routledge, 1995).
4. T.S. Eliot, *Notes towards a Definition of Culture* (Faber & Faber: London, 1949) p. 111.
5. Kingsley Amis, *Whatever became of Jane Austen and other essays* (Harmondsworth: Penguin Books, 1981) p. 198.
6. Polesel, 'Reform and Reaction', p. 553.
7. OECD Spain 2006 p. 23.
8. Benedetto Vertecchi, 'Vecchi e Nuovi Analfabeti', *La Revista del Manifesto*, no. 2, p. 36, January 2000.
9. Basil Bernstein and Brian Davies, 'Some Sociological Comments on Plowden' in *Perspectives on Plowden*, ed. R. Peters (London: Routledge and Kegan Paul, 1969).
10. For example, R. Alexander, *Policy and Practice in Primary Education* (London: Routledge, 1992); R. Alexander, *Culture and Pedagogy: international comparisons in primary education* (Oxford: Blackwell, 2001).
11. See the summary of French critiques in Duru-Bellat and van Zanten, *Sociologie de l'école*, pp. 121–2; for critiques of progressivism in the Spanish context, see below.
12. Rachel Sharp and A. Green, *Education and Social Control: a study in progressive primary education* (London: Routledge & Kegan Paul, 1975). Basil Bernstein, 'Class and pedagogies: visible and invisible', in *Language, Codes and Control* (London: Routledge & Kegan Paul, 1975).
13. Plowden Report, *Children and Their Primary Schools* (London: HMSO, 1967) pp. 194 and 188.
14. Ibid., p. 187.
15. Graham Murdock, 'The Politics of Culture' in *Education or Domination?* ed. D. Holly (London: Arrow Books, 1974) p. 101.
16. Searle, cited in Ken Jones, *Beyond Progressive Education* (London: Macmillan, 1983), p. 128.

17. LATE, *Race, Society and School: education in a multi-cultural society* (London, 1982).
18. H-J. Hahn, *Education and Society in Germany* (Oxford: Berg, 1998).
19. Max Jäggi, Roger Müller and Sil Schmid, *Red Bologna* (London: Writers and Readers, 1976, 1977) pp. 112–32.
20. Storia della Scuola Media Statale Paulo. Straneo di Alessandria http://icstraneo. scuole.piemonte.it/pagine_1m/storia.htm
21. Attilio Monasta, 'Italy', in *Education in a Single Europe* ed. Brock and W. Tulasiewicz (Routledge, 2002) p. 234. Monasta is quoting from the governmental regulation of 1979 *Programmi, orari di insegnamento e prove di esame per la scuola media statale.*
22. Paulo Virno, *A Grammar of the Multitude: for an analysis of contemporary forms of life* (Cambridge, MA: MIT, 2004).
23. Leaflet produced by students at the Liceo Berchet, Milan, 1968, quoted in Robert Lumley, *States of Emergency: cultures of revolt in Italy from 1968 to 1978* (London: Verso, 1990).
24. G. Porrotto, *Il Quadro Normativo del Progetto Moratti: prime realizazzioni e valutazioni*, www.anisn.it/scienzescuols/documenti.htm.
25. Olivier Vinay, 'Transformer l'école et la société–entretien avec Olivier Vinay', *L'Education et ses contraires*, Agone 29–30, 135–76, p. 159, 2003.
26. Derouet, 'Lower Secondary Education in France'.
27. P. Bourdieu and J-C Passeron, *Reproduction in Education, Culture and Society* (London: Sage, 1990).
28. José Jimeno Sacristán, 'The Process of Pedagogic Reform' in *Education Reform in Democratic Spain*, ed. O. Boyd-Barrett and P. O'Malley (London: Routledge, 1995) p. 118.
29. Ibid., p. 119.
30. For the classical statement of this position, see Basil Bernstein, 'On the Classification and Framing of Educational Knowledge' in *Class Codes and Control, Volume 3: towards a theory of educational transmissions* (London: RKP, 1975).
31. Colectivo Baltasar Gracián, 'El desmantelamiento de la enseñanza pública en España', *Crisis* 3, 2003.
32. Arco-Tirado Andjuan, José, L. and Miguel Fernández-Balboa, 'Contextual Barriers to School Reform in Spain', *International Review of Education* 49.6, 585–600, 595, 2003.
33. Antonio Gramsci, 'On Education' in *Selections from the Prison Notebooks*', ed. Q. Hoare and G. Nowell Smith (London: Larence & Wishart, 1970) p. 36.
34. Charity James, *Young Lives at Stake* (London: Collins, 1968).
35. 'Transformer l'école et la société: entretien avec Olivier Vinay', *Agone* 2003 no 29–30 pp. 145–76, p. 160.
36. HCE, 'Recommandations pour le socle commun;' DfEE, 'A Fresh Start' (The Moser Report) (London: DfEE, 1999). For England, the percentages are comparable to estimates made in 1945.
37. European Commission, *European Report on Quality of School Education: sixteen quality indicators* (Brussels: European Commission, 2000).
38. In the case of France, Pierre Merle calculates that the gap between the resources available to the least and the most 'scholarised' students actually increased between 1988 and 1998, *La démocratisation de l'enseignement* (Paris: La Découverte, 2002) pp. 86–91. There are even stronger disparities, of course,

in relation to family 'investment'. In relation to Spain, the Colectivo Baltasar Gracián has calculated that 'if the difference between the sectors of higher and lower incomes in terms of average total family spending is 1 to 3, in the area of spending on education it is 1 to 44'.

39. For figures, see Green et al., p. 161 and Moscati 'The Changing Policy of Education in Italy', *Journal of Modern Italian Studies* 3.1, pp. 55–73.
40. P. Willis, 'Footsoldiers of Modernity: the dialectics of cultural consumption and the 21st-Century School', *Harvard Educational Review* 78.3, p. 399.
41. For the problems of the *bachillerato*, see R. Teese, et al., *Equity in Education: thematic review – Spain: country note* (Paris: OECD, 2006), p. 35.
42. See Stephen Ball, *The More Things Change ... Educational research, social class and 'interlocking' inequalities* (London: Institute of Education, University of London, 2003); DfES, *Education and Inspection Bill* (London: The Stationery Office, 2006).
43. Jean-Michel Drevon, 'Surprises, étonnements et ravlissement', *'Ecole Emancipée* mai 2006, 90.7, pp. 15–16.
44. See, for instance, the frequent comments of Andreas Schleicher, head of the OECD's Education Indicators and Analysis Division. For example, William Pratt, 'Schools face new criticism', *Frankfurter Allgemeine Zeitung 17 September 2004*, (English edition).
45. For the extra provision made in England for 'gifted and talented' students, see the DfES website. www.standards.dfes.gov.uk/giftedandtalented. For the significance of the international comparisons of achievement made possible by the OECD's PISA project, see Laval and Weber and OECD, *School Factors Related to Quality and Equity – Results from PISA 2000* (Paris: OECD, 2005).
46. The civil servant Michael Barber, quoted in Robin Alexander, 'Excellence, Enjoyment and Personalised Learning: a true foundation for choice', in *Education Review* 18.1 Autumn 2004 pp. 15–33.
47. Haut Conseil d'Education, pp. 2–3.
48. Christian Laval, 'Socle des competences: l'utilitarisme scolaire et ses dangers' in *'Ecole Emancipée* mai 2006, numéro 90 pp. 15–16.
49. Quoted in Samy Johsua, *UNe autre école est possible* (Paris: Textuel, 2003), p. 44.
50. Sharon Gewirtz, *The Managerial School* (London: Routledge, 2002), p. 161.
51. See David Miliband, 'Choice and Voice in Personalised Learning' Speech to the DfEs/Demos/OECD conference on *Personalising Education: the future of public sector reform* (London: May 2004) pp. 3–4.
52. L. Sciascia, *The Moro Affair & The Mystery of Majorana* (Manchester: Carcanet Press, 1987) p. 18. See also Monasta's account, quoted above.
53. Maccarini, 'La réforme de l'éducation en Italie'.
54. See in this context Italo Florin, ' A proposito di OCSE/PISA e di qualità dell'istruzione' in the journal of the union federation CISL *Scuola Formazione* no. 11, November 2006. Noting that in the Trentino region, students who did well in the PISA tests performed worse in the tests set by the Italian national evaluation body, INVALSI – and vice versa, and that the first tested competences and the second tested knowledge, he concluded:

Before adopting a cultural model from outside our own tradition, whilst recognizing the validity of competence based education in line with the current UE orientation ... it would be wise to reflect on the specificity of our particular cultural heritage and seek to prevent its dissipation. There is an economistic conception of education underlying the competence model which leads to an erosion of pedagogic factors and subordination to a market logic where competition and success are the key terms. A good school is able to ensure both problem solving abilities and the competences necessary to deal adequately with contemporary economic transformations without relying on such models. ... But, as business culture is discovering and the renaissance of philosophy including recent experiments in 'philosophy in business' testify, there is more involved than just problem solving. There is a growing awareness of the dangers inherent in positivistic and overly pragmatic frameworks which have proven to be too mechanistic to deal adequately with complex systems. The PISA/OECD tests are useful but bear cultural codes which are neither neutral nor innocuous and it is well to recognize them as such in the interests of making more informed choices.

55. Legambiente, *Scuola e Formazione: Scuola Pubblica: liquidazione ... di fine stagione, cifre, dati, commenti sui tagli operati dal Governo ai danni scuola pubblica* February 2004. www.legambientescuolaformazione.it/.
56. Javier Doz Orrit, 'Problems of Implementing Educational Reform' in Boyd-Barrett and O'Malley, p. 83.
57. M. Brown et al., 'The Role of Research in the National Numeracy Strategy', *British Educational Research Journal* 29.5, 2003; and F. Smith et al., 'Interactive whole-class teaching in the National Numeracy and Literacy Strategies' Strategy' *British Educational Research Journal* 30.3, 2004 pp. 655–667; 395–411.
58. Andy Hargreaves, *Teaching in the Knowledge Society* (Buckingham: Open University Press, 2003).
59. See the call of the 'Stop Moratti' campaign, national conference, Florence 2004.

7
Symbolic Worlds

Our previous chapters have treated neo-liberalism as a design for a new kind of education, which has had significant, and contested, effects on institutions, practices and subjectivities. As Gramsci suggested long ago, for programmes of this sort to succeed, they must contain not only the element of design, but also a capacity for what can broadly be called persuasion. Persuasion entails the deployment of meaning-making resources, through which the world can be described, explained and evaluated. It also requires the establishment of material situations (for instance, quasi-markets) in which a particular logic of action pertains, such that the activities that seem to be safest and most productive for people to follow within the situations, are those that match a system of constraints and incentives that is 'wired into' them.

The material we assemble here is of three kinds. In the first part of the chapter, we sketch the ideological landscape into which neo-liberalism makes its intervention – a landscape where social democratic, republican and neo-conservative positions still have a part in delimiting the educational space in which questions of schooling's meaning, value and purpose are debated and contested. In the following section, we briefly set out the tenets of neo-liberalism's educational philosophy. Here we are dealing with an ideological system which is formally and copiously presented, alongside an equally systematic critique of preceding philosophies, which are then subject to refusal or recuperation. Finally, we move on to consider neo-liberalism's multifarious discursive practice, arguably the more potent part of its repertoire. In this section, we are concerned less with formally articulated analyses, judgements and recommendations than with a cluster of practices that act to position students, parents and teachers in such a way that particular sorts of discourse are encouraged, while others are constrained and sanctioned.

From this perspective, certification, choice, competition between schools, strategies of management, technologies which set out to measure the performance of the school are all not only means of bringing about institutional change, but are acts of meaning-making. They embed new and often implicit understandings of education's purposes, and of what participation in the schooling process necessarily and ineluctably involves. To control these processes is to occupy a hegemonic position within schooling. That is precisely the ambition of neo-liberal educational politics, which, in terms of both its symbolic and practical effects, works to determine the horizons of what can be thought and said in and about contemporary schooling.

Residual positions: equal opportunity and the School of the Republic

By the early 1980s, the beliefs that had sustained post-war reform had been undermined by economic and social crisis; the viability of the institutions created by reform was being called into question, not least by reformers themselves. Across Western Europe, reform pulled back, before reaching the objectives that had earlier been on its horizon. The non-selective transformation of German secondary education slipped off the social-democratic agenda. The English public schools remained unchallenged, and the regional spread of comprehensivisation remained uneven. In France, the secularist objectives of the left were set aside; the PSOE in Spain reached a compromise that embedded a state-subsidised private sector at the heart of the system. In Italy after 1980, the failure of the Italian Communist Party's (PCI) attempt at historic compromise, the large-scale repression of social movements following the Moro kidnapping and the inert governmental alliance of PSI and Christian democracy made practical action difficult and at a programmatic level ensured the stagnation of educational reform.

Paralysis at the level of government or political leadership did not mean that movements of reform or resistance ceased to operate. Nor did it involve the immediate disappearance of the intellectual and cultural traditions from which reform drew its inspirations, for these were not confined to the programme of any individual party, but were diffused throughout entire societies, defining for many the horizons of the educationally possible. As we shall see in the next chapter, child-centred and egalitarian traditions played such a role in England. In Italy, secondary schooling continued to take as an important and equivocal reference point, the Gentile reforms of 1923. From one perspective, the Gentilian model of the school rested on sharp class division. From another, it emphasised through the *liceo* an element of disinterested knowledge, distinct from and potentially critical of social interests.[1] In political terms, this was an ambivalent legacy: when the centre-left government of the 1990s attempted its market-centred reforms, the far right protested in the name of the 'loss of Italian culture' which would ensue.[2] But the *liceo* also did much to shape the cultural formation of a social movement which in the 1960s and 1970s had flooded into the faculties of literature, history and philosophy.[3] When Luigi Berlinguer began, in 1997, the process of change, and when the Berlusconi government sought to intensify it, the opposition which confronted them drew on several traditions. The historicist humanism associated with the *liceo* was fused with militant political traditions: the anti-fascism of the wartime resistance, and the tumultuous upsurges of the 1960s and 1970s. The effects of this history were still being felt in the twenty-first century, and were registered, negatively, in the rhetoric of Berlusconi. As Slavoj Zizek suggests, the premier's frequent recourse to a rhetoric of anti-communism was less an anachronistic hangover from the Cold War than a realisation that neo-liberalism would benefit from the success of 'an ongoing project to change the terms of a post-war European identity hitherto based on anti-Fascist unity'.[4]

Nowhere were the residual effects of embedded traditions more powerful than in France. Here, schooling, as Lelièvre argues, was deeply inscribed in the political space of the republic. It was 'at the heart of a political project concerning the social tie; it is the means by which a public, national space is constructed ... French schooling ... is a matter first and foremost of the republican state and its logic, not of civil society with its taking into account of particularism and particular interests, however legitimate these may otherwise appear ... That which unites must prevail over that which divides: the logic of civil society, the privateness of religion, cultural or ethnic communities, business'.[5] To this extent, the policies of expansion and equalising opportunity that were pursued by educational reform were underwritten by an ideology of political citizenship that greatly augmented their political force and social implantation.[6] Social republicanism of this sort has a complex character – there are many for whom it serves as a basis for criticising the supposed decline in standards for which the *collège unique* is responsible. But – grounded in a commitment to the state as a necessary and beneficent agent of change, widely and fervently supported among teachers, made manifest time and again in public protest – it gave the French school, for a period, the capacity to withstand a neo-liberal transformation of large sectors of the domestic economy, and a global educational climate in which very different priorities had developed. Such has been the power of these commitments that even those – like Ferry – who have the 'French exception' in their neo-liberal sights are compelled still to speak the language of social republicanism.[7]

Residual positions: neo-conservatism

Conservatism was never one and indivisible across Europe. The confessional nationalism of the Francoist state stood at some distance from the decentralised hierarchies of mid-century England; neither possessed the elaborated educational ideology of the remade West German system, in which the humanist elitism of *Bildung* was still a major force. It is possible, nonetheless, to speak for much of the earlier post-war period in terms of still-potent *national* conservatisms, which, addressing invariably gendered themes of tradition, nation, authority and allegiance, continued to pattern European schooling. Strongly implanted in elite education – the gymnasium, the public school – high cultural in its reference points and sustained in many cases by organised religion, Conservatism's influence has never been entirely extinguished. But from the 1960s onwards it was, challenged and to an extent displaced – elitist cultures could not thrive in mass education systems; commercial popular culture further eroded their base; attacks on selectivity and the knowledge traditions associated with it were often effective. Yet weakened though it was by an educational politics of egalitarianism and cultural diversity, Conservatism made from the 1970s onwards a spectacular though ultimately unsuccessful comeback. It did so first of all as a critique of the new. Primary education was struggling through a difficult process of transformation; so were the secondary and tertiary systems, which had become massified without a coherent programme for curricula, pedagogy and institutional pattern. This prolonged and in the event uncompleted period of transition allowed conservatism its second wind. Invoking memories of a golden age of education, in which academic values had prospered everywhere, the right supplied many of the resources for an impassioned and resonant critique of educational reform. In the process, especially in England, it played a crucial destructive role: it became, as it were, a solvent of the post-war settlement, only to be itself subsumed within a larger and more compelling programme of neo-liberalism.

Thatcherism: triumph and decline

Neo-conservative themes – traditionalist, xenophobic – were central to Thatcherism. They provided it with a populist discourse in which disenchantment with educational reform could be persuasively expressed. They offered a critique of an English school system allegedly dominated by libertarian, relativist, multi-culturalist forces; they supplied the elements of an alternative, in the form of a programme of intervention by an authoritarian state, in which social cohesion would be organised around a racialised Englishness and a freezing of gender roles in the mould of the 1950s. The critique, widely diffused by sympathetic media, was potent; it did much to discredit the more radical curricular experiments which had developed within the general process of reform; it succeeded in associating reform with a supposed decline in educational standards. But the alternative offered by the right was in many ways a failure. Conservatism's project was in tension with deep-seated social and cultural change: mass education could not be run on a programme of nostalgia. Its attempt to translate its cultural principles into a militant and centrally directed programme of curriculum transformation was defeated in 1993–4 by teachers' refusal to implement a testing system in which traditional values were embodied. Subsequently, as Thatcherite Conservativism began to decompose, the cultural right ceased to play a significant educational role. Neo-liberalism could always find a niche position for 'traditional education', as a marker of educational distinction in a marketised and differentiated system; but programmatic conservatism could not provide the basis for the relentless economising of the school at which its Blairite successor aimed.[8]

France and Spain

In France and in Spain, the fortunes of the right followed a similar trajectory. The campaigns against the Savary legislation of 1984–5, which would have incorporated church and private schools into the state sector, were the occasion for a mass protest whose scope exceeded the immediate issues of autonomy, to confront fundamental aspects of mass education in France – the supposed disorder of its classrooms, the new preferences of government for social integration rather than academic quality. Discontent was catalysed by the traditional right, but spread well beyond its borders. In the name of republican tradition, significant voices attacked teachers who cared more for pupils' happiness than for academic standards – in this sense the right was far from alone.[9] Likewise, a decade later in Spain, the partial and manifestly unsuccessful legislation of the Gonzales period gave the Aznar government the opportunity in the 1990s to denounce an 'unnatural, systematic and lethal'[10] system, hostile to choice, to educational standards, to Catholicism and to the integralism of the Spanish State. Scathing critique was followed by an attempt at legislation – a decree revising the content of the humanities curriculum, so as to defend Spain's 'historic patrimony' from dilution by regional interests. But, as in England, it was one thing to criticise the failings of reform, another to reconstruct education on traditionalist lines. Aznar's party found itself alone in its more conservative concerns: the proposal was defeated in the Chamber of Deputies. Its attempts to restore confessional teaching to a central position were initially more successful. But here, too, the People's Party (PP) found itself at an impasse: after its defeat in the elections of 2004, the future of its legislation became uncertain.

Aside from its contribution to the defeat of previous reforming project, conservatism brings one other gift to the table of contemporary policy. Its celebration of continuity and national tradition was often linked to xenophobia and the defence of an imperial past. Thatcher's talk of Britain in 1979 being 'swamped' by migrants and Sarkozy's description 25 years later of the protestors and rioters of the banlieus as 'racaille' indicated a continuity in the first element. A law passed in 2005 by the right-wing majority in the French National Assembly offered evidence of the second – it stipulated that the curriculum should 'recognise the positive role played by the French presence overseas, particularly in North Africa'. After 2001, with the declaration of the war on terror, and the rise of Islamophobia, the attitudes of governments moved on a path of convergence with conservative monoculturalism. 'It is in this context,' wrote Liz Fekete

> that we need to understand the new drive, across Europe, towards assimilation. Assimilation is being forced through by the adoption of a number of measures, which include the recasting of citizenship laws according to security considerations; the introduction of compulsory language and civics tests for citizenship applicants; codes of conduct for the trustees of mosques; a cultural code of conduct for Muslim girls and women who, in some areas of Europe, will be forbidden to wear the hijab in state schools and other state institutions.[11]

Neo-liberalism: the inheritor

Politically, neo-liberalism has benefited greatly from the conservative onslaught against the post-war settlement. Conservatism – especially the Conservatism of Thatcher – showed how the social forces that had created the settlement could be defeated, and how their achievements could be dismantled. Without this prior underlabouring, the contemporary economisation of education would be a much harder task. But traditional conservatism, with its outbursts of ethno-nationalism, its authoritarian gender politics and its suspicion of EU government is too regressive in its inclinations and too abrasive in its relations with educational interest groups to provide a globalised, free-market capitalism with a functioning educational programme.

The educational programme of neo-liberalism combines elements from very different traditions. Child-centred progressivism, post-1968 theories of workers' self-management and a revalorisation of technical education of a kind associated with communist productivism rub shoulders with elitism and with celebration of the entrepreneurialism of private business. To unpick the elements of this synthesis is to reveal something about the scope of neo-liberalism in education, which aims to provide a total programme, relating as much to classroom practices as it does to forms of institutional governance. Deconstruction can also suggest something of neo-liberalism's hegemonic force: it aims both to destroy previously powerful educational practices, and to assimilate them, and the social agents associated with them, into a new educational regime.

Neo-liberalism negates the past and repudiates the idea that education can be shaped by collective action, either popular or reactionary. Neither traditional conservatism, nor bureaucratically controlled selective systems nor social democratic egalitarianism are spared. Thus, rather than celebrating the achievements of its social democratic predecessors, the Blair government offers unrelenting criticism. Recruits to the DfES are told to assume that history begins with the 'year zero' of 1988, when the Conservatives' Education Reform Act was passed. Before that point, educational history is a record of failure. The governments of Attlee (1945–51) and Wilson/Callaghan (intermittently from 1964 to 1979) presided over a largely 'unskilled' working population that had possessed 'jobs for life' in local industries. A stagnant economy produced a school system in its own image. In the supposedly static society of the long boom, there was 'a general acceptance that only a minority would reach the age of 16 with formal skills and qualifications'. Comprehensive reform had not done enough to challenge this acceptance, and by setting 'social' as opposed to 'economic' goals it had contributed to stasis. Over-reacting to the failings of the selective system, and dominated by the 'ideology of unstreamed teaching', it had failed to differentiate among students and to 'link different provision to individual attitudes and abilities'. Hence mass illiteracy and slow rates of economic growth.[12]

Likewise the McKinsey consultant Jürgen Kluge has no hesitation in breaking from German tradition. Education should have less to do with *Bildung* than with the formation of human capital. From this starting point, it is possible to see that 'the bureaucratic embrace' of government and the 'institutional blindness' of educators has depressed the 'quality standards' of the German school. Constitutionally, education may be a civil right; but in practice 'our actually-existing schools' are incapable of responding to international competition.[13] In France, the Thélot report came to a similar conclusion about the republican tradition: its belief in the school as an effective agent of social and political equality was daily contradicted by the evidence of student behaviour; ideologies of citizenship misrecognised the classroom reality of 'incivility' and disruption. In this context, 'republican values' could no longer generate constructive educational strategies. Far better for the school to concentrate on matters of quality and effectiveness than that it should try to serve, impossibly, as some kind of repository of national values.[14]

Such critiques are usually silent about the social decay that has contributed to the crisis of the school – in 2003, the Education Minister Luc Ferry's book-length appeal to 'all those who love the school' contained no programme of social reconstruction and made no mention of unemployment or insecurity.[15] Neo-liberalism instead emphasises the replacement of exhausted traditions by modernisation – the transformation of curricula, pedagogies, governance, ownership, in line with what are seen as contemporary realities. Modernisation is justified by a system of inter-related maxims, constantly repeated at every level of education, from the classroom to the ministerial meeting. The societies of the EU are knowledge societies, in which competitiveness and wealth depend on innovation and flexibility. Information and the capacity to use it are essential. Education and training systems must provide the 'intangible capital' that is central to knowledge economies, but they cannot effectively do so because institutionally and pedagogically, they are outdated[16]. They must operate in a new way, to develop 'autonomous individuals', capable of constant 'reconversion' – the transmission of 'consolidated knowledge, traditions and habits' is no longer useful,[17] and indeed there is something 'dodgy' – to use the term of an English Secretary of State – about the idea of 'learning for its own sake'.[18] The school cannot develop this new type of human subject without itself being transformed: 'independent pupils' require 'independent schools'.[19] Schools will raise their levels of quality through a combination of operational autonomy, inter-institutional competition, and detailed national regulation and inspection. Strong institutional leaderships will create new cultures of achievement among teachers and students; governments will establish indicators that allow the precise measurement of school performance; regular inspections will provide a further measure of control, not just over teaching, but in relation to the management of the school and its relationship to external 'partners'. In these ways reform will no longer be an 'exceptional event' embodied in episodes of legislation; it will instead become 'a continuous process of revision, adjustment and improvement', inspired and legitimised by the models of management developed in the private sector, a force that New Labour's chief education policy adviser deemed 'uniquely capable of managing change and innovation'.[20]

This is the context in which new education programmes assimilate, utilise and recuperate positions and practices whose original impulses were far from neo-liberal. Bontempelli makes the point well. For liberals and socialists in the twentieth-century educational autonomy meant the independence of schools from outside interests such as the church or economic factors, and the defence of teacher initiative against bureaucratic or governmental interference. Autonomy of this kind, Bontempelli argues, 'was understood as an essential means of achieving … the acquisition of autonomous thought by students through the transmission of collective culture from one generation to another.' Today however

> autonomy means the destruction of public education. It is no longer the autonomy of the public education system but autonomy from that system … It has become synonymous with scuola-azienda (the school-business relationship) … It is the negation of the previous concept because education is no longer free from outside economic interests, culture is no longer free from pragmatic and contingent influences and teachers are no longer free in their work. The period when teachers have been literally submerged by bureaucratic and pedagogic restrictions regarding their work is paradoxically the era of so-called autonomy.[21]

Agnès van Zanten makes a similar point: decentralisation is now at the heart of the neo-liberal programme but some of its antecedents lie in movements of *autogestion*, critical of bureaucratic and fordist hierarchies.[22] There are other recuperations too. Theories of civil society are translated into free market terms.[23] Inclusion – that is, the strand of neo-liberalism which seeks to mitigate the worst effects of social and educational inequality – has been accepted, particularly in England, as a new form of egalitarianism. Some sorts of feminist critique have been answered by curricular programmes whose content owed little to the women's movement but whose success in promoting the achievement of girls in public examinations was demonstrated across most sectors of education. 'Creativity', once the watchword of a romantic critique of industrialism and of mass education, has been revalued as a quality vital to business innovation and to the communicative demands of informational capitalism.[24] Likewise, 'personalisation' has emerged as a central term in the remaking of secondary education, though in the process it has shifted from the repertoire of child-centred pedagogy to that of differentiation: personalised programmes of study are those which at the same time as they attend to 'individual need' – and thus are claimed to break from the collectivism of the past – serve also to segregate academic from vocational tracks. The same could be said of the respect which neo-liberalism pays to technical education. As Moscati points out in relation to Italy, the other side of Gentilian culturalism was an undervaluing of training, 'which has always been conceived as remedial training for students dropping out of other levels of the system'.[25] The Moratti reforms, by contrast, place training near their centre – while at the same time, they prepare for its regionalisation and privatisation.

In these senses, we can speak less of a cancellation of the discourses of social democratic and progressive reform than of their recombination, and of their insertion into a new economised ensemble of discourses, whose main point of reference is the need to ensure education's close compatibility with rapid, market-driven change. Educational discourse has thus been remade under the sign of capital; and in the process, social agents previously associated with egalitarian or emancipatory goals have found a new location. Industrial unions welcome the stress on training; sections of the teaching force think they see in programmes of access-oriented, creative and personalised education a means of pursuing their child-centred commitments. The neo-liberal project does not lack the element of consent, and the grand and overarching process of *trasformismo*, by means of which social democratic parties come to adopt neo-liberalism as a creed of their own, is enabled partly by the capacity of various groups to 'find themselves' – to see their evolving interests recognised – in the programme of modernisation.

Neo-liberalism as practice

But the success of neo-liberalism does not rest only upon consent. The process of converting an ambivalent educational logic into a set of unequivocal economised procedures requires force as well. Force has many elements, from the symbolic violence with which teachers are represented – *faule Säcke* in Gerhard Schröder's words, 'corporatist, conservative and reactionary', according to the champions of the PSOE's 1990 curriculum reform[26] – to the battery of legal measures required to convert public into private goods, citizens into consumers, (relatively) autonomous professionals into managed subjects. The unrelenting negativity of the media and the increasing frequency of legislation are the most visible faces of coercion. But neo-liberalism's position will finally be secured by more mundane activities – by the cluster of practices which, underpinned by managerial and academic authority, and by quasi-market disciplines, creates new identities and new purposes for those who work and study in education, so that they become more flexible, capable and reliable agents of the state's strategies. In establishing these routines of dull compulsion, European education systems necessarily move at an uneven pace, in which national government has to take account of the extent to which opposition is itself embedded in recalcitrant daily practice. England is in the vanguard here, in understanding as well as practice. 'Beliefs do not necessarily change behaviour,' wrote two of the architects of the New Labour school, 'more usually, behaviours shape beliefs.'[27] It is in the creation of new behaviours, and in the simultaneous production of new meaning-systems relating to schooling, that neo-liberalism is having striking effects.

Policy orthodoxy does not disguise its view that education systems must serve economic purposes. But this insistence is interwoven with other themes, much more attractive to educational constituencies. Central here – as Thélot suggests – is the question of 'quality'. Quality involves the continuous effort to raise the level of school performance relative to indicators that are not themselves subject to question: the essential thing is not that the school should reflect society's best values but that it should function well.[28] If policy succeeds in elevating 'quality' to such a transcendent position, then it can command debate – thus in Germany, the release of the OECD's comparative PISA statistics has helped create a general acceptance of the necessity of modernisation; while the lowly position of French universities in international league tables of research has likewise fuelled demands for change.[29] In England, this effort is incited more systematically and continuously by the annual publication of schools' test and examination results. 'Quality' and 'standards' are thus not only themes of policy debate; they also structure the daily life of the school. Performance indicators are the lens through which students' learning is perceived. Thus, in England, when 11-year olds arrive at their new secondary school, predicted grades for their 16+ examination results are available to the teacher; they enable the allocation of a student to a particular 'ability'-based set, and at the same time condition the school's expectations.[30] Interim reports compare progress with prior attainment. The success of a teacher in terms of students' achievement in national tests then becomes one of the issues at stake in a localised system of performance management. Just as the PISA indicators serve to manage national performance, and national league tables – in some countries – to measure the work of schools, so here the attainment levels of classes within the individual school have come to provide managers with an instrument for monitoring and directing the work of teachers.[31] The linking of performance to levels of pay, now well-established in England, offers managers a further instrument of control. Stephen Ball describes this process as the insertion of 'a new mode of power into the public sector', a mode which 'plays a key role in the wearing-away of professional-ethical régimes that have been dominant in schools and bringing about their replacement by entrepreneurial-collective régimes'.[32]

Decentralisation, in its many guises, has similar effects. Policy orthodoxy is fulsome in its praise of decentralisation, especially in relation to school autonomy. It 'empowers people, creates more innovation, and delivers services more attuned to client needs'.[33] But to see decentralisation in these terms is to overlook its aggressive, destructive dimension. Politically, it acts to inhibit the development of focused conflict, in which subordinate groups might collectively protest at a generalised level, or collectively generate alternative practices. The Conservatives who introduced local management of schools to England knew this: there would be far fewer protests at the Town Hall, and much more scope for strong school managements, empowered by national regulation, to control the workplace. The enduring resistance of French teachers to many aspects of decentralisation policy stems from an intuition of consequences like these: a system where policy and funding decisions are transparently made at central level encourages collective responses, and facilitates teacher, parent and student organisation; a localised system disaggregates, and in associational terms, disempowers collective actors. Zambeta and her colleagues write that decentralisation is a 'strategy to produce personal feelings of efficacy through participation, as well as a governing strategy that produces increasing loyalty to the system itself in a period when changes are being sought.'[34] But they know quite well that loyalty and participation are the products of a system that, has first of all, broken the back of collective organisation.

The compulsions exerted by new education systems work also to reposition parents and students. We are not talking here about a total sea change. It is plain from many accounts that even in the period of 'egalitarian' reform, middle-class parents worked to place their children in the best schools, accentuating class-based divisions in what were supposedly more uniform systems of provision.[35] Neo-liberalism's achievement is to convert this exceptionality into a rule. The British sociologist Mike Savage depicts a national landscape of deindustrialisation, from which 'the working class has been largely eviscerated as a visible social presence', no longer a 'central reference point in British culture'.[36] In this emptied space, rather than there being socially recognised tensions between class-specific practices, 'the practices of the middle class have increasingly come to define the social itself.'[37] Nowhere, according to Stephen Ball, is this more the case than in education. The quasi-market has not only given the middle class privileged access to educational resources; it has also served to obscure the processes by which class advantage works. The success of middle-class children is held to be related not to their class, but to the effective operation of markets, a universal process, and when parents deploy every cultural and financial advantage that they possess to secure for their children a future that is better than the future of others, this is not seen as a class strategy so much as rational and appropriate behaviour. Thus, after a period in which policy and significant elements of practice were orientated towards issues of equality – which involved a particular emphasis on working-class education – a new orientation dominates. School choice has become a universal principle, and in the process middle-class *mores* have become generalised.

This everyday triumph of the market order is one of neo-liberalism's most significant achievements. Outside England, it has yet to be generally replicated. In France, parental choice is undoubtedly a force, but not one that has general statutory recognition. In Germany, selectivity remains closely related to formal academic performance. In Italy, a tradition of familism[38] has contributed to patterns of class advantage in education, but 'choice' has not, even in the Moratti reforms, been installed as a basic educational principle. Spain is the only other country in which marketisation created powerful choice-based norms. The LODE of 1985 granted a definitive legal character to private, state-subsidised schooling, and since then – culminating in the Spanish Organic Law on Education (LOE) of 2006 – the extension of subsidy beyond the compulsory age-range, combined with a crisis of public education, has supported, legitimised and normalised a strategy of middle-class exit.[39]

Where parents have been repositioned by discourses of choice – in which not to be an active chooser is to display signs of a social pathology – students have been encouraged by their circumstances to view education in commodified terms. Taking human capital theory at its word, significant sections of the student population see education as an investment in their own future, the more so when legislation insists that they become fee-payers, contributing large sums to the cost of their learning. The idea that knowledge is a private good to be purchased from *scuole/aziende* is not universally popular among students – the French and German revolts of 2003 against the Bologna process demonstrated as much, and the demand for free education underpinned British students' 2004 protests against tuition fees. But the language of commodification is gaining ground. 'We cannot support the lecturers' strike,' said the students' union at one British university in 2004, 'as it is detrimental to the students' education. The students have lost a product – that is, a lecture they have paid for … We have urged our students to lobby the university for reimbursement of their fees for the lectures they have missed.'[40] Similar attitudes occur at other levels of education. In a mass system of certification, in which millions compete for advantage, student conceptions of educational purpose are shaped accordingly. There is much British research that demonstrates how school students, inhabiting a system of permanent assessment, develop a sophisticated awareness of what is necessary to obtain particular grades, value teaching which is focused on such an objective and criticise the irrelevance of other sorts of study.[41] Such awareness is positional: students seek not absolute performance, but performance that is better than that of others.

Fault-lines

The new educational order seeks legitimacy through its claims to deliver higher standards, individual prosperity and freedom of choice. These are powerful claims, which at particular levels of policymaking, and in particular countries, have become hegemonic. But this does not mean that they are secure. This is because of the kinds of problem that their dominance generates – new intensities of work and study, sharper inequalities, a conception perceived by many to be narrow and instrumentalist. These specific issues are part of a more general condition.

'The modern state', argues one group of authors, 'has come to need *weak citizenship*. It depends more and more on maintaining an impoverished and hygienised public realm, in which only the ghosts of an older, more idiosyncratic civil society live on. It has adjusted profoundly to its economic master's requirement for a thinned, unobstructed social texture, made of loosely attached consumer subjects.'[42] Overcommitted – by contrast even with the idea of a 'social Europe' promoted by Jacques Delors – to the perceived imperatives of economic competitiveness, the discourses that seek to legitimise educational neo-liberalism are models of weak citizenship, that mobilise no popular forces and, indeed, fear the notion of political mobilisation itself. In breaking from conservatism, and in attacking the aspirations of the social movements which helped give shape to the post-war system, neo-liberalism forsakes the most powerful forms of post-war collectivism, forms which nourished the imagination of the groups most actively pursuing – or resisting – educational change, and through which were created forms of subjectivity intimately related to citizenship and to a social contract. With the single and very dangerous exception of an aggressive assimilationism towards Muslim minorities, it shuns notions of collective identity and seeks to replace the various collectivisms of the past with a design for education in which cohesion is supplied by common participation in market-based transactions or standards-orientated programmes initiated by a managerial state. The next chapters, on curriculum and pedagogy, students and teachers, explore this design in more detail.

Notes

1. Massimo Bontempelli, *L'agonia della scuola italiana* (Pistoia: Editric CRT, 2000); Lucio Russo, *Segmenti e Bastonici Dove sta andando la scuola?* (Milan: Feltrinelli, 1998).
2. Rosalind Innes, *Italian Educational Reform: discourse and the production of compatible subjectivities*, MA Thesis, Macquarie University.
3. Checchi, *The Italian Educational System*, p. 9.
4. Slavoj Zizek, 'The Two Totalitarianisms', *London Review of Books* 27.6, 17 March 2005, p. 16.
5. Lelièvre, 'The French Model of the Educator State', p. 8.
6. See Alexandros Patramanis and Harris Athanasiades, *Globalisation, Education Restructuring and Teacher Unions in France and Greece: decentralisation policies or disciplinary parochialism?* Draft 2002. Published by the Globalisation and Europeanisation Network in Education (www.genie-tn.net).
7. Ferry et al., *Lettre à tous ce qui aiment l'école*.
8. See the account in Ken Jones, *Education in Britain* (Cambridge: Polity Press, 2003).

9. J-C Milner, *De l'école* (Paris: Editions du Seuil, 1984).
10. G. Esperanza Aguirre, 'Educaciòn y cultura: calida y libertad' (Speech given at the Club Siglo XXI Madrid) 26 de mayo de 1997.
11. Fekete, 'Anti-Muslim Racism and the European Security State', p. 19.
12. Department for Education and Employment, *Schools Building on Success* (London: Stationery Office, 2001) pp. 4–5.
13. Klüge, p. 1.
14. Brunner and Laronche, 'Ce que va proposer le rapport Thélot pour réformer l'école;' C. Laval, (2004) *L'Europe libérale aux commandes de l'école: a propos du rapport Thélot et du projet de loi d'orientation pour l'avenir de l'école*, website of the Institut du Recherches de la FSU http://institut.fsu.fr.
15. Ferry et al., *Lettre à tous ce qui aiment l'école*.
16. European Commission 1993, quoted in Nóvoa, p. 258.
17. Massimo Bontempelli, *Controlesscio-formazione – critica sulla riforma Moratti* www.cespbo.it.
18. Charles Clarke, Secretary of State for Education in the Blair government, quoted in Jeevan Vasagar and Rebecca Smithers, 'Will Charles Clarke have his place in history?' *The Guardian* 10 May 2003. (Although education has always had the function of preparing students for the labour market, it was considered by educationalists and teachers that pedagogy is structured by another logic than that of efficiency and profit.)
19. Klüge, p. 1.
20. Michael Barber, High expectations and standards for all, no matter what, Speech to North of England Education Conference January 1998. Quoted in Ken Jones, *Education in Britain* (Cambridge: Polity Press, 2003) p. 145.
21. Bontempelli, *Controlesscio-formazione – critica sulla riforma Moratti* www.cespbo.it.
22. Agnès van Zanten, *Un libéralisme éducatif sans frontières* in van Zanten ed. 2000.
23. Maccarini, 'La réforme de l'éducation en Italie: un exemple de gouvernance?'.
24. Department for Education and Skills/Department of Culture, Media and Sport *All Our Futures: creativity, culture and education* (London: The Stationery Office, 1999). See also L. Cillario's work on 'cognitive capitalism' *L'economìa degli spettri* (Rome: Manifesto Libri, 1996).
25. R. Moscati, 'The Changing Policy of Education in Italy', *Journal of Modern Italian Studies* 3.1, p. 65.
26. See Javier Doz Orrit, 'Problems of Implementing Educational Reform', in Boyd-Barrett and O'Malley, pp. 271–82.
27. Michael Barber and Vicky Phillips, *Fusion: how to unleash irreversible change: lessons for the future of system-wide school reform.* Paper to a DfEE Conference on Education Action Zones March 2000.
28. Christian Laval, L'Europe libérale aux commandes de l'école: a propos du rapport Thélot et du projet de « loi d'orientation pour l'avenir de l'école », Website of the Institut du Recherches de la FSU http://institut.fsu.fr 2004.
29. *Le Monde*, 23 janvier 2004.
30. Mary James, 'Measured Lives: the rise of assessment as the engine of change in English schools', *The Curriculum Journal* 11.3, pp. 343–64, 2000.
31. Jenny Ozga, *Measuring and Managing Performance in Education*, Briefing No. 27 (Edinburgh: Centre for Educational Sociology Edinburgh University, 2003) p. 1.

32. Stephen Ball, 'Global trends in educational reform and the struggle for the soul of the teacher', Paper presented at the British Educational Research Association Conference, Brighton, 1999.
33. OECD, *Reviews of National Policies for Education: Italy* (Paris: OECD, 1998) p. 77.
34. S. Lindblad, J. Ozga and E. Zambeta, 'Changing Forms of Educational Governance in Europe', *European Educational Research Journal* 1.4, pp. 615–24, 2002.
35. See, for instance, François de Singly, 'L'école et la famille' in A. van Zanten (ed.) *L'école: l'état des savoirs*, pp. 271–83.
36. Mike Savage, A New Class Paradigm? *British Journal of Sociology of Education* 24.4, pp. 535–41, p. 536, September 2003.
37. Ibid.
38. See the discussion in Paul Ginsborg, *Italy and Its Discontents* (London: Allen Lane, 2001) pp. 97–100.
39. Francisco Delgado, 'LOE: Escuela Pública, Escuela Privada, Religión y Pacto', *Crisis* 9 June 2005.
40. Polly Curtis and Katherine Courts, 'University strike action builds towards climax', *The Guardian*, 24 February 2004.
41. Martyn Denscombe, 'Social Conditions for Stress: young people's experience of doing the GCSEs', *British Educational Research Journal* 26.3, pp. 360–74.
42. 'Retort' Afflicted Powers; the state, the spectacle and September *11th*, *New Left Review* II.27, 5–22, p. 9, May-June 2004.

8
Human Resources: Students

Previous chapters have dealt with the advent of neo liberal ideology in relation to other formerly hegemonic, contested and contesting discourses. They have discussed transformations in curricula and pedagogy in the macro context of wide-ranging Europeanising reforms and traced the latter's uneven path through the erosion of collective identities and the emergence of a competitive individualism compatible with the knowledge economy. Here we attempt to sketch an outline of how all of this has impacted on contemporary student subjectivities, how they are constructed, disciplined and positioned in a context where economic discourses prevail and citizenship is weak; and how educational systems geared to the exigencies of the knowledge economy contribute to establishing the co-ordinates of a transformed and transforming symbolic framework. Of course, the extent to which any discourse is 'heard, believed and obeyed'[1] depends on a variety of factors – social, semiotic and cultural – as well as those pertaining to an economy where huge structural differences in sectoral unemployment and real expectations heavily influence credibility levels. These factors, though sufficiently common for us to speak of shared experiences across Europe, also differ according to national circumstance. The historical pre-eminence and to some extent uniqueness of the English experience in the context of neo-liberal change has been discussed at several points. But this uniqueness is not only confined to the speed with which a system of market managerialism has come into being; it also applies to other domains, especially those of the regulation of the social. The significance of its relative specificity seems to be linked also to a greater pragmatic and perhaps protestant/puritan predilection for hands-on social engineering, observable in the wider cultural dominance of political correctness, albeit often at a purely formal level, as well as in a myriad of discourses interpellating and regulating parents, educators and students. Thus, in England, 'equal opportunity', translated from the economic-social to the legislative-procedural level, is a principle institutionalised in data collection, institutional mission statements, school inspection reports and so on. At the same time a punitive culture of regulation imposes curfew orders on young people and imprisons parents when the truancy of their children is deemed to be excessive. Latin countries have not yet experienced such proceduralised political correctness, nor such intense regulation.

New subjectivities/old schools

Schools have always contributed to the fashioning of subjectivities, producing and re-enforcing dominant forms of social relations as well as, at times, sowing the seeds for their contestation and providing promises of social mobility. Depending on time and place, the discourses surrounding their socialising and disciplining functions have been more or less articulated, more or less finely honed, taking on explicitly strategic importance in exceptional periods such as national unification[2] or within dictatorial regimes (nazism, fascism, francoism) where their overt ideological function has been the production of 'national' or 'compatible' subjects. The neoliberal education policies of contemporary Europe are also often posed in similarly strategic terms – but as we have seen, it is not the development of a national identity or canonic cultural tradition which is proclaimed but rather the imperatives of live-or-die economic competition. Constant reiteration of this same admonitory refrain has dulled interrogation of its fundamental strategic premises, which consequently tend to be taken for granted or 'absorbed' rather than questioned. Thus in daily practice it is the details of the mosaic of educational changes necessary to meet the exigencies of the knowledge economy that are discussed and debated and in which students are embroiled rather than the grand project itself. Of course, this is also a consequence of the nature of the project and of the epoch. In previous times, whether or not they were decreed exceptional by national governments, educational systems had a fundamental philosophy or '*cultural axis*;[3] there were grand narratives and symbolic subjects to inhabit them. Now, as Allan Bloom remarked in relation to a similar crisis in American universities, there are no more heroes. We have instead a scenario of 'human resources' and a corporate auditing culture.

Transnational systems and schools without walls

Two important shifts have occurred here. With the change in the role of the nation state and the concomitant tendency towards the Europeanisation of education, the disciplining of student subjectivities in national terms has declined, leading to changes in the nature of cultural capital: on the one hand it has become globalised and unmarkedly, blandly 'Western';[4] on the other it is regionalised or localised. This process has, of course, not been even or without resistance. One controversial and complex instance of the powerful re-assertion of national identity lies in the 2004 French legislation regarding the ban on religious symbols in schools. Although considered by many, including advocates of secular education, as a futile attempt to dam the crumbling structures of an obsolete monocultural national identity, the legislation can also be seen as an index of the difficulties facing exponents of republican ideals in a globalised context where strong defence of nationally consolidated universalist principles is less compatible with neo-liberal globalising processes than are market-based valorisations of difference and the proliferation of multiple identities produced by the 'deregulation of the symbolic'[5]. As Balibar puts it, in an attempt to capture the nature of transitional times:

> the political construction of the national state brought about the devaluation of religious identity. Today, with the processes of transnationalization it is apparent that the relation between religion and politics has not been definitely resolved. The epoch of religious identifty is not over and the crisis of national identity has begun.[6]

A second major shift concerns the growth of the tendency – which Readings observed in North American universities a decade ago and which is increasing rapidly in England particularly – for educational institutions to become not just more and more *like* corporations but to increasingly take on the form of corporate services themselves. In this, and other ways – the link between schools and workplace learning, the establishment of 'partnerships' between schools and business and other interests – the walls between 'education' and 'society' are weakened. Rather than carrying out the functions of what Althusser in Fordist times called the 'Ideological State Apparatus' – with its famed 'relative autonomy' within an articulated social formation – schools become part of what the autonomist movement called the extended and diffuse *'social factory'*.[7] In the process, the Fordist separation between the ideological constitution of the subject in the family and in education and its later participation in a determinate sector of the economic sphere began to dissolve. Students are directly positioned within a modular and personalised universe where the old borders between life, work, training and leisure are increasingly blurred.

This displacement of learning and personal formation from the school to society, and particularly to the sphere of the mass media /infotainment/ICT industries in the formation of student identities, has been evident to those working in schools for some time.[8] Writing in an Australian context, Kenway and Bullen have suggested that 'we are entering another stage in the construction of the young as the demarcation between education, entertainment and advertising collapse'.[9] Writers in Western Europe have made a similar point with greater trepidation; they tend to claim that contemporary students are bereft of the more stable points of reference that existed in the life-world of a Fordist working class. These reference points are now supplied by other frameworks of meaning: 'never before have children arrived at school with such an organized, simplified and "mass" symbolic universe' claims one Italian educator.[10] Other theorists concur on the relative weight of schooling and the social. Pierre Lévy 's[11] work on collective intelligence privileges the wider social sphere rather than the role of formal education in accounting for new forms of subjectivity. Likewise, the crucial object of analysis for Beradi suggests an approach to learning that is very far from the ideas of self-development at the heart of *Bildung*: the focus here is on 'the creation of techno-social interfaces which generate preconstituted cognitive paths and influence social behaviour in such a way as to make it functional regardless of any particular individuality'.[12] Thus, while attempts to map this constantly evolving process are also in constant transformation, it would seem clear that there has been a weakening of the distinctly autonomous role of schools, in keeping with the hegemony of economic discourses which has accompanied the implosion of the Fordist social contract and the dissolution of its universal mass (culine) symbolic subject. Rather than functioning as a site where discourses relatively independent of other domains are produced and circulated, the educational sector has reworked pre-existing discourses, including formerly antagonistic ones, and also adapted more and more to those emanating from elsewhere. The effect has been what in Italy has been called the 'adeguamento' to the economic sphere.[13] Moreover, the hugely differentiated nature of contemporary educational options precludes in itself the kind of master discourses of yesteryear. As Collini points out, this has at least fortunately saved us from subjection to more 'deathless prose' on such topics as the 'Idea of the Tertiary Education Sector',[14] but has not delivered us from other rather more dangerous discursive attempts to fill the void at the centre of neo-liberal education. While the discourse of the technocratic, left-centre governments as well as that of Brussels is couched in the terminology of corporate culture, with its colourless if politically correct register, other political forces have attempted to exploit this vacuum by the implantation of a variegated spectrum of populist rhetoric, both religious and nationalistic.

Precarity

It is directly in the name of the knowledge economy, then, that students are everywhere exhorted continually to update their personal portfolios with increasing quantities of certification of increasingly diversified competences in what is becoming a desperately competitive obstacle race for increasingly improbable positions. On the one hand, modularity, personalised lifelong learning and accreditation promise seamless passages between school, work, leisure and life. On the other, the post-fordist globalised economy is in a credibility crisis with the collapse of the dot coms, international financial scandals, repeated failures of its major international organisms and increased white collar intellectual offshore outsourcing. Promise is thus combined with a tangible fragility: the casualisation or precarisation or permatemping of intellectual labour is proliferating. Increasing numbers of graduates are pressured into unskilled jobs, underemployment or unemployment[15] – or, in England, forced by a system of student finance now heavily reliant on loans to spend the first decade of their post-university lives paying back the debts they have incurred.[16] (By such means and with disciplinary effect, van der Pijl suggests, 'micro-economic rationality is restored in each individual's life cycle'.[17])

However, despite its individualistic meritocratic promises, and despite such apparent achievements as the acceleration in the academic performance of girls, the feminisation of work and the valorisation of difference, the knowledge economy is unable to deliver a just distribution of benefits. In real terms, the old story of privileged white men is still playing across Europe. Its current phase – seen by some as the passage from patriarchy to fratriarchy – retains characteristics such as access to better schools, better university courses, better jobs, quicker and better promotions, fewer redundancies and better salaries for a highly advantaged group and in many areas these privileges are increasing.[18] Conversely, projects of social inclusion repeatedly founder against the responses of excluded groups. Chapter 10 discusses the most strongly articulated forms of such opposition, but its less visible forms should also be noted. One of the most strongly attested findings of educational research in urban areas, for instance, is the existence of sub-cultures that are in some sense rejectionist in the face of the demands of the school. Archer and Yamashita write that 'working class, inner city and certain minority ethnic young men have been posited as problems within current social policy and educational discourses;' yet 'government policies and strategies may have little impact on increasing the boys' identification with, or engagement with, formal learning, since they do not address the boys' strong emotional attachment to ideas grounded outside the educational context'.[19] Thus it is not only the government that blurs or weakens the boundaries between education and other social milieux. The relationship between formal education and popular culture is, as ever, a two-way street, along which travel not only projects of regulation but forms of resistance.

Individualisation

The transition from fordism to post-fordism has been described as the transition from a dualistic conflictual system based on the antagonistic interests of capital and labour to a different order. The new order is characterised by the management or governance of diverse elements in societies which are pluralistic, but whose fundamental contradictions are no longer admitted let alone allowed to be challenged. Where there was a clearly defined social contract now there is the slippery terrain of individual private negotiation.[20] Collective security has given way to personal risk and where fordist monotony once reigned there is now a flux of constant change and instability. Thus, as Christian Marazzi has written and as those teachers know whose pay, as in England, is linked to performance:

> Salaries are highly individual: qualifications determine only a part of salaried income with an increasing part arising from performance on the job, from the zeal and interest shown during the work process, after the initial contract. In this way salaries are disassociated from the actual position occupied and lose their sectoral status to become increasingly individual.[21]

Schools actively contribute to individualisation. Personalised learning, for instance, is one of the many modes in which students are encouraged to see themselves as single players in a world which increasingly 'takes no prisoners', to conceive of themselves as projects to be managed and directed towards success. The fragmentation of learning paths, the development of mentoring and counselling, career orientation programmes, private tutoring, international learning packages (including the huge industry that has developed around the study of the English language) all contribute to a sense of knowledge and 'competence' acquisition in terms of augmenting one's personal arsenal for the battlefield of a competitive market economy. Middle-class families increasingly mobilise economic and cultural resources to further the singular chances of their privileged offspring, whose lives in the process, however, are often reduced to an intolerable series of learning experiences, while private education in many countries is seen by a much-wider social sector as indispensable in acquiring more than the basic package that public education now provides. All of these practices also work powerfully to institute a private relationship to knowledge and research, framing a world where intellectual property rights are perceived not as piracy but as the 'normal' and just rewards for individual effort.

Individualisation, in a field where the goal posts are increasingly movable,[22] also nurtures opportunism, calculation and what in Italy is known as 'spregiudicatezza', a concept seemingly emblematic of the spirit of neo-liberalism, embracing both 'admirable open mindedness and deplorable ruthlessness'.[23] This spirit has long been a feature of the world of business and finance; it has now become commonplace in schools at many levels. Even in countries which have thought of such practices as alien to their systems, there has been a significant increase in individual instances of cheating and plagiarism.[24] The problem also has institutional dimensions, with the 'tampering' of marks becoming an integral element of systems where funding or other incentives are in some way dependent on determinate results. In England this situation is still subject to formal condemnation. However, the war against cheating and plagiarism has been accompanied there by the introduction of forms of testing and examination where the questions set are highly predictable, where (in consequence) a large 'revision industry' has come into existence and where there rumbles a continuous controversy about the diminishing difficulty of public examinations. In Italy the phenomenon of cheating is so normalised that disapproval is limited to timid and sporadic campaigns regarding the 'examifici' where public exam papers are openly bought and sold. The bulk of such practices are left untouched amid general indifference – or else interpreted as benign forms of inclusion. The increasingly fuzzy demarcation between illicit practices, inclusion, 'dumbing down' and profit-making constitutes a kind of analytical blind spot of neo-liberal educational practice and is an extremely murky area, not the least in its impact on student mentalities.

Individualisation and differentiation

Both France and Italy have systems that are – apparently – somewhat more socially open than the English, with less reliance on exam grades for educational progression. But this distinction is superficial: entry to the grandes écoles of France is more restricted, socially, in the 1990s than it was in the 1960s;[25] and the myth of a career open to educational talents was strongly challenged by the youth riots of 2005. In Italy where differentiation still takes precedence over overt competition as the preferred cultural model of individualisation, the scenario is no less problematic. Possible social conflict is preventatively displaced through a decrease in state examinations[26] and a softer more inclusive policy within a normalised system of social and cultural difference. Differentiation works through a combination of formal democracy and blatantly unequal practices based on 'naturalised' 'normalised' 'inevitable' class differences and choices. Given the absence of any serious engagement with mass education in terms of curricula in the licei, the 'high culture' approach of the upper secondary school automatically precludes attendance by most 'working class' students. The deceptive softness of the Italian system has been criticised because of its failure to provide students with essential challenges necessary to their personal development. Umberto Galimberti, a prominent Italian psychoanalyst and social theorist, sees this policy as having important negative consequences for the formation of student identity:

> The abolition of these exams and generalized 'promotions' ... deprives students of necessary recognition, leaving them in a limbo with no criteria for distinction between right or wrong ... (it leaves them with) a sense of uncertainty, disorientation, a total lack of awareness not only of their own value but of their very identity.[27]

Of course, in such a strongly differentiated system, practices like these have a much more significant impact on the majority of (non-*liceo*) students. They could be seen as providing an excellent basis for the series of vocationally oriented, low status university courses that such students are encouraged to attend. *Liceo* students not only have more rigorous and discipline-based curricula but also have access to other cultural resources and have other expectations which usually include attendance at the more academically serious and prestigious university courses where entry examinations are often required.

Individualisation and equality

Individualisation and competition are intimately related, acting recursively one upon the other. As Ulrich Beck noted in 1986:

> The growing pressure of competition leads to an individualization among equals i.e. precisely in areas of interaction and conduct which are characterized by a shared background (similar education, similar experience, similar knowledge). Especially where such a shared background still exists, community is dissolved in the acid bath of competition. Competition ... causes the isolation of individuals within homogeneous social groups.[28]

In European schooling, the presence of vast extending networks of certification contributes to the dissolution of community and differentiation among equals by positioning students as necessarily discerning customers on the look out for the cutting edge which may just make the difference in a labour market where the most significant salary differentials are to be found precisely among those with similar formal qualifications.[29] And while there has been a general rise in the qualifications of individuals competing on the labour market this has been accompanied by a shift in their utilisation:

> Qualifications are increasingly used not for the competences they refer to but as a means of increasing one's chances on the labour market and thus as a mechanism for lessening the possibilities for those with lower qualifications'.[30]

Students and young people consequently find themselves in the double bind situation whereby ever higher and broader qualifications are essential in getting a job but often are not relevant to the work itself, which is unsatisfying and underpaid. Employers, moreover, exploit this situation through their non-recognition of the added value contributed by over-educated workers.

The complementary processes of differentiation and fragmentation of learning within and between schools can be seen within this framework as processes of individualisation among *non equals* where the rhetoric of choice has worked to mask and mystify the limits of economically, culturally and demographically based possibilities. As we have seen, despite the horizontal diversification in the educational market place, there has also been a strong tendency to vertical differentiation, with policy orthodoxy intending to channel more students into vocational training at an earlier age, or into the lower echelons of dumbed down 'academic' education. In the former particularly, high levels of integration with the world of work through 'stage' or work experience serve to discourage any residual perception on the part of these students that education is anything other than a means of inserting oneself in the labour market.

Individualisation does not only work to preclude the possibility of collective solutions to social problems such as unemployment and flexible hyper-exploitation. It also serves, in Marazzi's words, to displace social conflict onto 'conflict with ourselves against our exclusion, against the singularity of our very being'.[31] Competitive individualisation leads to the interiorisation of failure to achieve determinate goals as personal inadequacy with often-dramatic consequences in terms of psychological and physical well-being.[32] The English system with its emphasis on testing through a complicated metrics of benchmarking, constantly revised National Curriculum levels of achievement, performance indicators, targets, league tables, stargrades, where children and students are subjected to continual examinations whose results have serious consequences for their future life chances as well as present self-esteem, has led to significant increases in stress-related illnesses, which, however, are not uniformly distributed across different social groups. A 2003 study of this phenomenon noted that particularly high stress levels had been recorded for affluent girls and that the time period for the increase in stress for this group coincided with the period when girls began to outperform boys in almost every academic subject at every academic stage, i.e. 1987–99. The report suggests that the feminine tendency 'to please' makes girls more 'vulnerable' to school cultures where academic success is highly valued'.[33] Returning to Bourdieu, we could reframe this and hypothesise instead that it is perhaps the greater propensity of affluent girls to 'hear, believe and obey' determinate discourses, i.e. to respond to the compellingly competitive messages which assail them from within and without the school culture, and which, when these are almost inevitably unfulfilled, lead to their personal dissatisfaction, anxiety and illness. Despite the 'crisis in masculinity' and their generally lower academic performance,[34] boys have lower stress levels and the proportionally greater rewards bestowed on them for their achievements in the external world would seem to justify this relative lack of panic.

Legitimation crisis

To reproduce themselves school cultures of individualisation require an individualised perception on the part of the mass of the population of what processes underlie competition, success and failure. There are, however, inherent difficulties in maintaining this perspective; Hayek expresses the dilemmas involved:

> It is important that within a market framework individuals think that their well-being derives principally from their own efforts and decisions. Few things are as effective in making them efficient and energetic as this belief, which is why it is so encouraged by education systems and in public opinion generally. ... However this also undoubtedly leads to an excessive faith in the truth of this generalization on the part of those who fail and who consider themselves to be equal to those who have succeeded, thus inducing feelings of bitterness ... Therefore it is a real dilemma to decide just how far young people should be encouraged in the belief that their efforts will be rewarded or rather if it should be emphasized that inevitably only a few of the worthy will succeed while many others will fail.[35]

If Hayek is right, then there are clear limits both to meritocracy and to the argument that governments have employed to legitimise their policies: that a relentless focus of certification can deliver success for all those who assent to the rules of an examination-centred game. When the North African student complained that it was always those from the Maghreb who were steered toward vocational pathways – see page 101 – Hayek would have found his fears confirmed.

Certification

We have already discussed the increase in certification in terms of its role in the marketisation and commodification of education. Here we are interested in how the widespread normalisation of certification practices contributes to the moulding of student mentalities. In the early years of neo-liberalism, it was still possible to speak of the differences between a diploma, an award, a degree etc. on the one hand and external, non-academic certification on the other, thus maintaining an increasingly tenuous difference between students and consumers. However, the effects of the growing practice of accreditation of privately certified external knowledge packages together with the increasingly hegemonic presence of modular learning have significantly eroded this residual space, as well as contributing to the acceptance of the concept of all knowledge as quantifiable and objectively measurable, which is perhaps one of its more insidious long-term effects. It is interesting to see how the intrusion of certification into a realm previously dominated by disciplinary knowledge was initially regarded. An Italian philosophy teacher comments in these terms:

> Schools engaged in the obsessive certification of competences do not seem so absurd when observed from within the framework of the new labour market which requires workers ready to demonstrate their levels of utility and the abolition of collective contracts in favour of individual ones. From this perspective, certification of competences, dossiers, objective evaluation, entrepreneurship take on their real significance. At a practical level school certificates will have close to zero interest for employers but schools will have carried out an extremely important task in moulding student mentalities in terms functional for the market, in conceiving of themselves as individuals in competition with other individuals, totally lacking in critical spirit. Thus the autonomous school becomes a complicit tool in the erosion of workers rights which is the real and regressive essence of this moment of history.[36]

The implosion of the Weberian paradigm where credentials enjoyed a kind of fordist guarantee, and its replacement by the system of servile insecurity discussed above, where qualifications are necessary, but not sufficient, to success on the labour market, has led to an enormous expansion in the education sector. Constant differentiation, vertically and horizontally, is its logic as it mimics the promotional strategies of other consumer items in a saturated market. But for students cum consumers, positioned as shrewd (and often indebted) investors in their own futures, levels of certification, once achieved, are likely to be experienced as unsatisfactory, either inadequate or as excessive. This dissatisfaction in turn leads to the perpetuation of the familiar 'insatiable', interminable consumer cycle.

Certification is also closely related to the so-called decline in standards or dumbing down debate.[37] If students are now positioned as clients paying for a service there is obviously a strong tendency for that service to be 'delivered' successfully, particularly at lower levels. At higher levels, to ensure the relative scarcity and thus higher value of the product, higher levels of failure or lower levels of success are considered more appropriate.[38] This does not mean that 'dumbing down' is simply a question of educational dumping, of blind compliance with market mechanisms. It is also closely related to the need for inclusion and social cohesion in an economy based on high levels of permanent structural unemployment or underemployment and thus is often, particularly in England, served under the guise of widening educational access and anti-elitism. (Much to the irritation of elite schools, 16+ vocational qualifications were for a period 'double weighted', so that schools whose students take such qualifications gain a more favourable position in league tables of performance; this does not, of course, disrupt the certification economy at the level of entrance to the most prestigious universities.) In countries with strong classical traditions, Italy, France and Spain, the 'adeguamento' to standardised and simplified modular learning, aided by the immediate adhesion of the publishing lobby to this new market, has been relatively rapid but rather more 'cynical'. On the one hand, despite generalised rhetoric, its fullest application is to be found in vocational education and the lower section of academic study as well as low-status university courses, where in many instances reforms at zero cost, and widespread disdain for forms of pedagogy other than traditional transmission, have resulted in a mere lightening of the academic load and an emptying of its conceptual content. In this way, the reframing of 'standards' facilitates the mass participation necessary for social cohesion while not invading the protected elite spheres. The former is particularly important for lower-level university courses in Italy and Spain which need to rapidly make up ground in the output of 'graduates' in order to approach European statistical levels. But the process has not gone contested: Italian students, noting the disparity in quality between established courses and new, 'university lite' programmes, launched in October 2005 mass protests against inferior higher education.

Lifelong learning: a threat or a promise?

As our chapter on the EU suggested, lifelong learning is no mere sound bite or secondary slogan of the new system. Once disengaged from the reassuring familiarity that it derives from culturally induced 'spontaneous' associations with universal truths and progressive beliefs regarding personal evolution, and examined instead within a framework of society as a social factory *'sans dehors'*, the perspective shifts. The broad unlimited horizon of becoming which it seems to promise – in contrast to the distinct temporal and terminable phases assigned to education in previous epochs – slides towards a slightly claustrophobic sensation of paranoia: there is no respite from the necessities of constant and constrained adaptation for one's very survival. Lifelong learning becomes not only a solicitation of ever increasing subjective flexibility and updating of personal competences in order to avoid obsolescence in the labour market. It is part of a more profound process whereby our lifeworlds are saturated by the logic of productivity. It fills those dangerous gaps. Concomitantly, the term unemployment has been emptied of its previous meaning. It has now become a time of socially useful 'workfare', of retraining, of studiously seeking employment and self-improvement and of remaining on call. What is important is not so much one's abilities or even their productive deployment but one's mental disposition.

The concept of lifelong learning exhorts us to 'keep up', to continually 're-invent' ourselves or be lost. The sharper our perspective, the greater our foresight in predicting trends, of taking up opportunities, of responding adequately to the 'évènements' which afflict all aspects of our existence, the greater our chances of personal success. In this context calls for time out or *otium* or as protesting Italian students have termed it 'slow learning' are both extremely defensive and radically liberating. At one level they make a plea for passive resistance. At another, in rejecting the pervasiveness of the logic of productivity, they are claims not for a return to the fordist separation between work and leisure but for the necessary space for the free development of human creativity and autonomy. This, as Gorz points out, means autonomy not just within work processes but in relation to the work process as a whole:

> An autonomy which is not just technical, practical and professional but one which is cultural, moral and political, capable of contestation, radical and fundamental questioning, of redefinition of the meaning of work in its social, political and cultural context. It is this autonomy which defines the stakes in the antagonism between labour and capital in the era of the virtual economy.[39]

In this fight for high stakes, creativity has taken on renewed value in neo-liberalism but it is a constrained, circumscribed creativity,[40] far from both the romantic connotations of past eras or from present human possibilities outside the framework of capital accumulation. Within the same confines, the recognition of the centrality of unprogrammable, indeterminate, abstract, socialised intelligence or *general intellect*[41] to contemporary production and innovation is immediately beset by the drive to control and domination in the forms of certification, quantification, specialisation, and productivity. It is this contradiction at the heart of the system which explains a number of paradoxes: the Qualifications and Curriculum Authority's attempts to isolate and package the essence of creativity – 'Creativity: find it, promote it;'[42] and the constant presence of infinitely novel communicational and relational techniques and problem-solving skills in training and retraining programmes of all kinds. This contradiction also suggests that the debate about declining standards and dumbing down is based on a false problem, posed in fundamentally misleading terms. If it is *general intellect*, a product of the 'common', and not any specific *individual* competence or specialisation, which is the source of productive labour and innovation, then it is not the 'content' of education which counts for capital but rather the disciplining practices involved in a constrained creativity compatible with its current stage of development.

Particularly in universities, students have at points rebelled against this onslaught on their autonomy and critical capacities. Gorz quotes German students in 1997, who centred their protests on a counterposition of old cultures and new: 'We don't want to be functionally programmed human machines ... we demand unconditional and unlimited access to *Bildung*.'[43] Similar sentiments animated the French and German protests against the Bologna process in 2004. The following year, Italian students during the university occupations stated their opposition to 'the political privatization of schools and of knowledge'. The large numbers of students who have mobilised on this basis have acted, especially in France, as catalysts of wider protest. Disciplined though they are by the pressures of debt and competitiveness, they serve in some circumstances as a rallying point of opposition that raises questions as much cultural as economic, and that at points has a retrospective appreciation of the educational cultures of the past. It is on such a mix of themes and affiliations, and the ways in which they are mobilised – along with others – in opposition to global policy orthodoxy that we will shortly focus.

Notes

1. Pierre Bourdieu, *Language and Symbolic Power* (Cambridge: Polity Press, 1991) p. 73.
2. Ibid., pp. 48–9.
3. Massimo Bontempelli, *L'Agonia della scuola italiana* (Pistoia: Editrice C.R.T, 2000).
4. Bill Readings, *The University in Ruins* (Boston: Harvard University Press, 1996); J. Hillis-Miller, *Black Holes* (Stanford, CA: Stanford University Press, 1999); Serge Latouche, *L'occidentalizzazione del Mondo*, (Turin: Bollati Boringhieri, 1992).
5. Dany-Robert Dufour, *L'art de réduire les tetes - sur la nouvelle servitude de l'homme libéré à l'ère du capitalisme total*, (Paris: Denoel, 2003).
6. Etienne Balibar interview in Il Manifesto, 4 September 2004. Balibar was one of many French intellectuals to sign the petition', 'Yes to secular education, no to emergency laws'.
7. See the work of Toni Negri and Michael Hardt, *Labor of Dionysos: a critique of the state-form* (Minneapolis-London: University of Minnesota Press, 1994); *Empire* (Boston: Harvard University Press, 1999); *Moltitudine*, (Milan: Rizzoli, 2004). Negri uses the work of Foucault and Deleuze and Guattari in tracing this passage from disciplinary society to the society of control. 'Disciplinarity fixed individuals within institutions but did not succeed in consuming them completely in the rhythm of productive practices and productive socialization; it did not reach the stage of permeating entirely the consciousness and bodies of individuals ... By contrast, when power becomes entirely biopolitical, the whole social body is comprised by power's machine and developed in its virtuality'(*Empire*, p. 24).
8. *Empire*, p. 33, 'The communications industries integrate the imaginary and the symbolic within the biopolitical fabric, not merely putting them at the service of power but actually integrating them into its very functioning'.
9. Cited in Stephen J. Ball, *Education For Sale! The Commodification of Everything?* (London: King's Annual Education Lecture, Kings College, 2004.
10. Scipione Semeraro, *Le nuove pedagogie crescono nei territori asimmetrici*, in Carta, vol. 5, no. 36, 2003.
11. Pierre Lévy, *Intelligenza Collettiva* (Milan: Feltrinelli, 1996).
12. Franco Berardi (Bifo) *Il sapiente, il mercante, il guerriero, Dal rifiuto del lavoro all'emergere del cognitariato* (Rome: Derive Approdi, 2004).
13. 'The norm is now money, but since money has absolutely no principles or identity of its own, it is no kind of norm at all. It is utterly promiscuous and will happily tag along with the highest bidder'. Terry Eagleton, *After Theory* (London: Allen Lane, 2004) p. 16.
14. Stefan Collini, 'HiEdBiz', *London Review of Books* 25.21, November 2003.
15. Mona Chellot, 'Education leads to temping and unemployment: France's precarious graduates', *Le Monde Diplomatique*, May 2006.
16. *The Guardian*, 3 January 2005. Maurizio Zenezini, 'Università e mercato di Lavoro', in *La Rivista del Manifesto*, Dec, 2001. Zenezini cites figures of 32% of graduates in England and Italy as working in jobs which do not require a degree. In France, in the period from 1985 to 1995 the same category rose from 12% to 25%. His sources are L. Borghans and A. de Grip ed.,

The Overeducated Worker?, Edward Elgar, Cheltenam, 2000; and D. Clerc, *Condamnés au Chomage?* (Paris: Syros, 1999). Saskia Sassen's work on Global Cities and Survival Circuits is also useful in challenging the dominant reading of the globalised economy as one based on highly educated labour.

17. Kees van der Pijl, 'A Lockean Europe', *New Left Review* 36, 9–37, January–February 2006.

18. For France see T.B. Smith, *France in Crisis: welfare, inequality and globalisation since 1980* (Cambridge: Cambridge University Press, 2004); for Italy see Sabina Minardi, 'Uomo sul lavoro vinco io', *L'espresso* 27 January 2005.

19. L. Archer and H. Yamashita, 'Theorising Inner City Masculinities', *Gender and Education* 15.3, 115–32, p. 115, 2003.

20. Marco Revelli, *Le Due Destre* (Turin: Bollati Boringhieri, 1996).

21. Christian Marazzi, *Il posto dei Calzini,la svolta linguistica dell'economia e i suoi effetti nella politica*, (Bellinzona: Casagrande, 1999).

22. Guido Rossi, *Il Conflitto Epidemico*, (Milan: Adelphi, 2003). This text explores the structural basis of corruption in contemporary capitalism.

23. Perry Anderson, 'Land without Prejudice', *London Review of Books* 24.6, 21 March 2002. Anderson provides an extremely interesting comment on the history of the term from its original enlightenment connotations to the present.

24. Rebecca Smithers, 'Crackdown urged on web exam plagiarism', *The Guardian* 22 November 2005. Rebecca Smithers: 'Exam papers should be scanned by specialist computer software as part of a crackdown on internet plagiarism by A-level and GSCE pupils in their compulsory coursework, the government's watchdog will urge today.'

25. Maria Fernandez Mellizo-Soto, 'Education Policy and Equality in France: the socialist years', *Journal of Education Policy* 15.1, 11–17, 2000.

26. At the moment there are two, at 13 and 18, but the direction of the reform seems to point to their eventual abolition, as residues of an obsolete system.

27. U. Galimberti in *La Repubblica*, 5 February 2005.

28. Ulrich Beck, *Risk Society* (London: Sage Publications, 1992) p. 94.

29. Zenezini, 'Università e mercato di Lavoro'.

30. Ibid.

31. Marazzi, *Il posto dei Calzini*, p. 24.

32. See Richard Wilkinson, *The Afflictions of Inequality* (London: Routledge, 1996); Andrea Beckmann and Charlie Cooper, 'Conditions of domination: reflections on harms generated by the British state education system', *British Journal of Sociology of Education* 26.4, 475–89, 2005.

33. 'The Trouble with Girls', *Observer Review*, June 1 2003.

34. PISA figures confirm this with some exceptions. In France, at the very highest levels, boys are not outperformed.

35. Cited in A. Conti, *Da un mondo all'altro.Il divenire azienda dell'università e il divenire università dell'azienda*, in *Posse: Il Lavaro di Genova*(Rome: manifestolibri) p. 106.

36. F. Bentivoglio, *Il disagio dell'inciviltà*, edizione (Pistoia: CRT, 2000).

37. Frank Furedi, *Where have all the Intellectuals Gone?* (London: Continuum, 2004); S. Collini, *op.cit.*

38. Ball, *Education For Sale!*, p. 2. Ball refers to the 'deafening silence' on this aspect of certification processes in England.

39. André Gorz, 'Miseria del Presente,ricchezza del possibile', Interview in *Tute bianche* ed. A. Fumagelli and M. Lazzarato (Rome: Derive Approdi 1999) p. 135.
40. Lorenzo Cillario, *L'economia degli Spettri* (Rome: Manifestolibri, 1966).
41. This concept derived from the fragment on machines in the *Grundrisse* has been at the centre of the Italian debate on post fordism. See the works of Negri, Virno, Marazzi, Beradi, Fumagalli, Revelli and Castellano.
42. Qualifications and Curriculum Authority, London http://www.ncaction.org.uk/creativity/.
43. Gorz, 'Miseria del Presente,ricchezza del possibile', p. 137.

9
The Agency of Teachers

In a previous chapter, we quoted Gramsci's observations on the difficulties of transformative change: it is not enough to design a programme; one must also attend to the capacities of those who will carry it out. This is a principle with which current policy orthodoxy is well acquainted. Most ministries of education accept the maxim of American policy analyst Erik Hanushek that 'the most productive reforms are almost certainly ones that improve the quality of the teaching force;'[1] and devising models of regulation, management and practice through which the work of a new generation of teachers can be linked to policy priorities is central to what they do. However, attempting such a remaking of the teaching force encounters immediate problems. The force that currently exists is ageing and often reluctant to adopt new practices. Newer generations may be more biddable but they are difficult to recruit and – so the experience of the last decade suggests – have high rates of resignation. In an attempt to deal with such difficulties, the OECD launched in 2003 a project entitled 'Attracting, Developing and Retaining Teachers'. Part of the project involved reviews of the condition of teaching and teachers in member countries, in which perceptive analysis of local situations – in Germany and Italy, for instance – was linked to a common, transnational model of the remade teacher.

We discuss this model at a later point. Here we want to suggest something of the depth at which programmes of change are required to work. In relation to Germany, the OECD review team wrote of a:

> kind of malaise within the teaching profession. We heard much about lowering of social esteem, unjust criticism by politicians, increasing burdens and worsening working conditions. ... [But] there is some evidence that teachers' psychological concerns are connected

not so much with excessive situational demands but rather with the intensification of demands in the sense of forced decision-making and pressure for action ... and [this situation] enhances a subjective feeling of being powerless.[2]

A background report to the OECD on teachers in Italy made comparable points, identifying a profound crisis of teacher morale and suggesting a great disjuncture existed between the programmes elaborated by policy and the condition of the people required to be its agents. Teachers experience 'widespread uneasiness, crisis of identity, deterioration of self- image and of the image offered to public opinion and, finally, the weakened trust of students and their families'.[3] Hence the paradox of teaching:

> The more school becomes a crucially important institution in the *knowledge society* ... the more teachers feel like belonging to a class the prestige of which is in decline.[4]

Implicit in judgements like these is a kind of historical pathos: teacher identities were formed through the experience of the *liceo* and the elementary school, and remade through the hopes of democratisation that sustained the movements of the 1970s. Now they find themselves suffering from a kind of *mal du siècle:* the private is valued above the public, the teacher's vocation is demeaned, and for an entire professional group the time is out of joint. These judgements suggest that the policy and tactics of government agenda for the teaching force cannot be sketched, as it were, on a blank sheet, but must be constructed through an encounter with the cultures of teaching that became embedded in Western Europe in the post-war decades.

Autonomy

For much of this period, teachers' work in important respects escaped overt policy direction. Regulation might specify basic curricular requirements, the organisation of school time and teachers' responsibilities to management. But beyond that, even in the most regulated of systems, teachers enjoyed a kind of protected autonomy in terms of their classroom work. In Italy, for instance, the academic freedom of teachers was formally safeguarded in the post-war constitution. In West Germany, it was grounded in the authority provided by a very long period of initial training, and by success in competitive examinations. In England, its foundations rested more nebulously on custom and practice. Everywhere, though – including at a later point Spain – teachers' autonomy was underpinned by contractual arrangements that awarded teachers, once permanently appointed, a degree of job security unusual in the workforce as a whole. Civil service status, in France, Germany, Italy and Spain ensured that it was only in exceptional circumstances that established teachers could be dismissed. In England, a consensus between teachers' unions and local employers had the same effect. This secure workforce, though often, as in Italy, strikingly underpaid, was only lightly managed.[5] Head teachers were not appointed for their managerial expertise, and had few sanctions or incentives at their disposal: salary levels related to seniority rather than 'competence' or 'performance'. Inspection regimes were not intrusive, and the absence both of market-based competition and popular involvement in school governance meant that parental demands and criticisms were not strongly felt.[6]

This situation was legitimated by teachers' claim to be uniquely capable of adapting curricula and pedagogy to student needs, and to embody the kinds of freedom that democratic societies should celebrate. ('In this country,' declared the National Union of Teachers in 1960, 'the teacher has the inalienable right to decide what to teach and how to teach it.'[7]) Secondary teachers – especially those in selective secondary schools – could base this claim on their specialist subject knowledge; primary teachers, less securely, could rest it on their understanding of children's learning processes. However, these claims to autonomy – though hard won against governments that had in the pre-war period possessed much stronger directive powers – provided only an ambivalent advance. Part of the problem here was the uncodifiability and uncertainty of teachers' work, in classrooms whose demands inflected the processes of teaching and learning in what were felt to be unpredictable and idiosyncratic ways. Teachers' self-image was built on such a perception; particularly in primary education and mass secondary education, they saw teaching as an individual craft and themselves as 'lone fighters' (Germany) or 'artisans' (France), who managed uncertainty by combining unprogrammable personal qualities, such as charisma, with a knowledge born of practical experience.[8] But the converse of these claims was that teaching could not gain uncontested entry to the category of 'profession;' in the absence of a sure and authoritative knowledge base, linked to a university discipline, it lacked a measure of credibility. This later became a source of vulnerability in cases where governments turned to a policy of greater central regulation of classroom practice, but for a long period, post-war teachers' claims were generally accepted by governments: as Lawn puts it, of England, 'teachers were professionals, fostered by the state, partners in the deliberation of policy.'[9]

These 'partners' of policy development were in most instances part of a reforming bloc, that pushed, post-1960, for the further democratisation of education. In France individual members of the FEN provided much of the cadre of the left-wing parties, while the Federation itself had an important policy influence. The energies of the Spanish *alternativa* supplied the PSOE with much of the programme that it implemented in the 1980s. In a more diffuse way, the cohorts who entered teaching around 1968 brought with them an interest in popular education, with an anti-authoritarian axis and a stronger orientation towards political militancy. The reforms achieved at governmental level – the Italian *decreti delegati* of 1974, for instance – strengthened the capacities of these cohorts to implement curricular reform through local action.

Diversity

From this angle, teachers might appear as the vanguard of educational and cultural change. Broadening the perspective, however, complicates the picture. Ideologies of social progress through educational reform were interlinked with other positions that were less obviously radical. A professionalism that sought to put teachers' educational choices beyond the reach of popular dialogue was one such position. Another centred on the school's role in connecting social origins to occupational destinations: the child-centred ideologies that flourished in the 1960s and 1970s tended not to address such structural questions, and as a result often coexisted with quite conservative understandings of 'ability', 'differentiation' and the other concepts and mechanisms that the school required to carry out its traditional role. Thus, in relation to Spain, Guerrero writes of 'the demonstrable consensus of teachers – under pressure to maintain academic quality – that favours compartmentalisation according to achievement'.[10] Of France, as Bourdieu and Passeron noted, formal ideologies of egalitarianism were accompanied by practices of academic differentiation that favoured advantaged social groups.[11] The neo-liberal critique of the 'low expectations' that schools had of their students is to this extent not without foundation. In every country, the massification of secondary education was lived by great numbers of teachers as a time of difficulty, in which concerns over student behaviour and motivation eclipsed issues of a more programmatic kind.

Teachers were also inhibited by institutional, status and gender divisions. The differences between the identities of secondary and primary teachers ran deep. The OECD noted in 1998 that in Italy 'until now, secondary school teachers have been trained at university, elementary school teachers at ... upper secondary cycle level' and this situation, mapped on to gender differences, was replicated elsewhere. In all countries, the organisation of the teaching force rested on a distinction between those in possession of a university degree and those without, the majority of whom taught in the primary sector, and the majority of whom were women. (The percentage of women teachers in any given sector, it has been noted, is in inverse proportion to the prestige and pay levels of that sector.[12])

This tiered teaching force was also subject to other sorts of division. Demographic and budgetary fluctuations have led to periods of significant teacher unemployment – in West Germany, for instance, in the 1980s and in the deindustrialising eastern Länder of Germany post-2000.[13] In Italy, this was a chronic problem. The over-supply of qualified graduates produced for a huge number of teachers and would-be teachers – an estimated 440,000 in 2004 – a situation of long-standing 'precariousness'.[14] Precarity involved a tortuous and fragmented career route – supply teaching, frequent legal battles, unpaid work in private crammers, frequent courses of training to accumulate the 'points' that might make secure employment possible in a teaching force which is appointed partly on the basis of success in competitive national examinations and partly through chaotic local procedures. This mix of systems provided, moreover, conditions in which the much-noted clientilism of Italian society could flourish, as teachers sought the assistance of a sponsor to improve their position in a labour market that was not completely decipherable, or to obtain prior access to exam papers for the national *concorsi*. In its severity, this experience is peculiarly Italian, but as we suggest below, precarity – if not as yet clientilism – is increasingly familiar in other parts of Europe.

Finally, in this catalogue of division, there is the question of trade unionism. A definition of effective trade unionism in an educational context would include such elements as organisational unity, mass membership, a capacity to defend members' interests and contribute in some broad sense to socially inclusive reform. In no country are all of these minimal conditions met. With the possible exception of Germany, teacher unionism is characterised by organisational diversity, based on sectoral divisions and/or political orientation. English levels of unionisation are high, though unions are excluded from negotiation on central issues such as pay. In other countries (France, Italy and Spain), paid-up membership is less than 50% of the teaching force – though unions demonstrate their respective levels of support in national workplace ballots to determine representation on local and national negotiating committees. In broader terms, the capacity of unions to defend members' interests (over jobs, pay and working conditions) and to maintain historic commitments in the midst of neo-liberal change has been severely tested. As we suggest in the following chapter, the record here is a very mixed one.

In with the new

Modernisation has several dimensions. Politically, it is an exercise in delegitimation and relegitimation. As Christian Laval wrote of the discursive strategies of the Raffarin government, they sought to 'bury' the education-based protest movement of 2003 through an appeal to different sources of legitimacy. Seeking an alternative to the voices of professionals and parents, Raffarin had recourse to three sources of counter-authority – to public opinion (through a staged 'great debate' on educational futures), to the judgements of 'experts' (set out in the Thélot report) and to the deliberations of elected representatives, expressed through the 'Fillon' law, which followed swiftly on the heels of Thélot. Belatedly mimicking the strategies of English policymakers in the 1970s and 1980s, Raffarin hoped in these ways to loosen the grip of teachers on the process of policy formation' and in this way substantially to modify a pattern of relationships between teacher organisation and national government that had endured for the previous five decades.[15]

In another dimension, modernisation involves a new discourse about the nature of teachers' work. In this context, Martin Lawn's summary of policy discourse in 1990s England has now a wider application:

> Professionalism as an employer discourse has almost entirely disappeared ... The overtones of a responsible group, working within the state, are no longer necessary or even valid. Teacher professionalism is now being redefined as a form of competent labour, flexible and multi-skilled; it operates within a regulated curriculum and internal assessment system in a decentralised external market. The dominant version (of professionalism) is now a notion of individual responsibility and incentive reward legitimised by an ... idea of efficient service and performance incentive.[16]

Thus policy discourse signals the replacement of relatively unregulated cultures of teaching with the strongly directed forms of practice whose impact we trace in the sections that follow. But it is important to understand that this strategy, which entails giving 'professionalism' a new meaning, is not limited to ideological advocacy, nor is it advanced only in the form of designs for the definition, management and direction of teachers' work.[17] Important though these are, their effect depends on their interfacing with another side of policy, and strategic vision at this point combines with harsher measures. The modernisation of teaching occurs in a context where managerial force and material constraint exercise a powerful influence, and where a combination of flexibilisation and in some cases casualisation work to reshape teacher identities.

Contexts of constraint

Educational funding – it should never be forgotten – takes a smaller share of GDP than was generally the case in the 1970s. The neo-liberal programme of deficit reduction, inflation control and balanced budgets provides a powerful set of constraints, whose effect on teacher numbers, on pensions and pay and on material resources has been to wear down teachers' capacity for autonomous initiative, and thus make more likely the success of reprofessionalising projects. In 2002–3, the Raffarin government overturned the teacher supply policy agreed to by its Socialist predecessor: it cut teacher numbers, announced a policy of filling only half the vacancies created by retirement and increased the number of temporary – i.e. precarious – staff.[18] The transfer of large numbers of school-workers out of state employment and civil service status, to the pay-rolls of the regions had a similar, precarising effect. When, in 2005, the de Villepin government announced plans to make teachers cover the classes of their absent colleagues, the position of these precarious layers became still more difficult: the imposition of flexibility on permanent staff would lessen the job opportunities of 'casual' teachers. In Germany, the hours of work of teachers increased, and class sizes grew larger. In many Länder, new teachers were employed only on the basis of one-year or part-time contracts, with a lower entry salary than in previous times.[19] In Spain also, in a strategy initiated in the early 1990s, precarisation became integral to plans for cost reduction. Demographic change in the cities, and the growth of the private sector, supplied pretexts for cuts in teacher numbers. The term 'temporary teacher' – previously related to a common short-term experience among those waiting for permanent status – now designated an employment situation that could stretch for up to 10 years. The teaching force became multiply divided – between the secure and the precarious, the public and the private sector, the displaced (those who had lost tenure through school reorganisation) and those unaffected. In addition, the devolution of educational control to regions which differed greatly in their ability and willingness to fund education created important divergences in salaries, pensions and working conditions, as well as barriers to mobility across regional boundaries.

In England, where government spending on education has increased since 1997, material constraints are codified in legislative and contractual provision, the effect of which is to place the organisation of teachers' time at the disposal of local managements. Since 1987, the length of teachers' working year has been specified, as have obligations to carry out activities in 'directed time' and to cover for absent teachers. Since 1988, with the introduction of financial autonomy, 'hire and fire' decisions have been devolved to school level – with the rate of teacher redundancy increasing sharply. More recently, in 2004, a 'workload agreement' signed by most of the teacher unions introduced a new element of flexibility: teachers would be supported by, and would direct the work of, 'teaching assistants' – not necessarily qualified – who would in some cases cover unsupervised classes, as well as relieve teachers of administrative work. The National Union of Teachers opposed what it saw as a move to deskill the teaching force, and its introduction has been fraught with budgetary difficulties. But it remains central to government plans for the reorganisation of teachers' work, in which the use of ancillary workers, and computer-based resources for individualised learning, are significant factors.

Policy in England, with its clear intention of placing teachers within a clearer and hierarchically organised set of relationships, in which a long chain of 'line management' responsibility connects heads, deputies, middle managers, classroom teachers and classroom assistants, is thus in the vanguard of European developments. Performance-related pay is one marker of this status. Since 2003, teachers have been performance managed: to cross a pay threshold and proceed up the pay scales teachers must demonstrate to head teachers that they have 'grown professionally' and made 'sustained and substantial progress'.[20] By contrast, Italian proposals to this effect were defeated by teacher opposition, and in Germany, by 2004, the extent of PRP was limited to two pilot projects.[21] Nevertheless in terms of general orientation towards stronger management, England is hardly alone. In Spain, the practice of electing the school director, established by the PSOE reforms of the mid-1980s and even then hedged with qualifications, was ended by the legislation of 1995, which transferred the director's lines of accountability 'upward' to local administrations. Pélage has noted a growing tendency in France for head teachers to be appointed for their managerial rather than their educational expertise.[22] Even so, the pace of change is often slow. In Germany, where cultures of teaching have been inhospitable to managerialism, the OECD study team found in 2004 that

> the identity of school leaders is still basically associated with class teaching. Principals tend to see themselves more as head teachers rather than as school managers and leaders. Teachers generally perceive the principal as 'first among equals', raised from the ranks and paid a bit more to coordinate the work of the school.

This was an identity which the reporters wished to transform: collegial structures and consensual processes tended to place obstacles in the way of the drive towards to 'quality assurance and evaluation'[23] that was the raison d'etre of new types of management, the complexities of whose strategies for remaking teachers we will now explore.

Developing teachers' potential

The attempts to reduce the cost, alter the conditions, and increase the managed flexibility of teachers' work are complemented by other measures of modernisation, relating to curriculum and pedagogy. At this point, the authoritarianism that necessarily accompanies enforced change acquires a new emphasis. The rhetoric of reform is still written, as it were, in the imperative, but the focus now is on 'upskilling' and the development of teachers' potential. 'The time has long gone,' declared a document of the English Ministry of Education (DfEE) in 1998, 'when isolated professionals made curriculum and pedagogic decisions alone, without reference to the outside world'.[24] Instead, teachers needed to take 'personal and collective responsibility for improving their skills', to seek to base decisions 'on evidence of what works in schools', to welcome the contribution that parents and business can make to a school's success and to 'promote innovation'. These conceptions were embodied, in England, in a highly specified and regulated form of initial teacher education, in programmes of 'continuous professional development' that were likewise subject to government approval, and in an approach to research that directed public funds towards pragmatic, 'evidence-based' studies.

Outside England, though less strongly steered by government, programmes of teacher development were turned in a similar direction, though often with an acknowledgement of the difficulties of change. The OECD reviewers suggested that the

> methodological skills and the general teaching competencies of German teachers are less developed than their subject knowledge, and they are not sufficiently prepared to develop students' learning competencies, to individualise teaching, to enhance self-regulated learning, to motivate students by using active methods, to initiate complex projects for learning, or to organise learning in cooperative teams.[25]

Reviewing Italian education, an OECD background paper addressed similar issues and called for 'changes such as greater autonomy and responsibility, teamwork and teaching methods based not on the transmission but on the acquisition of knowledge'. At the same time, however, the organisation accepted that it would take 'years' for such changes to be assimilated – an expectation that has proved to have been realistic. Likewise, in Spain, the LOGSE of 1990 attempted to shift 'the focus of pedagogic action from the transmission of knowledge to the processes of learning', while also placing a strong emphasis on the pastoral function of the teacher.[26] However, as Orrit noted, the meeting, in times of austerity, between proposals for pedagogic change and the reality of Spanish schools was something of a 'shock encounter', and to stress the pastoral role of teachers was also to project them unprepared into the front line of conflicts between home and school.[27]

The softness of management

The powers of management and the mechanisms of policy thus relate to softer issues than those of employment and salary. Schools have become increasingly complex in their functions. Co-ordinating the different aspects of their work requires a more sophisticated approach to management than bureaucratic-professional traditions can provide. All the French research on school effectiveness, writes Pelage, 'underlines the necessity of promoting the collective dimension of the institution and of achieving a condition of *"travailler ensemble"* among categories of personnel who have up until now kept themselves at a distance.'[28] But this work of functional co-ordination is over-determined by a political emphasis. The human resources of the school must be mobilised behind policy agendas, and for this task – as the knighthoods awarded to English head teachers demonstrate – local leadership is vital. In the words of an EC document, decentralisation offers a means of 'taking the political debate on quality down to lower levels of the education system'. At these lower levels 'stakeholders' can be 'empowered' by 'making them more responsible for defining what they understand by quality in education and giving them 'ownership' of their part in the education system.'[29] It is at this point that 'leadership', as opposed to mere 'management' becomes important. Leadership provides the inspiration and the glue for the enterprise of *'travailler ensemble'* so as to achieve the objectives laid down by policy.

Leadership also has a strong cultural dimension. The theories of business organisation favoured by reformers make much of issues of 'culture' – of the norms, values, procedures and rituals that are unique to individual organisations. In such accounts, culture is highly plastic and amenable to direction from above – issues of cultural conflict are downplayed. To 'turn around' a school from failure to academic success is, in these narratives, a work of cultural transformation. Managers must therefore become cultural leaders, working on emotions and relationships as much as systems and regulations. They must identify and then transform the culture of their organisation, so that it is based on a commitment to 'quality', as that term is defined by the policy agenda. This mission, conceived as one of personal vocation, is everywhere celebrated in the discourse of school reform. The job of an educational leader, said Blair's policy advisor, is – Moses-like – to take teachers to a promised land, from which they will not want to return.[30] Or, as van Zanten more analytically puts it, 'the legitimacy of bureaucratic hierarchies is dismissed in favour of the personal vision and capacity to mobilise individuals and to organise group work by an educational leader.'[31]

Interpreting change

Policy orthodoxy, then, constitutes far more in relation to the work of teachers than simply a regressive programme aiming at the inculcation of 'basic skills'; neither does it rely solely on managerial force. Susan Robertson, summarising OECD work in this area, brings out very clearly the demands made in policy design for qualities of quite another kind – innovation, collectivity, complexity and sophistication, summarised by the OECD in these terms:

> The creation and application of professional knowledge on the scale and in the time-frame demanded by 'schooling for tomorrow' makes

demands at the individual and system levels. At the level of the individual teacher, there needs to be a psychological transition from working and learning alone with a belief that knowledge production belongs to others, to a radically different self-conception which, in conformity with interactive models, see the production of knowledge with colleagues as a natural part of a teachers' professional work. At the system level ways have to be found to bring teachers together in such an activity.[32]

The 'underlying thrust' of this analysis, she comments, is that the 'dominant model of the teacher working alone' – of the teacher as artisan, we could say – 'is no longer viable in a society where knowledge production, its distribution and consumption are central'.[33] In the past, teachers' claims to professionalism rested upon tacit knowledge and were linked to strategies for maintaining an autonomy that was individual in character; but it is precisely these claims that are now 'seen to have contributed to an underdeveloped body of knowledge about teaching and learning'. From this perspective, there is something archaic about teachers. The 'demands of an imagined knowledge economy' are that they should work collaboratively, to produce authoritative, generalisable, evidence-based knowledge about how learners learn, and about 'effective' teaching. Policy orthodoxy, however, believes that as yet they lack the capacity to do so.

We can find similar analyses replicated at the level of individual countries. Researchers committed to a modernising programme have commented on what they see as the backwardness of educational culture in Spain, where collaboration between teachers, and the diffusion of pedagogic culture, are both underdeveloped.[34] Likewise, the report written for the OECD on teachers in Italy begins by noting a discrepancy between the reforming energies displayed by legislation and the reception of new policies at the level of the school:

At present, it seems that the entire professional staff is in a stand-by position, or defending the 'conquests' made in the '70s. This position, which was also defined [as] 'immobilism', is perhaps due to the fact that the majority of teachers do not clearly perceive the advantages of change yet, while the guarantees and opportunities of the present situation are evident. However, this uncertain role, which derives from an ancient tradition, is the most critical aspect. Even from the '20s of the last century teachers were already considered more as intellectuals and 'artists' than professionals capable of resolving problems connected with learning.[35]

Accordingly, as traditional intellectuals, teachers have 'been asked to do everything, in the name of a generic educational idea according to which school should give a response to all the unresolved problems of society'. In consequence, they have 'not been able to produce [themselves as] a professional group; ... their social vocation was solicited instead.'[36]

In this situation, which lacks a true 'pedagogic culture' and in which teachers have 'lost their way', new policies are seen as potentially liberating. Decentralisation, for instance, offers the opportunity for democracy and innovation;

> [It] introduces a deep innovative element. It sanctions that hierarchic logics are over - as they were characterised by the principles of authority and superordination - and affirms the logics of participation - characterised by equality and cooperation. The State "protection" traditionally applied ... to schools, is substituted by the legal status recognized to school networks, units or groups of institutes of adequate size. The bureaucratic control which complicated didactics, is substituted by a service of assistance and advice in favour of the initiatives of school innovators. The headmaster (school manager) substitutes the authoritative and centralising model, with a diffused *leadership;* this new decision-making decentralised model aims at appreciating the teaching staff resources and at improving the school service quality.[37]

Thus policy orthodoxy presents itself not as a constraining force, but as an enabling one; not individualistic, but collective; not 'authoritative' but participatory. It corresponds, in other words, to the possibilities opened up by the undermining of the 'authoritative' state by decentralisation, and proposes a way of working that is more capable than bureaucratic centralism or old professionalism of meeting teachers' need for satisfying, productive work. Yet despite the apparent attractiveness of this offer, the accounts offered by OECD reviewers – and by university-based researchers – suggest that teachers have responded to it, at best unevenly, and in many cases with individual scepticism and collective opposition.[38]

A recent history of late twentieth-century Italy, which is alive not only to the miseries of Italian schooling but also to the cultural achievements that are embodied in it, provides material for understanding why teachers' responses to the attractions of this programme are not best understood in nostalgic or conservative terms. For the historian Paul

Ginsborg – as for the OECD – the condition of upper secondary schooling in the 1990s was disappointingly archaic; secondary schooling as a whole was 'largely populated by a demoralized staff lacking incentives;' it reproduced, more strongly than other education systems, patterns of social inequality.[39] But at the same time – a point made by Ginsborg, but not by the OECD – 'among the 900,000 dissatisfied, demoralized and poorly paid Italian schoolteachers ... there were tens of thousands who retained a sense of urgency in encouraging school students to reflect critically on the modern world.'[40] Their inspiration, he suggested, was likely to stem from the educational movements of the 1970s, that from one point of view amounted to no more than a (democratic) modernisation *manqué*, but from another contributed to a concrete sense of educational possibility – from which perspective the type of modernisation offered by the OECD was lacking. It seemed to be less an example of policy orthodoxy's liberating powers than an illustration of a policy that spurned ideas of democracy and egalitarianism. From this point of view, modernisation demonstrated what one tendency in Italian critical thought termed the contradictions of a knowledge economy that on the one hand requires innovation and experiment, and on the other sees such qualities as destabilising, and seeks through intensive strategies of management to control them.[41]

This perspective on change helps explain why cultures of teaching have not been remade along the lines that policy desires, and retain a certain impermeability to reform, relatively immune so far to the effects of government programmes on their relationships with students and on their teaching methodologies. At the political level, at least up until the end of the Berlusconi period in 2006, it was difficult to find evidence of teacher support for the Moratti reforms. Trade unions and social movements, though they did not defeat the legislation, at least established a climate among teachers in which her proposals were regarded with extreme scepticism, as a weak Italian variant of neo-liberalism. The attempts of Berlusconi's centre-left successors to continue in the spirit of Moratti met militant opposition in the strikes of November 2006.[42] It is difficult, at least, to see ground-level evidence of the changes that policy orthodoxy calls for.

Impact and response

Ineffective so far in Italy, have new leadership and management strategies succeeded elsewhere in remaking the cultures and working practices of teaching? In Germany, also, the answer would seem to be 'not yet'. For a number of years, the German press has carried articles by business groups, SPD and even Green politicians calling for an increase in the quality and effectiveness of education – with a higher degree of curriculum specification, competition between schools and a stronger system of inspection heading the list of desirable reforms. Such changes are not possible, it is thought, without a transformation of the teaching force, of a kind that holds few attractions for teachers: 'civil servant status' argues OECD reviewers, 'characterised by extensive job security and limited mechanisms for teacher evaluation and feedback is not the employment status that best achieves this objective.'[43] The generation of teachers which began work in the 1960s and 1970s and which is now nearing retirement age is out of sympathy with these demands, and with the whole *Zeitgeist* of economisation that underlies them. Compared with Italy, however, public protest is scarce and comes into the open only in response to particularly strong provations – such as the introduction of university fees. It is as if the old discourses of reform are being worn out, piecemeal, step by step, without one single conflict appearing to be decisive. Sticking to them, the GEW, fears, runs the danger of being out of tune with the times, and the teachers' union has therefore consistently worked 'to prevent the worst case scenario', by an acceptance of that which is second worst.[44] Even so, a thorough-going transformation of the teaching force is some way off: as Hanushek realised, there is no quick fix to the problem presented by the working practices of teachers.

In France, research tends to suggest that the refocusing of teachers' activity that policy orthodoxy calls for has had a significant impact. Vincent Lang, writing in 2001, suggested – in the manner of OECD reviewers – that the resources of older professional cultures are demonstrably insufficient to deal with new educational and social contexts, and that this failure has created space for the development of a new type of professional mobilisation – a mobilisation that is linked to a 'broadening of the frame of reference of pedagogy'. Similarly, he noted with the establishment in 1989 of university-level teacher-training institutions, 'a break from an academic type of teacher education and from an abstract type of qualification' towards an engagement with actually existing educational problems.[45] Pélage, arguing along similar lines, suggests that the new education is not simply a construction from above: head teachers who attempt to transform their school in line with its principles find support among at least a section of their staff.[46] Such teachers can make a new kind of claim for recognition, founded neither on the 'high culture' of lycée teachers nor on the domestic and citizenly virtues propagated in the primary school, but – as Lang suggests – on the blending elements of autonomous decision-making with a body of knowledge about teaching and learning authorised and promulgated by state agencies. In this context, Lang writes of a professionalism that is a work of some complexity, new in French education, that valorises both the 'autonomous, performative individual' and the 'relational aspects of an organisation', and that is willing to adapt to new externally defined norms at the same time as being able to construct a 'know-how' related to 'locally identified difficulties'.[47]

Accounts like these capture something of the ambitions of reprofessionalisation and of the commitments of its supporters. But like Italian accounts of new cultures of teaching, they tend to overlook the destructive element of change. As elsewhere, the attempts to establish new models of teaching are simultaneously an assault on the old, and are experienced by teachers as a kind of violent deskilling. In response to a series of circulars from the Minister of Education, de Robien, two French teachers wrote in 2007:

[He writes] as if the process of teaching could be reduced to the operationalising of a just a few prefabricated tools. What is at stake here is the very idea of the teacher as someone capable of conceiving educational ideas and skilfully putting them into practice. The endless succession of circulars seeks to transform this teacher into just an executant of ministerial directives, under the control of the headteacher/manager.[48]

Against this degradation of teachers' work – by means of which teachers become 'polyvalent' knowledge workers, delivering curricula designed elsewhere through teaching strategies that are improvised, untheorised, survivalist responses to particular local situations – the writers evoke the qualities of a different period, when teachers (they argue) possessed an identity based on subject expertise and on substantive knowledge of pedagogic theory. They thus mobilise in opposition to de Robien the intellectual and cultural dimensions of an earlier perspective on knowledge and pedagogy: to this extent, positions developed in the 1970s and 1980s remain an important reference point. Van Zanten, in her account of teachers in disadvantaged schools, likewise suggests that in some respects this earlier orientation has endured. She emphasises, though, that what is involved here is not only a conflict between teachers and government, but a clash at school level between different orientations to the work of teaching:

Conflicts between 'old' and 'new' teachers are more likely to arise, both because there are important ideological cleavages between the professional ethics of the two groups and because solidarity appears as an essential dimension for professional success. Old and stable teachers are much more orientated towards a 'humanitarian' ethic that gives meaning to their activity in 'disqualified' school contexts, even when pupils do not make any significant achievement progress. Most young and mobile teachers just develop survival strategies, some of them based on the use of managerial techniques, to cope with situations they hope are transitory; theirs is a much less ideologically informed professional ethic.[49]

There is anecdotal evidence from other places to suggest that the generational divergence that van Zanten describes is not confined to France. Local branch officials in the NUT, for instance, comment on the difficulties of mobilising the newer generation of London teachers – 'every year activists would leave the branch and there'd be slightly more activists leaving the branch than we'd be managing to create new ones.' They also perceive generational differences, stemming from 'everything that's happened in government policy over the last twenty years', at the level of classroom work. The effects of an 'eroded' classroom autonomy were felt in the conservatism of younger teachers:

> Where ... the new breed of teachers are least political is in relation to what they do in a classroom and the lessons that they teach ... They'll be political [outside] about GM crops or about the [Iraq] war or about anti-deportation campaigns, but they'll think that what they have to do in their history lessons is teach the Black Death and the Peasants' Revolt as if these things had no connection whatsoever with now here.[50]

But generational differences, though real, may be overstated. Curricular radicalism has declined across generations, not simply between them. In London, with the erosion of effective trade unionism, teachers' capacity to affect decisions about the daily routines of the school and the classroom was generally constrained; when one researcher talked in the mid-1990s to teachers in a school that had previously enjoyed a reputation for radical curricular initiative, she found that they 'made hardly any mention of present engagement with wider political struggle as educational activists' – instead a discourse organised around 'accountability, access and achievement' prevailed.[51] Writing a few years later, Bottery found that teachers' saw their job as 'centrally concerned ... with the "kids" or "the subject"; other issues were regarded as little more than intrusions, and any which involved taking a wider vision as also politically dangerous'.[52] Conversely, where teacher mobilisation has occurred – notably in France and Italy – younger teachers have participated fully.[53] In such mobilisations, the commitments of earlier generations – to an educational mission in some sense egalitarian, solidaristic and critical – are echoed, perhaps even more intensely than before. The professional ethic may be, in van Zanten's terms, 'less informed' but the sense of educational crisis is acutely developed.

The field of teaching is thus a complex one. Policy orthodoxy involves both reskilling elements and measures to control, standardise and simplify the teacher's work. Teachers' responses to new policies and difficult practical situations include adaptation, despair, survivalism, reasoned critique, appeals to now-marginalised traditions and – more rarely – depictions of an alternative future. In these complexities, we can see reflected the wider patterns of educational conflict which we trace in our final chapter.

Notes

1. Erik A. Hanushek, *Economic outcomes and school quality* (Paris: International Institute for Educational Planning, 2005) p. 17.
2. OECD, *Attracting, Developing and Retaining Effective Teachers – Country Note for Germany* (Paris: OECD, 2004) p. 39.
3. Alessandro Cavalli, *Gli insegnanti nella scuola che cambia* (Bologna: Il Mulino, 2000).
4. OECD, *Attracting, Developing and Retaining Effective Teachers: country background report for Italy* (Paris: OECD, 2003) p. 7.
5. 'The economic framework is the sad part of the teaching profession' notes the OECD background report on Italian teachers 2003, p. 87.
6. This situation has not passed without criticism – for instance, this comment from a German parents' organisation: 'There is no evaluation culture. Evaluation is considered mainly to be a threat. There is no feedback culture. Feedback from the students about instruction, and feedback from the parents about the school are generally non-existent. Everything that happens in classes and how it happens is not transparent enough. Many teachers see themselves as teachers who convey a specific subject. They do not see themselves as experts who assist the children in learning' (Paper from *Landeselternrat der Gesamtschulen*, North Rhine-Westphalia, May 2003, quoted in OECD, Country Note Germany, p. 29).
7. Editorial, *The Schoolmaster*, 30 September 1960, quoted in Gerald Grace, 'Teachers and the State in Britain', in Martin Lawn and Gerald Grace, *Teachers: the culture and politics of work*, (Lewes: Falmer Press, 1987).
8. Duru-Bellat and van Zanten, *Sociologie de l'école*, pp. 143–4; OECD, Germany 2004, p. 37.
9. Lawn, 2001: 175.
10. Guerrero, 'Professionalism, unionism and educational reform', p. 174.

11. P. Bourdieu and J-C Passeron, *Reproduction in Education, Culture and Society* (London: Sage, 1990).

12. Duru Bellat and van Zanten, *Sociologie de l'école*, p. 135 (In Italy, 'where teaching more than in the other European countries is a profession mostly carried out by women', teachers' pay levels are lower than the EU average. OECD, 2003 p. 106.)

13. Christoph Führ, *The German Education System since 1945: outlines and problems* (Bonn: Inter Nationes, 1997) p. 216. OECD, *Attracting, Developing and Retaining Effective Teachers: Country Note – Germany* (Paris: OECD, 2004) p. 16.

14. OECD, Country Background Report, Italy, 2003.

15. Christian Laval, 'L'Europe liberale aux commandes de l'ecole' www.ecoledemocratique.org, 8 December 2004.

16. Martin Lawn, *Modern Times? Work, Professionalism and Citizenship in Teaching* (Lewes: Falmer Press, 1996) pp. 112–13.

17. For a discussion of the re-profesionalisation that this involves, see Terri Seddon, 'Education: Deprofessionalised? Or deregulated, reorganised and reauthorised,' *Australian Journal of Education*, 41.3, pp. 228–47, 1997.

18. Duceux, 'Du rapport Thélot à la loi Fillon'.

19. See OECD, Germany (2004).

20. DfES guidance to head teachers, quoted in Richard Hatcher, 'Distributed Leadership and Managerial Power in Schools', Paper presented at the Society for Educational Studies and BERA Social Justice SIG Annual Seminar 'School Leadership and Social Justice' (London: 4 November 2004).

21. Piero Bernocchi, 'Behind the recent school protests in Italy', *Education and Social Justice* 3.1 44–7, 2000; OECD, Germany (2004).

22. Agnès Pélage – Les transformations du rôle du chef d'établissement d' enseignment secondaire' in van Zanten (ed.) 2004, pp. 219–27.

23. OECD, Germany (2004) p. 25.

24. DfEE, *Teachers – Meeting the Challenge of Change* (London: DFEE, 1998) para 13.

25. OECD, 2004, p. 29.

26. Javier Doz Orrit, 'Problems of implementation in Spanish educational Reform' in O'Malley and Boyd-Barrett *op. cit.* p. 92.

27. Orrit, pp. 92–3.

28. Pélage, 'Les transformations' p. 219.

29. European Commission, *European Report on the Quality of School Education* 2000, p. 10.

30. Barber and Phillips, *Fusion*.

31. Agnes van Zanten, 'Educational Change and New Cleavages between Head Teachers, Teachers and Parents: global and local perspectives on the French case', *Journal of Education Policy* 17.3 289–304, p. 291, 2002

32. OECD, *Knowledge Management in the Learning Society* (Paris: OECD, 2001) p. 71.

33. Susan Robertson, 'Re-imagining and rescripting the future of education: global knowledge economy discourses and the challenge to education systems', *Comparative Education* 41.2 151–70, p. 159, 2005.

34. J-L Arco-Tirado and J.M. Fernandez-Balboa, 'Contextual barriers to school reform in Spain', *International Review of Education* 49.6 pp. 585–600, 2003.

35. OECD, *Attracting, Developing and Retaining Effective Teachers: country background report for Italy* (Paris: OECD, 2003) p. 7 (language as in original English text).

36. OECD, 2003 Italy p. 104.
37. OECD, 2003 Italy p. 49.
38. In addition to the OECD reports on Germany and Italy, already quoted, see for instance, Pat Mahony and Ian Hextall, *Reconstructing Teachers: standards, performance and accountability* (London: Routledge Falmer, 2000); and *Equity in Education in Spain – Country Note* (Paris: OECD, 2006).
39. Paul Ginsborg, *Italy and its Discontents 1980–2001* (London: Allen Lane, The Penguin Press, 2001) p. 232.
40. Ibid., p. 53.
41. Anonymous, 'Quell' abraccio mortale con I "baroni"', *Il Manifesto* 15 December 2006.
42. Piero Bernocchi, 'La scuola immutata di Gattopardo Fioroni', *Il Manifesto* 6 October 2006.
43. OECD, 2004 Germany p. 49.
44. Hence the GEW's decision to retire its objective of 'eine Scule für Alle', on the basis that this kind of commitment, to comprehensive secondary education, is not 'communicable'. To the GEW, it seems more practicable to fight alongside McKinsey for a two-tier, rather than a fully integrated, secondary system, on the grounds that this is a step in the right direction.
45. Vincent Lang, 'Les IUFM et la professionalisation des enseignants', in van Zanten, 'Educational Change and New Cleavages between Head Teachers, Teachers and Parents' pp. 228–35, p. 229.
46. Pélage, 'Les transformations' *p.* 219.
47. Lang, 'Les IUFM et la professionalisation des enseignants', 228–9.
48. Renaud Bousquet and Véronique Ponvert, 'Un non toujours d'actualité', *L'Ecole Emancipée* janvier/février 14–15, p. 15, 2007.
49. Van Zanten, 'Educational Change and New Cleavages between Head Teachers, Teachers and Parents: global and local perspectives on the French case', p. 299.
50. Ken Jones and Farzana Shain, *Teacher Trade Unionism in Urban Contexts: the global and the local*, Paper to the European Conference on Educational Research, Lisbon 2002.
51. Lynne Raphael Reed, 'Reconceptualising equal opportunities in the 1990s: a study of radical teacher culture in transition', in *Anti-racism, culture and social justice in education*, ed. M. Griffiths and B. Troyna (Stoke-on-Trent: Trentham Books, 1995).
52. Mike Bottery, 'Globalisation and the UK Competition State: no room for transformational leadership in education?', *School Leadership and Management* 21.2, 198–218, p. 213, 2001.
53. Brigitte Perucca, 'Les syndicats sont toujours là ...'*Le Monde de l'Education* 317, pp. 22–3, September 2003.

10
Unconcluded

In this chapter we aim to chart the existing courses of opposition to neo-liberalism, and to suggest the themes and focuses of a productive future strategy. Any such discussion must take into account neo-liberalism's achievements, which are, in the first instance, not political or ideological but economic and social. Through neo-liberalism, technologies and social relations have been reorganised and social classes recomposed. In a capitalism described by Castells as 'informational' in character, labour has bifurcated: at one end of the market, demand for low-skilled labour has expanded; in other sectors, labour has become to a greater extent immaterial, cognitive, linguistic – at the same time as it is required to be flexible, self-renewing and accustomed (through debt, job insecurity, the under-provision of welfare and pensions) to a greater level of risk and precarity.[1] In these changed landscapes – which are always land-scapes of polarisation – education occupies a new and larger place – a site where capital is accumulated, social problems managed and skills and dispositions are produced more intensively and extensively than in earlier periods.

Economic change has been accompanied at the political level – specifically, here in terms of the politics of education – by a rescaling of policy production and decision-making capacity to which the establish-ment of supra-national institutions (most importantly the EU) has been key. As we have seen, for the EU, neo-liberal principles of competitive-ness and deregulation, in a world economy based to a large extent on free trade of goods and services, are central – albeit qualified by policies to manage the problems of the social and economic exclusion that attend economic change. At national level, governments – frequently citing EU policy or OECD/PISA data as legitimating factors – have embarked upon the transformations of institutional design and function that have been the subjects of our previous chapters. In the process, the victories won by European capital against labour in the 1980s and 1990s have enabled governments to rewrite the terms of educational agency, such that the social forces associated with previous periods of reform have tended to be pushed to the margins of influence, and other actors – autonomised school managers, public – private networks – have become prominent. Thus the scalar shifts in policymaking, towards a European level of governance and agenda-setting, that are noted by writers like Dale and Robertson, have developed through clashes between diverse and often antagonistic social actors.[2] Writing of the post-war period, Crouch insisted that issues of the institutional form, character, range and trajectory of social provision could best be understood in terms that recognised the influence upon them of contending political and social forces.[3] In this book, but with reference mainly to a later period, we have made a similar effort to relate the changing grammar of schooling to the unfolding of social conflict. But there is a difference. Crouch could credibly identify social arrangements that were in a significant and large-scale sense the creations of reforming movements; we, scanning the contemporary patterns of educational change, will detect no comparable achievements. Educational processes are still contested, of course, but policy-shaping initiative is very definitely held by the advocates of economising change.

Correspondingly, despite occasions of spectacular protest, those who have tried to contest the effects of political and economic change on work and learning have encountered difficulties of a severe kind. Some of these are 'ideational' and relate to the problems that opposition has in developing persuasive alternatives to dominant paradigms. Unger's comment on the programmatic insufficiency of opposition to neo-liberalism – 'we see in the world a universal political-economic orthodoxy contested by a series of local heresies' – is apposite, but it does not capture all the dimensions of the problem.[4] It is not just that educators in the radical tradition face a policy challenge, in which proposals for educational restructuring are advanced which up to now they have not demonstrated the capacities to answer with an alternative programme; there are also other and more fundamental problems than that, relating to unresolved questions of both political and social agency. Politically, the collapse of West European communism and the neo-liberalisation of social democratic parties have left an absence where opposition to market-centred orthodoxies might have appeared. Beyond the political level, occupational change, and the social and cultural transformations that have attended it, raise a question of social agency that, since it was first posed by writers such as Gorz and Hobsbawm at the end of the long boom, has not become less acute: in a new period, where the weight of the industrial working class is greatly reduced, and where that of workers in the service sector (public and private) has increased, what forces, and what alliances, might constitute the engine and the point of reference of movements of change?[5] The issues here – those of 'new social subjects' and their political consequence – would seem to have a strong educational dimension. Education is central to theorisations of informational capitalism, and from some perspectives the over-managed knowledge workers and the massified students created by the expansion (but not the democratisation) of institutionalised learning seem to embody an oppositional potential.[6] Yet for the most part the new mass worker is quiescent – and where it has acted, it has not been the catalyst of any enduring change.

Accommodation

To take stock of opposition is thus first of all to chart a recent history of set-back, which extends from policy commitments to discursive coherence, to the level of mundane, individual choices. At the policy level, one can justly speak of a process of *trasformismo*, through which parties and unions have accommodated – never without hesitation – to the new order. The record here is a consistent one: the support of the majority unions in Spain for the LOGSE and for the 2006 legislation of the Zapatero government; the Labour Party's acceptance of an endless succession of privatising initiatives; the attacks of the French socialist Allègre on jobs and his enthusiasm for a business agenda; the backing that the General Confederation of Italian Labour (CGIL) gave first to the Berlinguer reforms then in 2006 to the Prodi government's acceptance of much of the Moratti laws; the GEW's conviction that the OECD's agenda offers the best chance for the egalitarian transformation of German education. These evolutions and U-turns have contributed to a crisis of policy and strategic orientation, all the more profound because the effect of shifts at the level of policy has been compounded by a failure to respond to the potential revealed episodically by popular resistance. In Spain, the teachers' strikes of the late 1980s – based on egalitarian demands for pay parity – were settled by the unions on terms which reinforced hierarchies within the workforce. In England and Wales in 1993–4, a strongly supported teacher boycott of the testing system was allowed by union leaderships to culminate in minor changes to the National Curriculum. More recently, the French spring of 2003 undoubtedly demonstrated the resources for resistance still possessed by the school sector – but it also showed the reluctance of national leaderships to link school protests to a more general challenge to the government of the day. The protests of 2006 against the flexibilisation of the youth labour market achieved the withdrawal of the CPE legislation through which the de Villepin government aimed to do this. However, as we discuss later, they were unable to achieve a wider change. In its dénouement, the action was weakened by the unwillingness of the union federations which dominated discussions with the government to extend their agenda beyond a single issue; the creeping vocationalism of schooling that troubled the French educational Union, the FSU, and the school-student movement was not addressed.

In these contexts, the strategic activity of teachers – their capacity to initiate, shape and popularise new forms of educational practice – has been reduced. The intensified workloads of new models of schooling, themselves often a consequence of defeat, form a further obstacle to resistance. Thus opposition to neo-liberalism often takes individualised and scarcely articulated forms. Rates of early retirement express the growing withdrawal of a generation of teachers from the educational scene; low levels of union membership in most countries likewise demonstrate a scepticism and a demobilisation that are the bitter consequences of a collective aspiration, extending over some decades, that has now been blocked.[7]

In such circumstances, neo-liberalism has generally been confident that opposition to its programme can only take a vestigial, routinist character – to be dismissed, as Blair dismissed the opposition of teachers in England, as a 'force of conservatism'.[8] Likewise, the EU's Reiffers report of 1996 acknowledged 'the natural resistance' of the traditional public system' but is confident that it can be overcome by a 'combination of encouragement, goals, resources, consumer orientation and competition from the private sector'.[9] From this confident perspective, the educational cultures and commitments created by the movements of '1945' and '1968' are manageable and, without great difficulty, transformable. Crouch's question (see chapter 1) – whether 'the assembly of non-capitalist interests' created by post-war movements contains a 'potentiality for new action' – has for interests like Reiffers only a negative answer.

Problems of neo-liberalism

Any attempt at a balance sheet of opposition must take such judgements seriously: the successes of the neo-liberal programme are undeniable. But this scarcely means that it constitutes, as it were, the 'end of educational history'; nor does it mean that there is nothing to be said about opposition except to note its failures. As we suggested in chapter 2 – and as Commission documents repeatedly recognised – the EU's programme of post-Lisbon reform had by 2004 run into difficulty, and pro-market think tanks increasingly doubted the ability of national governments to implement change.[10] What was initially a confident blueprint for reform began to resemble, in several states, the contingent governance of a messy situation. In countries such as France and Italy the continuing calls from business and finance interests for further reform can be read more as signs of frustration than as contemplation of the next phase in a coherent programme.[11]

Part of the reason for the difficulties that reform has encountered is the inertial effect of established social arrangements. Italian corporatism, for instance, may not be the most progressive of forces in terms of its political positions, but it presents situations that have to be negotiated rather than swept away. Likewise, though trade unionism and social movements cannot, in most instances, set the terms of educational agenda, they can nevertheless mobilise an opposition that has significant social effects.

Kees van der Pijl argues that the ability of different European societies to submit to what he calls the 'discipline' demanded by the EU's neoliberal turn varies, and that the very pressures exerted by this discipline 'tend paradoxically to reactivate the specific heritage of each separate society in new combinations'.[12] 'Reactivation', though not a term that applies universally to the reception of EU policy by the populations of member states, illuminates very clearly the nature of some national-level responses, and the challenge they pose to attempts to develop an EU-inspired agenda. From the perspective it provides, a number of recent developments can be highlighted, including the social republicanism that has animated successive waves of French protests and the claims made by Italian opponents of educational reform that the education legislation of the Berlusconi government violated the terms of the post-war constitutional settlement. One basis for such counter-mobilisation is the continuing resonance of 'old' commitments – to equality and disciplinary traditions, democracy and professional self-definition. Such attachments have been prominent, for instance, in the 2005–6 protests of students in Germany, Spain and Greece against what is seen as the imposition through the Bologna process of an Anglo-Saxon model of higher education. Likewise, the French school students' 2005 protests were a defence of the *baccalauréat* as a national system of qualification – they perceived the *Loi Fillon* of 2005 as a fragmentising attempt to weight the value of the *baccalauréat* differently, according to the status of an institution. These critical responses represent commitments that are far from vestigial: as the French activist Daniel Bensaid has noted, 'every time the government has tried to reform the university or the condition of youth, it has experienced a setback'.[13] Their force is such that those who sponsor reform find it necessary to engage intellectually as well as politically with educational traditions that in the post-war period became embedded in national systems. Whether they are criticised as examples of the failures of egalitarianism or denounced in the form of 'forces of conservatism' (Tony Blair) or recuperated to an extent in a rhetoric of self-management or creativity, these traditions retain a presence in educational debate.

Van der Pijl notes not only the effect of 'heritage', but also its appearance in 'new combinations'. One might utilise this latter category to think about those 'non-traditional' social subjects which have played some part in recent educational conflict – in particular the school students and precarious groups who have been a strong presence in French movements – and whose perspectives, as we shall suggest below, in part overlap with those of established social actors, and in part diverge from them. Contrasting the Paris students of 2006 with those of 1968, Judith Revel commented that the earlier generation, still a force in French politics, demanded 'the right to be able to dream;' the latter – facing the highest rates of youth unemployment in the OECD countries – 'the right to be able to live'.[14] The contrast is too bold, but it nonetheless draws attention to the heterogeneity of opposition – both in ideological and in social terms – and to the diverse sources from which it can muster support.

National patterns

Foremost in its oppositional diversity and militancy is the experience of France. As Perry Anderson has pointed out, neo-liberalism has transformed the French economy – through privatisation, through the growth of financial markets and through the increasing foreign share in the ownership of French companies. 'The rolling impact of these transformations,' he predicts, 'will be felt for years to come'.[15] This is surely right; but Anderson also draws attention to a counter-movement which, in the political field at least, is of comparable power. Public services in France are not only a technical mode of delivering goods to citizens, but a bond of social solidarity.[16] Attachment to these services runs deep. It helps explain why 'among the masses, neo-liberalism *à la française* has not caught on' and why from 1983 onwards, 'the French electorate has unfailingly rejected every government that administered this medicine to it'.[17] Electoral rejection has been accompanied by more active forms of protest: in 1986, against the 'modernisation' of higher education; in 1995, with over six weeks of action that engulfed the public sector, against changes to social security; in 2003, against – *inter alia* – pension reform and decentralisation; in the spring of 2005, the school students' movement against the Loi Fillon and the successful campaign against the ratification of the European Constitution. Education has often been at the centre of this turbulence: strikes against cuts, localisation of contracts and worsening conditions of work have triggered campaigns with a national resonance and a strong basis of support at local level, among parents especially. Just as important was the function of these actions in the recomposition of teacher activism: the strikes and protest movements of the 1980s established habits of direct democracy, embodied in *assemblées générales* and national co-ordinations, that transgressed the bureaucratic procedures of trade unionism as it then existed, and helped to connect teacher organisation with a much broader social movement.[18]

From the point of a view of a Reiffers, perhaps even these various acts of resistance could be seen as no more than extended defensive reflexes – ultimately, though with more difficulty than in other cases, manageable. But this would entail overlooking not only the evident political impact of such movements, but also their capacity to generate new frameworks of thought and action in which historic commitments were combined with an emerging understanding of the impact of global processes – and with the emergence, too, of new categories of protestors. The commitments were strongly felt and poignantly expressed. 'Nos vies valent plus que leurs profits,' went a slogan on the demonstration organised by the European Social Forum in Paris in 2003, and it was this sense of a disintegrating *habitus* and of an achievement both institutional and ethical now placed in danger that helped to animate the strikes of that year. Bertrand Geay wrote of the strike-generated *assemblées générales* of school workers and citizens that they were lived by their participants as a kind of 'retour à l'essentiel'. In defiance of neoliberalism, the founding principles of public education were reactivated, and knowledge and the conditions of its diffusion became matters for public appropriation.[19] For one trade unionist what the 2003 strikes called into question was the entire 'social choice' of the Jospin and Raffarin governments. The immediate causes of the protests were specifically located, in controversies over decentralisation, job cuts and pensions, but beyond these issues lay questions that, for many defenders of the public school had an existential nature. Behind Raffarin's limited measures of decentralisation lay an urge to replace a collective system of provision with a differentiated hierarchy of schools; changing the pension provisions for younger teachers was an instance of a wider policy of de-collectivisation. The strikes, for many of their participants, were a rejection of these 'logics which reinforced individualism and the breaking of links between generations of educators'.[20] In Samy Johsua's words, the 2003 action demarcated a frontier between one system of values and another.[21]

2006

The same could be said, *a fortiori*, of the 2006 mobilisations against the *Contrat Première Embauche* in the spring of 2006, the product of two decades of organised activity, inside and outside education. These too were symbolic as well as substantive confrontations between defenders of the French social model, and the political class that aimed to dismantle it, and were built around a sense of solidarity that was an end as well as a means. The frequent mass mobilisations became 'weekly rendez-vous' where 'the employed, the unemployed, parents and grand-parents' joined up with students from schools and universities.[22] But this emphasis on continuity did not obscure a newer element. The precarity of youth is at the heart of the French social crisis, and the movement against the CPE demonstrated this in the strongest of ways. The trigger for the movement was the legislative response of the de Villepin government to the *banlieue* uprisings of late 2005. The response included both an educational dimension, labelled 'equal opportunity', that strengthened academic/vocational tracking at 14, and an element of employment law that aimed to increase the chances of employment by flexibilising the youth labour market – that is, by making it easier for companies to take on, and lay off, young workers.

Proposed in January, the CPE had within two months given rise to an immense opposition. Tuesday 7 March saw demonstrations in 160 towns and cities, involving a million people, most of them students and school students. From the 7th onwards, most French universities were occupied. By 18 March, a movement of students and workers had been created, with a million and a half people on the streets; and in the demonstrations of Tuesday 4 April, this number doubled again.[23] At least 750,000 took to the streets in Paris, 250,000 in Marseilles; there was a mass strike by workers in the public sector. As protest took more dramatic forms, with roads blocked and railway stations occupied, the government gave in and on 10 April announced the withdrawal of the law.

The movement against the CPE showed that the extension of neo-liberalism to the public sector remained an immensely controversial and uncertain project. But its course and outcome also suggested something of the uncertainties of opposition, at several levels. The first problem, here, was constituted by internal divisions which related not just to differences in political opinion but to deep gulfs in social experience. Movements for change in the post-war period saw themselves as modernising forces, and gave modernisation what was in broad terms an egalitarian content. The past was seen in terms of obscurantism, classroom authoritarianism and privilege. For those in the twenty-first century who continue to work in this tradition, the terms of the counterposition have changed. The 'past' signifies a period of partial democratisation and social reform, a resource to be defended. Yet for many of those marginalized youth who have hurled their energies into protest, the attachment of social movements to an imagined 'good time', when structural reforms brought about improvements in the condition of the masses, is itself part of the problem. In the words of one participant:

> We (the students) are struggling against the system because to us it seems unequal; they (the youth of the banlieues) are fighting because the system excludes them *a priori* ... And they also consider us to be part of the system (which is true), and therefore they direct their hatred towards everybody, including us. For them, even the rebellious part of the system still belongs within it. ... For me the violence (of the banlieue youth) is not part of our action, but it poses the problem of how to renew the dialogue with these people, so that their struggle lends weight to ours.[24]

Secondly, there is the problem of the movement's political scope and continuity. The concessions that ended the mobilisation were the least the government could have offered, and amounted to much less than what many protestors wanted. A national assembly of students in Dijon called for the cancellation of Fillon's entire legislation on equal opportunities, an amnesty for those arrested during the 2006 riots in the *banlieues* and changes in new laws on immigration.[25] Teachers, students and parents traced a direct line between government intentions for the labour market and its school policy, which aimed to strengthen tracking; in the words of one lycéen, 'we're mobilising not only against the new employment law, but against the new legislation on "equal opportunities;"' and in those of a Sorbonne student, 'the withdrawal of the CPE is an important demand, but it is not the principal grievance of those who have launched this movement'.[26] A major difficulty in securing these demands was that of representation – the movement was a vast and turbulent social force which relied for its negotiating capacity on organisations which had much more limited aims. Linked to this was a problem of political expression and continuity: for all its momentary impact, the movement was not easily translated on to the political plane – the 2007 presidential elections were contested, in the main, by candidates who favoured a neo-liberal transformation of the social model, and Sarkozy's victory opened a new phase in the attempt to dismantle the French social model.[27] As one protester commented, governments refuse to ever consider closed the question of the social model's future; after enormous efforts of mobilisation have achieved concessions, the French government will, after a brief pause, want to play 'extra time' to achieve a result in its favour.

Italy

In several respects, the French pattern of an opposition to neo-liberalism that is conceptually explicit and socially well-grounded is matched by Italy. Here, too, national policies are understood by their critics as examples of global policy trends. But the comparison should not be overdone. The leftist writer Rossana Rossanda pointed out that precarity, which had ignited French protest, had become institutionalised in Italy without significant opposition: it was the norm in all but the biggest organisations in the services sector, was a fact of life in education and involved 2.5 million workers across the country. Unions and centre-left parties tended to confine themselves to denunciations of the phenomenon, while in effect they encouraged a process of *arrangiarsi* – of personal accommodation to circumstances perceived as unalterable.[28]

Likewise, in education, the logic of reform tended to win a degree of acceptance. Maccarini cites a survey of Italian teacher opinion to the effect that institutional autonomy and curricular flexibility were in principle welcome to Italian teachers.[29] There was much more scepticism, however, about other aspects of the decentralising project: the new managerial role of heads and the devolution of control to regional level. But while the major educational unions were steering the ambivalences of this position towards a general toleration of the decentralising project of the centre-left, the much smaller Cobas-Scuola was able, if not to lead a massive opposition, then at least to organise significant protest actions and to supply a popular language in which to understand educational change. Not only Cobas, but the CGIL and its centrist counterparts CISL and the UIL, began to talk of the enterprise school ('la scuola azienda') and the commodification of learning, of the threat of privatisation and the growth of hierarchical structures within teaching.[30] That this shift occurred had not only to do with the persuasive powers of Cobas but with a growing perception of the historic scale of the change which the Berlusconi government intended. The Moratti reforms were seen as harbingers of privatisation and austerity; of an institutional and a cultural transformation of the Italian school, by means of which national knowledge traditions would be replaced by competences, and lateral lines of communication between teachers involved in a common educational project would be redrawn to emphasise the vertical transmission of government initiatives. Belatedly, at the end of 2004, the Italian unions came together to oppose Moratti, in a campaign which included a national strike. The demands of the action were couched in defensive terms. Citing the constitution, the unions sought to protect collegiality and teacher autonomy, to oppose regionalised decentralisation and to put an end to plans to shorten the primary school day. Sections of the Italian movement sought to go further and to organise around the defence of education a wider-reaching campaign. The university occupations in which tens of thousands of university students were involved in the autumn of 2005 attempted to express just such an alternative, criticising the exclusionary policies of Moratti and demanding the introduction of a national law demanding the right to study and free access to knowledge.[31]

From the perspective of such movements, it seemed that Berlusconi's centre-left successor – the Prodi government, supported by the major union, the CGIL – intended no more than a modification of his reforms. A national strike and demonstration, in November 2006, provided an occasion for opposition to be voiced to the Prodi programme, especially over issues of precarity and labour market reform. The immediate impact of protest, dividing the national council of the CGIL, suggested that policy orthodoxy, whether in educational or more general form, would not entirely dominate Italian politics.[32]

England, Spain and Germany

With a right-wing majority secured – it seems – in France, and with the Prodi government having achieved a disorientation of the Italian left, the prospects for opposition to reform have been clouded. Movements of opposition in England, Spain and Germany are more problematic still. In England, the weakness stems from the defeat of local and national teacher militancy in the 1980s. Having won a prolonged battle over pay and conditions, Thatcher's government swiftly introduced in 1988 legislation which codified the principles of a market-orientated managerialism. Teachers were able to defeat, in the early 1990s, Conservative attempts to centre the 1988 curriculum on traditionalist themes, but not to challenge the structure or dynamic of the new order. Conservative and New Labour legislation has strengthened the regulation of curriculum and pedagogy, deepened patterns of selection and marketisation and opened the school system to private interests without encountering, at national level, any significant opposition. Resistance has thus taken for the most part an episodic and localised form. Teachers' unions have occasionally mobilised around salary issues; the largest, the NUT, has opposed the introduction of unqualified personnel to teaching. Local coalitions have campaigned against the privatisation of particular local education authorities, or the transfer of schools to private control.[33] As a background to this very uneven pattern of action there exists a generalised discontent among teachers and some parents with a school régime that is heavily dependent upon testing, inspection and intrusive management. Likewise, there remain currents of opinion for which 'equal opportunity' remains a central reference point. Policies which further compromise this principle are still capable of provoking widespread challenge: in 2004, legislation to charge tuition fees to university students gave rise to national protest, and escaped defeat in Parliament by a narrow margin.

By comparison, however, with France and Italy, England has only a fragmented sense of what is at stake in conflicts over educational change. This is partly, no doubt, a result of the famous local distaste for systemic explanations, but a more proximal cause lies in the greater speed at which educational transformation has worked post-1988 in England, and its deeper level of embeddedness: the decisive battle came early, and in its aftermath, the routines of neo-liberal education became established. Habituated to pursuing change through a relationship of partnership with government, those forces most associated with educational reform were unable to develop more combative approaches. At school level, detailed government specification combined with the directiveness of local managements meant that the resources with which to think and practice another sort of education were diminished.

In the case of Spain, the relative weakness of opposition is less a consequence of 'frontal' defeat than of a long process of disorientation.

After the death of Franco, there were great expectations of democratic, egalitarian change. These expectations were realised only in the inadequate and underfunded forms of LODE and LOGSE, which – for all the support of the left and centre-left – failed to inaugurate a mass system of good quality education, and discredited educational progressivism through associating it with neo-liberal reform (see chapter 1). Divisions among the teaching force exacerbated these problems: the untenured and precarious sector expanded. LOGSE's incorporation of a section of elementary education within the secondary sector raised the status of some teachers; at the same time, many of those working at the higher levels of secondary teaching were repelled by reforms which they saw as lowering educational standards. From 1996, the conservative PP government worked on these discontents, presenting itself to teachers as a force that could restore the quality of education – while simultaneously it increased subsidies to the private sector and sought to restore Church influence and the homogenising traditions of the centralist state. In the face of these measures, there occurred both a strong level of regional resistance – to curriculum centralisation – and a certain muted revival of older reforming traditions; alliances between unions and parents' organisations supportive of the public sector were re-established. The PSOE (Zapatero) government of 2004 presented itself as a force that could resolve such tensions. It suspended the education laws formulated by its PP predecessor, and declared itself in favour of a great 'education pact' between contending forces.

Embodied in a law – the Ley Orgánica de Educación of 2006 – the pact amounted to a significant 'reconsensualising' of educational politics, the main beneficiaries of which were the right. The law endorsed the agreement made with the Vatican by the post-Franco government in 1979, by means of which the place of Catholic teaching had been guaranteed; and it extended the subsidies granted to the *concertados* to cover pre-school provision. In return, public authorities gained more control over the admissions procedures of the subsidised sector. Most of the educational unions – the exception, *STES-intersindical*, gained votes in the elections for workplace representation later in the year – alongside the main party of the left, *Izquierda Unida*, supported the law, arguing that 'in the interests of consensus and dialogue, in order to make possible a policy with guarantees for the future, all the groups must put in abeyance some of their aspirations'.[34]

In relation to England and Spain we can speak of 'early' neo-liberalisations – one the result of a Conservative offensive, the other of a more complex process of social democratic *trasformismo*. Each has created difficult conditions for counter-mobilisation. The German case is different again, but has proved no less problematic for opponents of neo-liberalism. Post-war German capitalism created a welfare state whose Bismarckian referents were always strong: the interests of labour were attended to, but the state – aiming more at stability than equality – worked against the kind of working-class driven policy radicalisation that occurred in other countries. Education in the Federal Republic – and in the unified German state – has proved resistant to egalitarian reform, and afforded relatively little space for curriculum experiment. In such conditions, a movement capable of contrasting neo-liberal precepts with an embedded counter-practice was unlikely to develop. The slow and piecemeal neo-liberalisation documented in chapters 1 and 4 provoked little – organised – opposition. Nor was the dividing line between this 'modernising' process and the policy designs of the Greens and of sections of the SPD a strong one: the centre-left hopes to graft its ambitions for a non-selective system of secondary education on to a programme of wider change which owes much to the OECD/*Deutsche Bank* critique of an obsolescent model of schooling. In such a situation, an educational programme which is explicitly anti-neo-liberal in its orientation has been slow to develop. This does not mean that it is entirely absent. Humanist traditions – in this case, those of *Bildung* – have supplied the intellectual resources for student mobilisation against the EU-driven harmonisation of university curricula; and the steps towards neo-liberalism (deregulation of sections of the labour market; co-payment in the health sector) embodied in Schröder's Agenda 2010 aroused protest. This was partly because of their real effects and partly because of Schröder's symbolic rupture with the German social model of employment protection and social welfare.[35] Protest, however, has hardly been of French proportions: even though unemployment rose to 20% in parts of East Germany, and the youth labour market collapsed, demonstrators could be counted in thousands rather than millions.

What has been achieved?

The terms of the new educational settlement remain those set by policy orthodoxy, and to speak of the achievements of resistance necessitates some modesty. Nowhere has the process of neo-liberalisation been halted, and even where governments – like Juppé's in 1995 – have been defeated, there has always been a successor ready to take things on. Even so, the capacities of opposition are neither negligible nor stagnating. Appeals made in the name of equality and non-commodified education have mobilised hundreds of thousands across Europe in a chain of protests which has not yet been broken. Resistance has undoubtedly forced a level of caution upon governments, and sometimes achieved concessions or delays. (At supra-national level, the fact that 'education services' have not yet been incorporated into the GATS agreement also provides evidence of the strength of opposition.[36]) The suspension of PP's LOCE legislation in Spain, and the failure of the Berlusconi government to complete its reforming project owed something to the hostility of the education sector. Even New Labour, without budging from its overall policy ambitions, has decreased some of the workload pressures upon English teachers.

The hesitant pace of reform – punctuated by outbreaks of opposition, hindered by policy failure – thus speaks of a continuing dissent, even in those societies which have experienced 20 years of acculturation. It marks an important negative achievement on the part of opposition. But this baseline of resistance – whose co-ordinates are set by the social conquests of an earlier period – does not delineate a strategy sufficient to challenge over the long term the existing order, nor a programme that can serve as a persuasive alternative to it. Any movement that seeks to become a significant social actor, challenging this order, must interrogate its own resources and recent achievements, probing their political effectiveness and intellectual force. From this point of view, some landmarks stand out.

The first is the emergent though belated Europeanisation of opposition. In chapter 2, we traced the accelerating coordination of the policies of national governments, and the increasing scope and penetration of policy instruments devised by the European Commission, the EU and the OECD. As Nóvoa points out, governing elites – without any encountering any significant check – have been able to construct at continental level 'categories of thought, of organising language and proposing solutions, which become the dominant schemes for approaching educational problems'.[37] Enticed by a rhetoric which claimed that the construction of a 'social Europe' was under way, neither the European TUC nor its educational counterpart was effective in countering this discursive hegemony – still less in attempting action against it. Only with the global rise of the movement against neo-liberalism did a substantial challenge occur. The terms of this challenge were in the first instance discursive. 'Our heads have been stuffed with neo-liberalism,' Bernard Cassen has commented, '[and] the overwhelming conviction at present is that, politically speaking, nothing can be done'.[38] The role of associations like Cassen's ATTAC, of the demonstrations at Nice, Prague and

Genova, and of the World and European Social Forums, has been to overturn this assumption: the purpose of the slogan 'another world is possible' is precisely to say that 'we are not condemned to neo-liberalism, that we can envisage other ways of living and organising society than those we have at present'.[39] A collective assertion of this sort, which is global in the range of its critique, in the form in which it is manifested and in the scale of its aspirations, has opened a political space in which opposition can assemble. The coming together of those who have written this book – and the existence of a readership which might find it relevant – is one aspect of such an assembly. More significantly, the European Social Forums of Florence, Paris, London and Athens have moved in their discussions of education from an initial exchange of experiences to a call for Europe-wide action, to 'reaffirm the right of education for everybody and the obligation of public institutions to concretise such a right in a system free from confessional bonds and not subordinated to logics of the market'.[40] At a more general level, opposition to the statecraft of European elites is for the first time taking a cross-national form: the various referenda on Maastricht took place within separate national frameworks; the terms of the challenge to the European Constitution, which sought to write free-market principles into the DNA of the continent, are debated across frontiers.

With this experience in mind, we can look again at the political relationship between national tradition and internationalisation, at least in relation to France. The protests of 1995–2006 were in a strong sense *national* phenomena. Their reference points were supplied by national-popular traditions of social republicanism, by which they were profoundly shaped: the idea that the domain of the 'social' should in all circumstances submit to the imperatives of 'the economic', accepted in England, remained controversial across the channel. In the context of the anti-globalisation movements of the 1990s, these traditions were reinflected and national ills were understood as symptoms of a wider project. It was the rising of 1995 which helped identify the new face of free-market capitalism and gave it a public name – 'neo-liberalism'.[41] The slogans of 2003 – 'the school is not a business', 'education is not for sale' – were signs that this understanding of a pervasive process of marketisation and privatisation had passed into the language of educational protest. Likewise the movement of 1995 was among the first to establish that neo-liberalism must be addressed at a level beyond the national. From the experience of the mid-1990s came Bourdieu's call for a European Assembly of the social movements,[42] and the founding of the anti neo-liberal ATTAC. Most importantly, French organisations – among them ATTAC, *Le Monde Diplomatique* and, in education, the Féderation Syndicale Unitaire – took a lead in the practical organisation of a global response to neo-liberalism: the World Social Forum and the European Social Forums have depended in part on French initiative. This cross-border interweaving of experiences makes it difficult to uphold the distinction made by a writer like Michael Hardt between national, state-focused responses to globalised policies, and the transnational approaches associated with a politics of the multitude: French protests have depended on a combined mobilisation of social categories – public and private sector workers, students, the unemployed, the precarious, and have linked both discursively and practically to an international 'movement of movements'.

As these last points imply, the beginnings of a process of Europeanisation from below have been accompanied by the popularisation of an analytical framework, now circulating well beyond the groups which gave it an initial impetus. Cobas-Scuola speaks of its success in placing Moratti's reforms 'under a magnifying glass',[43] so as to demonstrate the logic of privatisation that underlies apparently small-scale institutional reforms. Likewise *Le Monde de l'Education* notes that in the French strikes of 2003, the texts of writers like Hirtt and Johsua were quoted in the debates of the *assemblées* and reproduced in mobilising leaflets.[44] It was thus the radical left which helped to construct the position from which the coherence of neo-liberalism was demonstrated, and its likely trajectory identified. Work of this sort, circulated at a time when the Delors project of a 'Social Europe' has been displaced among policymakers by an emphasis on flexibility – with the loss of worker rights that the term tacitly implies – and the requirements of competitiveness, has begun to bring about something of a discursive shift in the world of European labour. The draft 'Bolkestein' directive of the EU, aimed at driving down wage costs through opening up national service industries to competition acted in 2005–6 as a shock to European labour organisations, and opened up a space in which anti-globalisation discourse offered resources for analysis and opposition – a Europe-wide demonstration against Bolkestein was one of its outcomes.

A third achievement has recently begun to take shape: the emergence of a youth movement, mobilised around questions of precarity and acting within the field of education. The potential of such a movement is great, not least because it shifts the centre of mobilisation and argument away from a beleaguered defence of past achievements – which have difficulty in addressing the requirements of youth – and towards questions of social and economic alternatives. In this sense, the long-standing argument of Italian autonomists takes on a new relevance. A new social subject – or set of subjects – is in the process of emerging, involved in a massified education system, yet only partially integrated into the labour market and its institutions. The existence of such a subject, that produces its own forms of knowledge and identity, demands from education systems an approach to pedagogy and curriculum that – hampered by high workloads, scarce resources and tight managerial control – its teachers cannot provide. As the anti-CPE movement suggests – *de facto* alliances between new social subjects and professional groups committed to the defence of public education can produce movements on a very large scale.

These achievements and experiences – a certain level of Europeanisation, the popularising of analysis and critique, the emergence of new social forces – are significant, but of course insufficient. Even in France, they are much less strongly implanted than those of an earlier era. In social and political conditions marked by the strong presence of working-class interests, the educational movements of 1945–80 were often successful in colonising educational space, and in creating there a set of practices and institutional forms which could sustain a broadly egalitarian project. No such prospect of stabilisation is open to current movements; on the contrary, neo-liberalism is programmatically committed to denying them space. Thus, in the absence of a commanding general challenge to neo-liberal governments, educational militancy, even at its strongest, has taken episodic form. Such episodes are often very intense, and seem to moderate commentators to be quite incomprehensible: the 2003 wave of occupations of French universities against the Bologna process was viewed in *Le Monde* as inexplicably excessive; the British mainstream press described the French events of 2006 in terms of a nostalgia for a superseded social model.[45] But viewed as a protest against the 'universe of neo-liberalism' their meaning becomes clearer. Likewise, the direct democracy of the 2003 *assemblées* and of the mass protests from below which have periodically occurred in Italy[46] speak of a desire to pose against capital the experience and values of a whole 'world of labour'. A crisis of representation in which the historic parties of the working class have associated themselves with privatisation and the rest of the neo-liberal agenda is thus momentarily resolved by mobilisations where democracy is both method of action and counter-systemic objective.[47]

These outbursts are passionate reaffirmations of value, purpose and solidarity. But in the absence of a wider movement to reject neo-liberalism, and of a significant political force to the left of neo-liberalised social-democratic parties, they cannot be decisive – indeed, their immediate effects can be exhausting. In most places, opponents of neo-liberalism in education now operate in a dense and hostile environment: legislation, institutional change, managerial authority and regulation both formal and informal have created powerful and embedded norms. To challenge this system requires episodic mobilisation certainly – for without it no wider movement can be born – but it also requires, in the middle term, the ability to identify central points of weakness in their opponents' programme, and to suggest alternative approaches to the questions it cannot resolve. A successful counter-hegemony depends to this extent on a war of ideological position, as well as a war of mass protest and manoeuvre.

Opposition has critique in plenty. It has an analysis of the processes which drive educational change. It has an understanding of their problems: neo-liberal policies – presented by their supporters as the answer to the exhausted project of universal, high-level education – have themselves been unable to resolve questions of educational failure on a large scale, and even to successful students have offered a narrow and unsatisfying education. Opposition draws from a tradition of educational and social conquests won within the framework of national education systems, and it has a new understanding of the necessity of working now in a wider, global framework, with different kinds of social actor. In thinking of alternatives, it possesses both a sense of the value of its own past achievements, and of their present insufficiency: 'a common school for all, certainly,' writes Jean-Yves Rochex 'but what kind of school, and for what kind of society?'[48] The questions are central. Answering them, in a form which is drawn not from the 'blank sheet' of the educational philosopher, but from the practice of generations of educators, is important if opposition – rather than 'mere' critique – is to have a future.

Notes

1. Manuel Castells, *The Rise of the Network Society* (Oxford: Blackwell, 1996); Christian Marazzi, *Il posto dei calzini* (Turin: Bollati Bolinghieri, 1997).
2. Roger Dale (forthcoming, 2007) 'Constructing Europe through Constructing a European Educational Space', *Education et Sociétés* 18; Robertson, 'Re-imagining and rescripting the future of education'.
3. Crouch, *Social Change in Western Europe*.
4. Roberto Mangabeira Unger, *What should the Left Propose?* (London: Verso, 2005) p. 8.
5. Andre Gorz, *Goodbye to the Working Class* (London: Pluto Press, 1982); Martin Jacques and Francis Mulhern (eds). *The Forward March of Labour Halted?* (London: Verso, 1979).

6. Terranova and Bousquet, 'Recomposing the University'.
7. England is an exception here: though almost totally unionised teacher population is split between five different organisations, and union membership is often related to protection against the risks of the workplace, rather than the collective defence of pay and conditions.
8. Ken Jones, *Education in Britain* (Cambridge: Polity Press, 2003) p. 147.
9. Reiffers Report, *Accomplishing Europe through Education and Training* (Luxemburg: European Union, 1996) para 166.
10. Stockholm Network, 'The State of the Union: market-oriented reform in the EU in 2004' www.stockholm-network.org.
11. See, for instance, the report by Alessandra Ricciardi of the demands that business was making in 2006 of the new Prodi government. Ricciardi summarises the views of Mario Draghi, head of the Banca d'Italia, as a 'stop to increased investments in education and to hiring of extra staff, and support for increased competition between schools, privileging the better ones and giving financial support directly to the families'. Luca di Montezemolo, head of the employers' federation, the Confindustria, is quoted in support of Draghi: 'finally Draghi has spoken in favour of liberalisations; we need fresh air, we need to get rid of the corporations'. (*Italia Oggi*, 14 November 2006.)
12. K. van der Pijl, 'A Lockean Europe', *NewLeft Review* 2.36, pp. 9–37, January–February 2006.
13. Daniel Bensaid interviewed by Anna Maria Merlo, *Il Manifesto* 24 March 2006.
14. Judith Revel quoted in Giuliana Visco, *Il movimento anti-CPE tra autonomia studentesca e sindacati*, Paper to the Italian Political Studies Association, Bologna, September 2006.
15. Perry Anderson, 'Union Sucrée', *London Review of Books* 23 September 2004, 10–16, p. 12, 2004.
16. See Bernard Cassen, 'On the Attack', *New Left Review* 19, pp. 41–62, January–February 2003.
17. Ibid.
18. Danielle Czalczynski, 'De 68 à l'effet U', *L'École Émancipée* (NF 3) January–February 2007, pp. 30–31.
19. Bertrand Geay, 'Un processus de réattachement à l'institution', *Le Monde de l'Education* 317, p. 12, September 2003.
20. Strikers quoted by Brigitte Perruca, *Le Monde de l'education*.
21. Samy Johsua, 'Un mouvement plus antilibéral qu'altermondialiste' *Le Monde de l'Education* 317, p. 15, 2003.
22. Jean-Michel Drevon, 'Y en a ras le bol de ces guignols!', *Ecole Emancipée* 90.7, pp. 4–5, avril 2006.
23. See the account by Giuliana Visco, *Il movimento anti-CPE tra autonomia studentesca e sindacati*.
24. 'Cécile' interviewed by Giuliana Visco, *Il movimento anti-CPE tra autonomia studentesca e sindacati*.
25. Visco, *Il movimento anti-CPE tra autonomia studentesca e sindacati*.
26. 'André' a lycéen from Pau, interviewed in 'Paroles des lycéens', *L'Ecole Emancipée* 90.7 April 2006, p. 13; 'Cécile', interviewed by Visco, *Il movimento anti-CPE tra autonomia studentesca e sindacati*.
27. Sarkozy's programme for education is set out in: Nicolas Sarkozy, *Lettre de mission addressée à M. Xavier Darcos, Ministre de l' Education Nationale*

(Lettre de M. Nicolas Sarkozy, Président de la Republique) 5th July 2007 www.elysee.fr.

28. Rossana Rossanda, 'Pourquoi la révoltefrançaise n'a pas gagné en Italie', *Le Monde Diplomatique* pp. 4–5, May 2006.

29. Maccarini, 'La réforme de l'éducation en Italie, p. 182.

30. Cobas-Scuola, *National Assembly of Cobas Scuola – Theses of the National Executive* (Cobas: giornali dei comitati di base della scuola, 2004) 20, febbraio 2004, p. II.

31. Katrina Yeaw, 'Scuola per tutti, libero sapere per tutti: the student struggle in Italy', *Counterpunch* 14 October 2005 www.counterpunch.org. ('The opposition to the reforms is rooted in the fact that they will clearly divide whose who will attend liceo, the stepping stone for entrance into the university system and those who will go to professional institutes.')

32. Loris Campetti, 'Il Manifesto', *Conflitto e governo: la Cgil si divide* 23 November 2006.

33. Richard Hatcher and Ken Jones, 'Researching Resistance: campaigns against academies in England', *British Journal of Educational Studies* 54.3 329–51, 2006.

34. Fermin Rodriguez Castro, 'El desarme politico e ideologico de la izquierda ante la LOE', *Crisis* 11 3–19, 2006; Colectivo Baltasar Gracián, 'LOE: el peor de los pactos posibles' http://www.colectivobgracian.com/ June 2006.

35. 'We will have to curtail the work of the state, encourage more individual responsibility, and require greater individual performance from each person. Every group in the society will have to contribute its share.' Gerhard Schröder, 2004. Quoted in Pamela Camerra-Rowe, 'Agenda 2010: redefining German social democracy', *German Politics and Society* 22.1, 1–30, March 2004.

36. Antoni Verger and Xavier Bonal, 'Against GATS: the sense of a global struggle', *Journal for Critical Education Policy Studies* 4.1, 1–27, March 2006.

37. António Nóvoa, 'The restructuring of the European educational space: changing relationships among states, citizens and educational communities', in *Rethinking European Welfare*, ed. J. Fink, G. Lewis and J. Clarke (London: Sage, 2001) pp. 249–75, p. 251.

38. Cassen, 'On the Attack', p. 56.

39. Ibid.

40. 'Stop Moratti Committee', *Appeal to the London Social Forum*, October 2004.

41. The Zapatista movement in Mexico also worked to popularise the term.

42. Pierre Bourdieu, *Acts of Resistance* (Cambridge: Polity Press, 1998).

43. 'Sotto lente di ingrandimento' Cobas-Scuola document, P. vi.

44. Anonymous "Le tournant 'altermondialiste' de la contestation enseignante" "*Le Monde de l'Education* September 2003 pp. 13–15.

45. *Le Monde*, 23 janvier 2004; John Lichfield, 'If only this were a real French revolution', *The Independent* 21 March 2006.

46. Confederazione Cobas, *A new model of social self-organisation: from a refusal of passivity to the building of a movement against capitalist globalisation*, www.cobas.it 2003.

47. Georges Ubbiali, 'Solidaires, Unitaires, Démocratiques (SUD): renouveau du syndicalisme révolutionnaire' in *Journal of Modern and Contemporary France* 12.1 35–48, p. 49, 2004.

48. J-Y Rochex, 'Ni le pédagogisme ni le mythe républicain', *Le Monde de l'Education* 317, p. 17, September 2003.

References

Adonis, A. and Leese, R. (2007) 'A New Blueprint', *The Guardian*, 9 January.

Agalianos, A. (2006) 'Crossing borders: the European dimension in educational and social science research' in *The World Yearbook of Education 2006: Education and Policy* ed. J. Ozga et al. (London: Routledge Falmer).

Alexander, R. (1992) *Policy and Practice in Primary Education* (London: Routledge).

—— (2001) *Culture and Pedagogy: international comparisons in primary education* (Oxford: Blackwell).

—— (2004) 'Excellence, Enjoyment and Personalised Learning: a true foundation for choice', *Education Review* 18.1, Autumn.

Alexiadou, N. (2005a) 'Europeanisation and education policy', in *World Yearbook of Education 2005: globalisation and nationalism in education*, ed. D. Coulby, C. Jones and E. Zambeta (London: Kogan Page).

—— (2005b) 'Social Exclusion and Educational Opportunity: the case of British education policies within a European Context', *Globalisation, Societies and Education* 3.1 101–25.

Alliance 90/The Green Party (nd) Program and Principles: *The Future is Green* http://archiv.gruene-partei.de/dokumente/grundsatzprogramm-english.pdf.

Amis, K. (1981) 'Whatever became of Jane Austen and other essays' (Harmondsworth: Penguin Books).

Anderson, P. (2002) 'Land without Prejudice', *London Review of Books* 24.6, 21 March.

—— (2004) 'Union Sucrée', *London Review of Books* 26.18, 23 September.

Anonymous (2003) "Le tournant 'altermondialiste' de la contestation enseignante" *Le Monde de l' Education*, September, pp. 13–15.

Anonymous (2006a) 'Berlin School Wants to Profit from Education', *Deutsche Welle*, 13 October 2006, www.dw-world.de.

Anonymous (2006b) 'No Solution other than Police Presence for Unruly Berlin School', *Deutsche Welle*, 1 April, www.dw-world.de.

Anonymous (2006c) '"Quell" abraccio mortale con I "baroni"', *Il Manifesto*, 15 December.

Antunes, F. (2006) 'Globalisation and Europification of Education Policies: routes, processes and metamorphoses', *European Educational Research Journal*, 5.1, 38–56.

Archer, L. and Yamashita, H. (2003) 'Theorising Inner City Masculinities', *Gender and Education* 15.3, 115–32.

Arco-Tirado Andjuan, José L. and Fernández-Balboa, Miguel (2003) 'Contextual Barriers to School Reform in Spain', *International Review of Education* 49.6, 585–600.

Attac-France (2004) *Décentralisation solidaire ou marchande* (Attac: Montreuil-sous-Bois Mai).

—— (2004) 'Une victoire contre la marchandisation de l'école', on the website www.attac.fr, 6 October 2004.

Babb, P. (2005) *A Summary of 'Focus on Social Inequalities'* (London: Office for National Statistics).

Balibar, E. (2004) Interview in *Il Manifesto*, 4 September.

Ball, S. (1999) 'Global trends in educational reform and the struggle for the soul of the teacher', Paper Presented at the British Educational Research Association Conference, Brighton.

—— (2003) *The More Things Change ... Educational research, social class and 'interlocking' inequalities* (London: Institute of Education, University of London).

Ball, S.J., Marques-Cardoso, C., Reay, D. Thrupp, M. 'Changes in Regulation Modes and Social Reproduction of Inequalities in Education Systems: Education Policy in England - Changing Modes of Regulation, 1945–2001, www.girset.ucl.ac.be(2002).

—— (2004) *Education For Sale! The Commodification of Everything?* (London: King's Annual Education Lecture, Kings College).

Ballarino and Checchi, *Sistema scolastico e disuguaglianza sociale; Se la scuola non ci rende uguali* La Republica 28 November 2006.

Balsera, Pauli Davila (2005)'The Educational System and National Identities: the case of Spain in the twentieth century', *History of Education* 34.1, 23–40.

Barber M. (2001) 'High expectations and standards for all, no matter what: creating a world class education service in England', in *Taking Education Really Seriously: four years' hard labour* ed. M. Fielding (London: Routledge).

Barber, M. and Phillips, V. (2000) *Fusion: how to unleash irreversible change: lessons for the future of system-wide school reform*, Paper to a DfEE Conference on Education Action Zones.

Barnett, C. (1986) *The Audit of War* (London: Macmillan).

Beck, U. (1992) *Risk Society* (London: Sage Publications).

Becker, G. (1964) *Human Capital: a theoretical and empirical analysis with special reference to education* (New York Columbia University Press).

Beckmann, A. and Cooper, C. (2005) 'Conditions of Domination: reflections on harms generated by the British state education system', *British Journal of Sociology of Education* 26.4, 475–89.

Béduwé, C. and Planas, J. (2003) *Educational expansion and the Labour Market* (Luxemburg: Cedefop).

Bensaid, D. (2006) Interviewed by Anna Maria Merlo, *Il Manifesto*, 24 March.

Bentivoglio, F. (2000) *Il disagio dell'incivilità*, edizione (Pistoia: CRT).

Berardi, F. (Bifo) (2004) *Il sapiente, il mercante, il guerriero, Dal rifiuto del lavoro all'emergere del cognitariato* (Rome: Derive Approdi).

Bernal, J.-L. (2005) 'Parental choice, social class and market forces: the consequences of privatisation of public services in education', *Journal of Education Policy* 20.6 779–92.

Bernocchi, P. (2000) 'Behind the Recent School Protests in Italy', *Education and Social Justice* 3.1 44–7.

—— (2006) 'La scuola immutata di Gattopardo Fioroni', *Il Manifesto*, 6 October.

Bernstein, B. (1975a)'Class and Pedagogies: visible and invisible', in *Language, Codes and Control* (London: Routledge & Kegan Paul).

—— (1975b) 'On the Classification and Framing of Educational Knowledge', in *Class Codes and Control, Volume 3: towards a theory of educational transmissions* (London: RKP).

Bernstein, B. and Davies, B (1969)'Some sociological comments on Plowden', in *Perspectives on Plowden* ed. R. Peters (London: Routledge and Kegan Paul).

Bertola, G. and Checchi, D. 'Sorting and Private Education in Italy' Departmental Working Paper 2001–21, Department of Economics, University of Milan (2001).

Blair, T. (1995) 'The Power of the Message', *New Statesman*, 29 September.

—— (2004a) quoted in the *Times Educational Supplement*, 2 April.

—— (2004b) *Speech to National Association of Head Teachers*, 1 May.

Blanden, J., Gregg, P. and Machin, S. (2005) *Intergenerational Mobility in Europe and North America* (London: Centre for Economic Performance, London School of Economics).

Block, R. and Klemm, K. (1997) *Lohnt sich Schule? Aufwand und Nutzen: eine Bilanz* (Reinbek: Rowohlt Taschenbuchverlag).

Blossfeld, H.P. and Shavit, Y. (1993) *Persistent Inequality: changing educational attainment in thirteen countries* (Boulder: Westview Press).

Boltanski, L. and Chiapello, E. (2006) *The New Spirit of Capitalism* (London: Verso).

Bontempelli, M. (2000) *L'agonia della scuola italiana* (Pistoia: Editrice, CRT).

—— (2003) *Controlesscio-formazione – critica sulla riforma Moratti* www.cespbo.it.

Boselli, R. (2005) 'Contre Feux', *L'Ecole Emancipée* 18–19 December.

Bottery, M. (2001) 'Globalisation and the UK Competition State: no room for transformational leadership in education?', *School Leadership and Management* 21.2, 198–218, p. 213.

Bourdieu, P. (1991) *Language and Symbolic Power* (Cambridge: Polity Press).

—— (1998) *Acts of Resistance* (Cambridge Polity Press).

Bourdieu, P. and Passeron, J.-C. (1990) *Reproduction in Education, Culture and Society* (London: Sage).

Bousquet, M. and Terranova, T. (2004) 'Recomposing the University', *Mute* 28 Summer/Autumn, www.metamute.com.

Bousquet, R. and Ponvert, V. (2007) 'Un non toujours d'actualité', *L'Ecole Emancipée* janvier/février, pp. 14–15.

Boyd-Barrett, O. and O'Malley, P. (1995) *Education Reform in Democratic Spain* (London: Routledge).

Brine, J. (2006) 'Lifelong Learning and the Knowledge Economy: those that know and those that do not – the discourse of the European Union', *British Educational Research Journal* 32.5, 647–66.

Brown, M., Askew, M., Millet, A. and Rhodes, V. (2003) 'The Key Role of Educational Research in the Development and Evaluation of the National Numeracy Strategy', *British Educational Research Journal* 29.5, 655–67.

Brown, P. (2003) 'The Opportunity Trap: education and employment in a global economy', *European Educational Research Journal* 2.1, 141–79.

Brulavoine, T. (2005) 'L'Acodomia aide l'état', www.ecoledemocratique, June.

Brunello, G. and Checchi, D. (2005) *School Vouchers, Italian Style* (Bonn: Institute for the Study of Labour).

Brunner, L. and Laronche, M. (2004) 'Ce que va proposer le rapport Thélot pour réformer l'école', *Le Monde*, 25 August.

Business Advisory Committee to the OECD (2004) *Briefing paper for the 2004 Meeting of Education ministers*, Dublin.

Camerra-Rowe, P. (2004) 'Agenda 2010: redefining German social democracy', *German Politics and Society* 22.1 March, pp. 1–30.

Campetti, L (2006) 'Conflitto e governo: la Cgil si divide', *Il Manifesto*, 23 November.

Capasso, G. (2005) 'Scuola Devoluta: regionalizzazione, territorialità', *Giornale di Cobas-Scuola* 26 March–April pp. 4–5.

Capital Strategies 'In focus: public sector professional services-boom time' http://www.capitalstrategies. co. uk/press/boomtime.pdf p. 3 (accessed May 2003).

Cassen, B. (2003) 'On the Attack', *New Left Review* 19, January–February, 41–62.

Castells, M. (1996) *The Rise of the Network Society* (Oxford: Blackwell).

—— (1998) *The Information Age: economy, society and culture Volume 3: End of Millennium* (Oxford: Blackwell).

Castro, Fermin Rodriguez (2006) 'El desarme politico e ideologico de la izquierda ante la LOE', *Crisis* 11, 3–19.

Cavalli, A. (2000) *Gli insegnanti nella scuola che cambia* (Bologna: Il Mulino).

CBI (2000) *In Search of Quality in Schools: the employers' perspective* (London: CBI).

—— *The Business of Education Improvement* (London: Confederation of British Industry).

Centre for Educational Sociology (2006) *Social-Class Inequalities in Education in England and Scotland*, Special CES briefing no. 40 (Edinburgh: CES, May).

CERI/OECD (2000) *Knowledge Management for the Learning Society* (Paris: OECD).

Charlot, B.(1994), 'La territorialisation des politiques educatives: une politique nationale', in *L'école et le territoire*, ed. B. Charlot (Paris: Armand Colin).

Chauveau, G. (2003) 'Les Rencontres de Observatoire des Zones Prioritaires', no. 40 avril – summarised in *L'Ecole Emancipée* Jan–Fev 2006, pp. 13–14.

Checchi, D. (2003) *The Italian Educational System: family background and social stratification* (Università degli Studi diMilano, Dipartimento di Economica Politica e Aziendale).

Chellot, M. (May 2006)'Education Leads to Temping and Unemployment: France's precarious graduates', *Le Monde Diplomatique*.

Choukri Ben-Ayed (2000) 'L'enseignement privé en France' in *L'école: l'état des savoirs* ed. A. van Zanten (Paris: la découverte).

Cillario, L. (1996) *L'economìa degli spettri* (Rome: Manifesto Libri).

Cimbalo, G. (2003) *Le regioni alla ricerca di una identità inesistente ... La strategia legislativa delle Regioni per la gestione differenziata del sistema scolastico* (Turin: G.Giappichelli).

Clarke, J. and Newman, J. (1997) *The Managerial State* (London: Sage).

Cobas-Scuola (2004) *National Assembly of Cobas Scuola – Theses of the National Executive* (Cobas: giornali dei comitati di base della scuola) no 20 febbraio, p. ii.

Colectivo Baltasar Gracián (2003) 'El desmantelamiento de la enseñanza pública en España' *Crisis* Issue 3.

—— (2006) 'LOE: el peor de los pactos posibles', http://www.colectivobgracian. com/.

Collini, S. (2003) HiEdBiz, *London Review of Books* 25. 21, 6 November.

Confederazione Cobas (2003) *A new model of social self-organisation: from a refusal of passivity to the building of a movement against capitalist globalisation*, www.cobas.it.

Confindustria (1998) *Verso la scuola del 2000. Co-operare e Competere: le proposte di Confindustria* (Document presented by Carlo Callieri, vice-president of the Confindustria to Luigi Berlinguer, Minister of Education, 30 April), www.confindustria.it.

Conservative Policy Unit (2002) *No Child Left Behind* (London: Conservative Party).

Conti, A (2001) *Da un mondo all'altro. Il divenire azienda dell'università e il divenire università dell'azienda*, in *Posse: Il Lavaro di Genova* (Rome: manifestolibri).

Corbett, A. 'Secular, free and compulsory: republican values in French education' in *Education in France: continuity and change in the Mitterrand years 1981–1985* ed. A. Corbett and B. Moon (London: Routledge) pp. 5–21.

Crouch, C. (1998) *Social Change in Western Europe* (Oxford: Oxford University Press).

Croxford, L. and Raffe, D. (2005a) 'Education Markets and Social Class Inequality: a comparison of trends in England, Scotland and Wales' (Edinburgh: Education and Youth Transitions Project October) unpublished paper.

—— (2005b)'Secondary school organisation in England, Scotland and Wales since the 1980s', Discussion Paper for Seminar on *Policy Learning in 14–19 Education*. Joint seminar of *Education and Youth Transitions Project* and *Nuffield Review*, 15 March.

Curtis, P. and Courts, K. (2004) 'University strike action builds towards climax', *The Guardian*, 24 February.

Czalczynski, D. (2007) 'De 68 à l'effet U', *L'École Émancipée* (NF 3) January–February.

Dale, R. (2004) 'Forms Of governance, governmentality And the EU's Open Method Of Coordination' in *Global Governmentality* ed. Wendy Larner and William Walters (London: Routledge).

—— (2005) 'Globalisation, knowledge economy and comparative education', *Comparative Education* 41.2, 117–49.

De Queiroz, J.M. (2000) 'Pédagogie et Pédagogues contre le Savoir', in *L'école: l'état des savoirs* ed. A. van Zanten (Paris: la découverte) pp. 375–80.

De Singly, F. (2001) 'L'école et la famille', in *L'école: l'état des savoirs*, ed. A. van Zanten (Paris: la découverte).

Del Campo, Carlos Prieto (2005) 'A Spanish Spring?', *New Left Review* 31 Jan–Feb pp. 42–68.

Delgado, F. (2005) 'LOE: Escuela Pública, Escuela Privada, Religión y Pacto', *Crisis* 9 June.

Demailly, L., Montray, B. and Tondellier, M. (2002) 'Analyse de l'évolution des modes de regulation institutionalisée dans les systeme éducatif francais'. Paper prepared for the research project *Changes in regulation modes and social production of inequalities in education systems: a European comparison*, March 2002, http://www.girsef.ucl.ac.be/France2.pdf.

Demeeulemeester, J-L and Rochat, D. (2001) *The European Policy Regarding Education and Training: a critical assessment*, Skope Research Paper no. 21, Autumn 2001. Centre on Skills, Knowledge and Organisational Performance (Oxford, Warwick: Oxford and Warwick Universities).

Denkschrift der Kommission, Zukunft der Bildung – Schule der Zukunft (1995) – *Schule der Zukunft Zukunft der Bildung* (Neuwied: Luchterhand-Verlag).

Denscombe, M. (2000) 'Social Conditions for Stress: young people's experience of doing the GCSEs', *British Educational Research Journal* 26.3 pp. 360–74.

Department of Education and Science (1976) *School Education in England: problems and initiatives* (London: DES).

Derouet, J.-L. (1996)'Lower Secondary Education in France; from uniformity to institutional autonomy' in *Education in France: continuity and change in the Mitterrand years 1981–1985* ed. A. Corbett and B. Moon (London: Routledge).

Deutsche K-G and Walter, N. (2003) *Mehr Wachstum für Deutschland: Die Reformagenda* (Frankfurt: Campus Verlag).

Department for Education and Employment (DfEE) (1998) *Teachers – Meeting the Challenge of Change* (London: DFEE).

—— (1999) 'A Fresh Start' (The Moser Report) (London: DfEE).

—— (2001) *Schools Building on Success* (London: Stationery Office).

Department for Education and Skills (2002) *Investment for Reform*, chapter 5(London: DfES).

Department for Education and Skills (2004) *Departmental Annual Report 2004* (London: DfES).

Department for Education and Skills (2005a) *14–19 Education and Skills* (London: The Stationery Office).

Department for Education and Skills (2005b) 'Has the social class gap narrowed in primary schools? A background note to accompany the talk by Rt Hon Ruth Kelly, Secretary of State for Education and Skills: Education and Social Progress', 26 July 2005, (London: DfES). http://www.dfes.gov.uk/rsgateway/DB/STA/t000597/IPPR_Speech.pdf.

Department for Education and Skills (2006) *Education and Inspection Bill* (London: The Stationery Office).

DfES, (2006) Education-Business website. http://www.dfes.gov.uk/ebnet/business/.

Department for Education and Skills/Department for Culture, Media and Sport (1999) *All Our Futures: creativity, culture and education* (London: The Stationery Office).

Dion, D-P. (2006) 'The Lisbon Process: a European Odyssey', *European Journal of Education*,40.3, 295–313.

Drevon, J.-M. (2005) 'Banlieues: il y a le feu!', *L'Ecole Emancipée* pp. 10–11, December.

—— (2006a) 'Surprises, étonnements et ravlissement', *L'Ecole Emancipée* mai 90.7, pp. 4–5.

—— (2006b) 'Y en a ras le bol de ces guignols!', *L'Ecole Emancipée* 90.7, avril pp. 4–5.

Dubet, F. (2004) 'The French Education System: institutional transformation or neo-liberal shift?', *Newsletter of the Institutional Institute for Educational Planning* (Paris: IIEP-UNESCO) April–June pp. 12–13.

Duceux, N. (2004) 'Du rapport Thélot à la loi Fillon', *Critique Communiste* 174 Hiver pp. 12–22.

Dufour, D. (2003) *L'art de réduire les têtes- sur la nouvelle servitude de l'homme libéré à l'ère du capitalisme total*, (Paris: Denoel).

Dugas, J. (2005) 'Les "3000" à Aulnay', *L'Ecole Emancipée* 90.4 decembre p. 13.

Duru-Bellat, M. (2002) *Les inégalités sociales à l'école: genèse et mythes* (Paris: PUF).

Duru-Bellat, M. and Kieffer, A. (2000) 'Inequalities in educational opportunities in France: educational expansion, democratisation or shifting barriers?', *Journal of Education Policy* 15.3, 333–52.

Duru-Bellat, M. and Suchaut, B. (2005), 'Organisation and Context, Efficiency and Equity of Educational Systems: what PISA tells us', *European Educational Research Journal* 4.3 pp. 181–94.

Duru-Bellat, M. and van Zanten, A. (2006) *Sociologie de l'école* (Paris: Armand Colin).

Dutercq, Y. (2000) 'Administration de l'éducation: nouveau contexte, nouvelles perspectives', *Revue Française de Pédagogie* 130, mai.

Eagleton, T. (2004) *After Theory* (London: Allen Lane).

Edwards, T. and Tomlinson, S. (2002) *Selection isn't Working: diversity, standards and inequality in secondary education* (London: Catalyst).

Eliot, T.S. (1949) *Notes towards a Definition of Culture* (London: Faber & Faber).

Ertl, H. (2006) European Union Policies in Education and Training: the Lisbon agenda as a turning point? *Comparative Education* 42.1 pp. 5–27 p. 12.

Esperanza Aguirre, G. (1997) 'Educaciòn y cultura: calida y libertad', Speech given at the Club Siglo XXI Madrid, 26 May.

Estève, G. (2000) Flashback on a 45-Day Campaign: the teachers' strike in the south of France *Education and Social Justice* 2.3, pp. 51–5.

ETUC (2004) 'The EU's Lisbon Strategy', www.etuc.org.

European Union Education and Training 2010 website http://ec.europa.eu/education/policies/2010/et_2010_en.html.

European Coalition of Cities Against Racism (2005) *Study on Measures Taken by Municipalities for Further Action to Challenge Racism through Education* (Graz: ECCAR) Occasional Papers, www.etc-graz.at.

European Commission (1993) White Paper, *Growth, Competitiveness, Employment* (Brussels: European Commision).

—— (1995) *Teaching and Learning: towards the learning society*, White Paper on Education and Training (Brussels: European Commission).

—— (2000) *European Report on Quality of School Education: sixteen quality indicators* (Brussels: European Commission).

—— (2001a) *The Concrete Future Objectives of Education Systems* (Brussels: European Commission).

—— (2001b) White Paper, *European Governance* 2001 http://europa.eu.int/comm/governance/governance_eu/nat_policics_cn.htm.

—— (2004) *Education et formation 2010: l'urgence des réformes pour réussir la stratégie de Lisbonne* (Brussels: European Commission).

—— (2005a) 'Implementing the "Education and Training 2010" Work Programme: 2005 Progress Report – France' (Brussels: European Commission).

—— (2005b) 'Implementing the "Education and Training 2010" Work Programme: 2005 Progress Report – Spain' (Brussels: European Commission).

European Council (2000) Conclusions of the European Presidency Council in Lisbon, 23–4 March.

European Round Table (1989) 'Education and Skills in Europe', *Inquiry by the European Round Table into Education and Training in Europe* (Brussels: European Round Table of Industrialists).

Eurydice (2000) 'Private Education in the European Union: organisation, administration and public authorities' role', December www.eurydice.org.

Fekete, L. (2004)'Anti-Muslim Racism and the European Security State', *Race & Class* 46.1, 3–29.

Felouzis, G. and Perroton, J. (2005) 'Un New Deal pour l'école', *Le Monde Diplomatique* décembre, pp. 14–15.

Felstead, A., Gallie, D. and Green, F. (2004) *Work Skills in Britain 1986–2001* (Nottingham: DfES).

Ferry, L., Darcos, X. and Haignère, C. (2003) *Lettre à tous ce qui aiment l'école: pour expliquer les réformes en cours* (Paris: Odile Jacob).

Flitner, E. (2004) 'Conditions culturelles et politiques du choix de l'école à Berlin', *Education et Sociétés* 14.2 33–49.

Florin, I. (2006) 'A proposito di OCSE/PISA e di qualità dell'istruzione', in *Scuola Formazione* no. 11, November.

Fondation Copernic (2003) *Europe: une alternative* (Paris: Syllepse).

Fortuna, S. (2004) *Università: una riforma per l'eccellenza* 'Il Sole-24 Ore' 14 February.

Freire, P. (1972) *Pedagogy of the Oppressed* (Penguin: Harmondsworth).

Führ, C. (1997) *The German Education System since 1945: outlines and problems* (Bonn: Inter Nationes).

Furedi, F. (2004). *Where have all the Intellectuals Gone?* (London: Continuum).

Geay, B. (2003) 'Un processus de réattachement à l'institution', *Le Monde de l'Education* no. 317, p. 12, September.

Geissler, R. (1996) *Die Sozialstruktur Deutschlands* (Opladen: Westdeutscher Verlag).

Gemie, S. (2004) 'Stasi's Republic: the school and the "veil": December 2001–March 2004' *Modern and Contemporary France* 12.3, pp. 387–97.

Gewirtz, S. (2002) *The Managerial School* (London: Routledge).

Gillborn, D. and Youdell, D. (2000) *Rationing Education: policy, practice, reform and equity* (Buckingham: Open University Press).

Ginsborg, P. (1990) *A History of Contemporary Italy: society and politics 1943–1988* (Harmondsworth: Penguin Books) p. 170.

Ginsborg, P. (2001) *Italy and Its Discontents* (London: Allen Lane).

Gorz, A. (1982) *Goodbye to the Working Class* (London: Pluto Press).

—— (1999) 'Miseria del Presente, ricchezza del possibile', Interview in *Tute bianche* ed. A. Fumagelli and M. Lazzarato (Rome: Derive Approdi).

Grace, G. (1987) 'Teachers and the State in Britain', in *Teachers: the culture and politics of work* ed. M. Lawn and G. Grace (Lewes: Falmer Press).

Gramsci, A. (1970) 'On Education', in *Selections from the Prison Notebooks* ed. Q. Hoare and G. Nowell Smith (London: Lawrence & Wishart).

Green, A., Wolf, A, and Leney, T. (1999) *Convergence and Divergence in European Education and Training Systems* (London: Institute of Education).

The Guardian, 3 January 2005. Maurizio Zenezini, 'Università e mercato di Lavoro', in *La Rivista del Manifesto*, Dic, 2001. Zenezini cites figures of 32% of graduates in England and Italy as working in jobs which do not require a degree. In France, in the period from 1985 to 1995 the same category rose from 12% to 25%. His sources are L. Borghans and A. de Grip ed., *The Overeducated Worker?*, Edward Elgar, Cheltenam, 2000; and D. Clerc, *Condamnés au Chomage?* (Paris: Syros, 1999). Saskia Sassen's work on Global Cities and Survival Circuits is also useful in challenging the dominant reading of the globalised economy as one based on highly educated labour.

Guerrero, A. (1995) 'Professionalism, unionism and educational reform', in O. Boyd-Barrett and P. Malley (eds) Education Reform in Democratic Spain (London: Routledge).

Hahn H-J. (1998) *Education and Society in Germany* (Oxford: Berg).

Halsey, A.H. (1972) (ed.) *Educational Priority: EPA problems and priorities* vol 1 (London: HMSO).

Hanushek, E. (2005) *Economic Outcomes and School Quality* (Paris: International Institute for Educational Planning).

Hargreaves, A. (2003) *Teaching in the Knowledge Society* (Buckingham: Open University Press).

Hart, S., Dixon, A., Drummond M. J. and McIntyre, D. (2004) *Learning without Limits* (Buckingham, Open University Press).

Harvey, D. (2005) *A Brief History of Neoliberalism* (Oxford: Oxford University Press).

Hatcher, R. (2003) 'Changing the School system in England: business agendas and New Labour's education policies', Paper presented at the COFIR conference 'Formazione "glocale": un' altra educazione e imPossible?' Arezzo March.

—— (2004) 'Distributed Leadership and Managerial Power in Schools', Paper presented at the Society for Educational Studies and BERA Social Justice SIG Annual Seminar 'School Leadership and Social Justice', London, 4 November.

—— (2005) 'The Distribution of Leadership and Power in Schools', *British Journal of Sociology of Education* 26.2, 253–67.

Hatcher, R and Jones, K. (2006)'Researching Resistance: campaigns against academies in England', *British Journal of Educational Studies* 54.3, 329–51.

Haut Conseil de l'Education (HCE) (2006) 'Recommandations pour le socle commun' 23 mars http://www.hce.education.fr/.

Henry, M., Lingard, B., Rizvi, F. and Taylor, S. (2001) *The OECD, Globalisation and Education Policy* (Oxford: Pergamon).

Hillis Miller, J. (1999) *Black Holes* (Stanford: Stanford University Press).

Hingel, A. (2001) *Education Policies And European Governance: Contribution to the Interservice Groups on European Governance* (Brussels: European Commission).

Hirtt, N. (2002) 'Im Schatten der Unternehmerlobby. Die Bildungspolitik der Europaischen Kommission', *Widersprüche* 83, 37–51.

—— (2004) 'Three Axes of School Marchandisation' *European Educational Research Journal* 3.2, 442–53.

—— (2005) *Education et formation 2010: comment Mme Reding a fait accelerer la cadence,* www.ecoledemocratique.org 7 March.

—— (2006) *PISA 2003 et les résultats des élèves issus de l'immigration en Belgique,* www.ecoledemocratique.org June.

Hobsbawm, E.J. (1994) *Age of Extremes: the short twentieth century 1914–1991* (London: Michael Joseph).

Hyman, P. (2005) *1 out of 10: from Downing Street vision to classroom reality* (London: Vintage Books).

INED (1970) *La Population et l'Enseignement* (Paris: PUF).

International Labour Organisation (1998) *World Employment Report 1998-9: employability in the global economy – how training matters* (Geneva: ILO).

Innes, R. (1998) *Italian Educational Reform: discourse and the production of compatible subjectivities* MA Thesis, Macquarie University.

IUCCI (2003) 'La Sperimentazione della Moratti: un bilancio negativo (e costoso)' www.rassegna.it/2003/speciali/scuola/noratti2htm.

Jackson, B. and Marsden, D. (1962) *Education and the Working Class* (London: Routledge and Kegan Paul).

Jacott, L. and Rico, Antonio Maldonaldo (2006) 'The Centros Concertados in Spain, parental demand and implications for equity' *European Journal of Education* 41.1, 97–111.

Jacques, M. and Mulhern, F. (eds) (1979) *The Forward March of Labour Halted?* (London: Verso).

Jäggi, M., Müller, R. and Schmid, S. (1976) *Red Bologna* (London: Writers and Readers).

James, C. (1968) *Young Lives at Stake* (London: Collins).

James, M. (2000) 'Measured Lives: the rise of assessment as the engine of change in English schools' *The Curriculum Journal* 11.3, 343–64.

Jenkins, S., Micklewright, J and Schnepf, S. (2006) *Social Segregation in Secondary Schools: how does England compare with other countries?* (Essex: Institute for Social and Economic Research, University of Essex) January.

Jessop, B. (2005) 'Cultural political economy, the knowledge-based economy, and the state' in *The Technological Economy*, ed. D. Slater and A. Barry (London: Routledge) pp. 144–66.

Johnson, R. and Steinberg, D. (2004) 'Distinctiveness and Difference within New Labour' in *Blairism and the War of Persuasion: Labour's Passive Revolution* ed. D. Steinberg and R. Johnson (London: Lawrence and Wishart).

Johnson, R. and Walkerdine, V. (2004) 'Transformations under pressure: New Labour, class, gender and young women' in *Blairism and the War of Persuasion: Labour's Passive Revolution* ed. D. Steinberg and R. Johnson (London: Lawrence and Wishart) pp. 114–33.

Johsua, S. (2003a) 'Un mouvement plus antilibéral qu'altermondialiste', *Le Monde de l'Education* no. 317, September.

—— (2003b) *Une autre ecole est possible* (Paris: Textuel).

Jones, K. (1983) *Beyond Progressive Education* (London: Macmillan).

—— (1989) *Right Turn: the Conservative revolution in education* (London: Hutchinson).

—— (2003) *Education in Britain* (Cambridge: Polity Press).

—— (2004) 'An old future; a new past: Labour remakes the English school' in *Blairism and the War of Persuasion: Labour's Passive Revolution* ed. D. Steinberg and R. Johnson (London: Lawrence and Wishart).

Jones, K & Shain, F. (2002) *Teacher Trade Unionism in urban contexts: the global and the local*, Paper to the European Conference on Educational Research, Lisbon.

Klausenitzer, J. (2002a) 'Investitionen in das "Humankapital": PISA und die Bildungspolitik der OECD'. Website of the Bund demokratischer Wissenschaftlerinnen und Wissenschaftler / BdWi 15 July, www.bdwi.de/forum/archiv/.

—— (2002b) PISA – einige offene Fragen zur OECD-Bildungspolitik *Widersprüche* 85 September 2002 55–69.

—— (2004) 'Altes und Neues Anmerkungen zur Diskussion über die gegenwärtige Restrukturierung des deutschen Bildungswesens' http://www.links-netz.de/.

Kluge, Jürgen 'Schluss mit der Bildungsmisere: Ein Sanierungs Konzept' Frankfurt, Campus Verlag (2003) p. 1.

Kok, W. (2004) The Kok Report, *Facing the Challenge: the Lisbon strategy for growth and employment. Report from the High-Level Group chaired by Wim Kok* (Luxemburg: European Communities).

La Vérité (1940/1978) no. 2, 15 septembre, Reprinted in facsimile (Paris: Etudes et Documentation Internationales).

Lang, V. (2000) 'Les IUFM et la professionalisation des enseignants', in *Sociologie de l'école* (Paris: Armand Colin) pp. 228–35).

Lange, B. and Alexiadou, N. (2006) 'New Forms of European Union governance in the education sector – a preliminary analysis of the implementation of the Open Method of Co-ordination (OMC) in the UK'. Paper to the European Conference on Educational Research Geneva.

Latouche, S. (1992) *L'occidentalizzazione del Mondo* (Turin: Bollati Boringhieri).

Laval, C. (2004a) *L'école n'est past une entreprise* (Paris: La Découverte).

—— (2004b) *L'Europe libérale aux commandes de l'école: a propos du rapport Thélot et du projet de loi d'orientation pour l'avenir de l'école*, Website of the Institut du Recherches de la FSU http://institut.fsu.fr2004.

—— (2006) 'Socle des competences: l'utilitarisme scolaire et ses dangers', in *L'Ecole Emancipée* mai 90.7.

Laval, C., Weber, L., Baunay, Y., Cussó, R., Dreux, G. and Rallet, D. (2002) *Le nouvel ordre éducatif mondial* (Paris: Nouveaux Regards/Syllepse Paris).

Lawn, M. (1996) *Modern Times? Work, Professionalism and Citizenship in Teaching* (Lewes: Falmer Press).

Lawn, M. (2001) 'Borderless Education: imagining a European educational space in a time of brands and networks' *Discourse* 22.2. pp. 173–184, p. 175.

Le Monde Dossier (2006) *Egalité des chances, une expression, un principe et une loi* 1 December.

Legambiente (2004) *Scuola e Formazione: Scuola Pubblica: liquidazione ... di fine stagione, cifre, dati, commenti sui tagli operati dal Governo ai danni scuola pubblica*, February 2004. www.legambientescuolaformazione.it/.

Lehmann, R. Peek, R and Gänsfuß, R. *Aspekte der Lernausgangslage und der Lernentwicklung von Schülerinnen und Schülem, die im Schuljahr 1996–7 eine fiunfte Klase an Hamburger Schülen besuchten* available from http://www.hamburger-bildungsserver.de/lau/lau5/.

Lelièvre, C. (2000) 'The French Model of the Educator State', *Journal of Education Policy* 15.1, 5–10.

Lévy, P. (1996) L'*Intelligenza Collettiva* (Milan: Feltrinelli).

Lichfield, J. (2005) 'TV Offensive fails to halt French drift to No vote', *The Independent* 18 May.

—— (2006) 'If only this were a real French revolution', *The Independent* 21 March.

Lindblad, S., Ozga, J. and Zambeta, E. (2002) 'Changing Forms of Educational Governance in Europe', *European Educational Research Journal* 1.4, 615–24.

Lindenberg. D. (1970) *L'internationale communiste et l'école de classe* (Paris: Maspero).

Lohmann, I. (2006) 'Jedes Schule ein kleines Unternehmen', *Freitag*, 4 August www.freitag.de.

London Association for the Teaching of English (LATE) (1982) *Race, Society and School: education in a multi-cultural society* (London: LATE).

Lumley, R. (1990) *States of Emergency: cultures of revolt in Italy from 1968 to 1978* (London: Verso).

Maccarini, A. (2004) 'La réforme de l'éducation en Italie: un exemple de gouvernance?' *Education et Sociétés* 14.2, 167–88.

Mahony, P. and Hextall, Ian (2000) *Reconstructintg Teachers: standards, performance and accountability* (London: Routledge Falmer).

Mahony, P. Menter, I. and Hextall, I. (2004) '*Building Dams in Jordan, Assessing Teachers in England: a case study in Edu-business*', *Globalisation, Societies and Education* 2.3, 277–96.

Marazzi, C. (1999) *Il posto dei calzini: la svolta linguistica dell'economia e i suoi effetti nella politica* (Bellinzona: Casagrande).

Maroy C. (ed.) (2007 forthcoming) *Ecole, régulation et marché. Une analyse de six espaces scolaires locaux en Europe* (Paris: Presses Universitaires de France, coll. Education et Sociétés).

Mamon, S. (2004) 'Mapping the attainment of black students', *Race and Class* 46.2, 78–91.

Mellizo-Soto, Maria Fernandez (2000) 'Education policy and Equality in France: the socialist years', *Journal of Education Policy* 15.1, 11–17.

Merle, P. (2000) 'Le concept de démocratisation de l'institution scolaire: une typologie et sa mise à l'épreuve' *Population* 55.1, 15–50.

—— (2002) *La Démocratisation de l'Enseignment* (Paris: La Découverte).

Milano, S. (2001) *La Pauvreté Absolue* (Paris: Hachette Litterature).

Miliband, D. (2004) 'Choice and Voice in Personalised Learning' speech to the DfEs/Demos/OECD conference on *Personalising Education: the future of public sector reform*, May, London.

Milner, J.-C. (1984) *De l'école* (Paris: Editions du Seuil).

Minardi, S. (2005) 'Uomo sul lavoro vinco io', *L'espresso*, 27 January.

Monasta, A. (2002) 'Italy' in *Education in a Single Europe*, ed. Brock and W. Tulasiewicz (London: Routledge).

Moscati, R. (1998) 'The Changing Policy of Education in Italy', *Journal of Modern Italian Studies* 3.1, 55–73.

Murdock, G. (1974) 'The Politics of Culture' in *Education or Domination?*, ed. D. Holly (London: Arrow Books).

Negri, T. and Hardt, M. (1994) *Labor of Dionysos: a critique of the state-form* (Minneapolis-London: University of Minnesota Press).

—— (2004a) *Empire* (Boston: Harvard University Press).

—— (2004b) *Moltitudine* (Milan: Rizzoli).

Nóvoa, A. (2001) 'The restructuring of the European educational space: changing relationships among states, citizens and educational communities' in *Rethinking European Welfare* ed. J. Fink, G. Lewis and J. Clarke (London: Sage) pp. 249–75.

OECD (1987) *Structural Adjustment and Economic Performance* (Paris: OECD).

—— (1995a) *Governance in Transition* (Paris: OECD).

—— (1995b) *Governance in Transition: public management reforms in OECD countries* (Paris: OECD).

—— (1998a) *Human Capital Investment: an international comparison* (Paris: OECD).

—— (1998b) *Reviews of National Policies for Education: Italy* (Paris: OCED).

—— (1999) *Measuring Student Knowledge and Skills: a new framework for assessment* (Paris: OECD).

—— (2001a) Investing in Competencies for all (communiqué) Meeting of OECD Education Ministers, Paris 3–4 April.

—— (2001b) *Knowledge Management in the Learning Society* (Paris: OECD).

—— (2001c) (Arnal, E., Ok, W. and Torres, R.) Labour Market And Social Policy – Occasional Papers no. 50, *Knowledge, Work Organisation And Economic Growth* (Paris: OECD).

—— (2002a) *Education at a Glance* (Paris: OECD).

—— (2002b) 'Rethinking Human Capital', *Education Policy Analysis* (Paris: OECD).

—— (2003) *Attracting, Developing and Retaining Effective Teachers: country background report for Italy* (Paris: OECD).

—— (2004) *Attracting, Developing and Retaining Effective Teachers – Country Note for Germany* (Paris: OECD).

—— (2005) *School Factors Related to Quality and Equity – Results from PISA 2000* (Paris: OECD).

Orrit, Javier Doz (1996) 'Problems of Implementing Educational Reform' in Boyd-Barrett and O'Malley, pp. 271–82.

Ostermann, H. and Schmidt, U. (1998) 'Education, Training and the Workplace' in *Modern Germany: politics, society and culture* ed. P. James (London: Routledge).

Ozga, J. (2003) *Measuring and Managing Performance in Education*, Briefing no. 27 (Edinburgh: Centre for Educational Sociology Edinburgh University).

Ozga, J. and Gewirtz, S. (1994) 'Sex, Lies and Audiotape: interviewing the education policy élite', in *Researching Education Policy: ethical and methodological issues* ed. D. Halpin and B. Troyna (Lewes: Falmer Press).

Papadopoulos, G (1994) *Education 1960-1990: the OECD Perspective* (Paris: OECD).

Parsons, E. Chalkley, B. and Jones, A. 'School Catchments and Pupil Movements: a case study in parental choice' Educational Studies 26.1 March 2000 pp. 33–48, p. 47.

Paterson, L. (2003) *Scottish Education in the Twentieth Century* (Edinburgh: Edinburgh University Press).

Patramanis, A. and Athanasiades, H. (2002) *Globalisation, Education Restructuring and Teacher Unions in France and Greece: decentralisation policies or disciplinary parochialism?* Published by the Globalisation and Europeanisation Network in Education (www.genie-tn.net).

Pélage, A. (2001) Les transformations du rôle du chef d'établissement d' enseignment secondaire' in *Sociologie de l'école*, M. Duru-Bellat and A. van Zanten (Paris: Armand Colin) pp. 219–27.

Perucca, B. (2003) 'Les syndicats sont toujours là ...', *Le Monde de l'Education* no. 317 September 22–3.

Philogenverband Nordrhein-Westphalen (1964) *Leitsätze für eine organische Ausgestaltung des gegenwärtigen Schulwesens* (Düsseldorf: Schwann) quoted in S. Robinsohn and J. Kuhlmann (1967) 'Two Decades of Non-reform in West German education' reprinted in D. Phillips (ed) (1995) *Education in Germany: tradition and reform in historical context* (London: Routledge).

Planells, Antoni Verger (2005) 'GATS, Privatisation and Education: when education becomes a marketable commodity', Paper prepared for International Higher Education and Research Conference Melbourne.

Plowden Report (1967) *Children and Their Primary Schools* (London: HMSO).

Polesel, J. (2006) 'Reform and Reaction: creating new education and training structures in Italy', *Comparative Education* 42.4, 549–62

Porrotto, G. (2002) *Il Quadro Normativo del Progetto Moratti: prime realizazzioni e valutazioni* www.anisn.it/scienzescuols/documenti.htm.

Poulantzas, N. (1978) *State, Power, Socialism* (London: NLB).

Pratt, W. (2004) 'Schools face new criticism', *Frankfurter Allgemeine Zeitung* 17 September, English edition.

Prost, A. (1987) 'The Educational Maelstrom' in *The Mitterrand Experiment: continuity and change in Modern France* ed. G. Ross et al. (Cambridge: Polity Press).

Pyke, N. (2004) 'Bring Back Banding' (interview with Tim Brighouse) *The Guardian*, 8 January.

Qualifications and Assessment Authority (2000) *QAA News* 6 September (London: QAA).

Qualifications and Curriculum Authority, London http://www.ncaction.org.uk/creativity/.

Readings, B (1996) *The University in Ruins* (Boston: Harvard University Press).

Reay, D. and Lucey, H. (2003) 'The Limits of `Choice': Children and Inner City Schooling', *Sociology* 37.1, 121–42.

Reed, L.R. (1995) 'Reconceptualising equal opportunities in the 1990s: a study of radical teacher culture in transition' in *Anti-racism, culture and social justice in education* ed. M. Griffiths and B. Troyna (Stoke-on-Trent: Trentham Books).

Reiffers Report (1996) (Report of the Study Group on Education and Training) *Accomplishing Europe through Education and Training* (Luxemburg: European Commission) p. 71.

Retort (2004) 'Afflicted Powers; the state, the spectacle and September 11th', *New Left Review* II 27, May–June, 5–22.

Reuter, L.R. (2002) 'Privatization of education: the case of Germany', *Education And The Law* 14, 1–2.

Revelli, M. (1996) *Le Due Destre* (Turin: Bollati Boringhieri).

Richardson, B. (ed.) (2005) *Tell it Like it is: how our schools fail black children* (Stoke-on-Trent: Trentham Books).

Robertson, S. (2005) 'Re-imagining and rescripting the future of education: global knowledge economy discourses and the challenge to education systems', *Comparative Education* 41.2, 151–70.

Rochex, J.-Y. (2003) 'Ni le pédagogisme ni le mythe républicain', *Le Monde de l'Education* no 317, September.

Rossanda, R. (2006) 'Pourquoi la révolte française n'a pas gagné en Italie', *Le Monde Diplomatique* May pp. 4–5.

Rossi, G. (2003) *Il Conflitto Epidemico* (Milan: Adelphi).

Russo, L. (2000) *Segmenti e Bastonici Dove sta andando la scuola?* (Milan: Feltrinelli).

Sacristán, José Jimeno (1995) 'The Process of Pedagogic Reform', in *Education Reform in Democratic Spain* ed. O. Boyd-Barrettand and P. O'Malley (London: Routledge).

Sarkozy, R. (2007) *Lettre de mission addressée a M. Xavier Darcos, Ministre de l' Education Nationale (Lettre de M. Nicolas Sarkozy, président de la République)*, 5th July.

Savage, M. (2003) 'A New Class Paradigm?', *British Journal of Sociology of Education* 24.4, 535–41.

Schnepf, S. (2002) *A Sorting hat that fails? The transition from primary to secondary school in Germany'*, Innocenti Working Paper 92 (Florence: UNICEF Innocenti Research Centre).

School of Barbiana (1969) *Letter to a Teacher* (Harmondsworth: Penguin).

Sciascia, L. (1987) *The Moro Affair & The Mystery of Majorana* (Manchester: Carcanet Press).

Scuola di Barbiana, (1967) *Lettere a una Professoressa* (Firenze: L.E.F.).

Seddon, T. (1997) 'Education: deprofessionalised? Or deregulated, reorganised and reauthorised', *Australian Journal of Education*, 41.3, 228–47.

Semeraro, S. (2003) 'Le nuove pedagogie crescono nei territori asimmetrici', *Carta*, 5.36.

Sharp, R. and Green, A. (1975*) Education and Social Control: a study in progressive primary education* (London: Routledge & Kegan Paul).

Shavit, Y. and Westerbeek, K. (1998) 'Educational Stratification in Italy: reforms, expansion and equality of opportunity', *European Sociological Review* 14.1, 33–47.

Smith, F., Wall, K. and Mroz, M. (2004) 'Interactive whole-class teaching in the National Numeracy and Literacy Strategies' Strategy' *British Educational Research Journal* 30.3, 395–411.

Smith, T. B. (2004) *France in Crisis: welfare, inequality and globalisation since 1980* (Cambridge: Cambridge University Press).

Smithers, R. (2005) 'Crackdown urged on web exam plagiarism', *The Guardian*, 22 November.

STES-i (2006) 'Reports from National Education Networks: Spain' in *Bulletin on Educational Systems in Europe*, prepared for European Educational Network of the European Social Forum, Athens.

Stockholm Network (2004) 'The State of the Union: market-oriented reform in the EU in 2004', www.stockholm-network.org.

'Stop Moratti Committee', *Appeal to the London Social Forum*, October 2004.

Supiot, A. (2005) 'Refeudalising Europe', *London Review of Books*, 21 July, pp. 18–21.

Teese, R., Aasen, P., Field, S. and Pont, B. (2006) *Equity in Education: thematic review – Spain: country note* (Paris: OECD).

Toynbee, P. (2006) 'Religious schools are indoctrinating and divisive. The people don't want them. So why are MPs backing them?' Friday 14 April, *The Guardian*.

Ubbiali, G.(2004)'Solidaires, Unitaires, Démocratiques (SUD): renouveau du syndicalisme révolutionnaire', *Journal of Modern and Contemporary France* 12.1, 35–48.

UNESCO/World Education Forum (2000) *Country Reports: Italy*.

Unger, Roberto Mangabeira (2005) *What should the Left Propose?* (London: Verso).

Unicef Innocenti Report Card (2002) *A League Table of Educational Disadvantage in Rich Nations* (Florence: UNICEF, Innocenti Research Centre).

Unison (2002) *A Web of Private Interest: how the big five accountancy firms influence and profit from privatisation policy* (London: Unison).

—— (2005) *PFI – against the public interest: why a licence to print money can also be a disaster* (London: Unison).

Van der Pijl, K. (2006) 'A Lockean Europe', *New Left Review* II 36 January/February.

Van Zanten, A. (2000a) *L'école: l'état des savoirs* (Paris: La Découverte).

Van Zanten, A. (2000b) *Un libéralisme éducatif sans frontières* in *L'école: l'état des savoirs* ed. A. van Zanten (Paris: la découverte) .

Van Zanten, A. (2002) 'Educational change and new cleavages between head teachers, teachers and parents: global and local perspectives on the French case', *Journal of Education Policy* 17.3, 289–304.

Van Zanten . A. (2005)New Modes of Reproducing Social Inequality in Education: the changing role of parents, teachers, schools and educational policies', *European Educational Research Journal* 4.3, 155–69.

Vasagar, J. and Smithers, R. (2003) 'Will Charles Clarke have his Place in History?', *The Guardian*, 10 May.

Verger, A. and Bonal, X. (2006) 'Against GATS: the sense of a global struggle', *Journal for Critical Education Policy Studies* 4.1, March, pp. 1–27.

Vertecchi, B. (2000)'Vecchi e Nuovi Analfabeti', *La Revista del Manifesto* no. 2, January.

Vinay, O. (2003) 'Transformer l'école et la société: entretien avec Olivier Vinay', *L'Education et ses contraires* Agone 29–30, 135–76.

Virno, P. (2004) *A Grammar of the Multitude: for an analysis of contemporary forms of life* (Cambridge: MIT).

Visco, G. (2006) *Il movimento anti-CPE tra autonomia studentesca e sindacati*, Paper to the Italian Political Studies Association Bologna.

Weber, L. (2003) *OMC, AGS: Vers la privatisation de la société* (Paris: Syllepse).

Whitfield, D. (2001) *Public Services or Corporate Welfare: the nation state in the global economy* (London: Pluto Press).

Wilkinson, R. (1996) *The Afflictions of Inequality* (London: Routledge).

Willis, P. (2003), 'Footsoldiers of Modernity: the dialectics of cultural consumption and the 21-Century School', *Harvard Educational Review* 78.3, 390–416.

Wolf, A. (2002) *Does Education Matter? Myths about education and economic growth* (Harmondsworth: Penguin).

—— (1999) *Education Sector Strategy* (Washington: World Bank).

World Bank (2002) *Constructing Knowledge Societies: new challenges for tertiary education* (Washington: World Bank).

Yeaw, K.(2005) 'Scuola per tutti, libero sapere per tutti: the student struggle in Italy', *Counterpunch*, 14 October, www.counterpunch.org.

Young, M (1999) 'Some Reflections on the concepts of social exclusion and social inclusion: beyond the third way' in *Tackling Disaffection and Social Exclusion* ed. A. Hayton (London: Kogan Page).

Zenezini, M.(2001) 'Università e mercato di Lavoro', in *La Rivista del Manifesto*, December.

Zizek, S. (2005) 'The Two Totalitarianisms', *London Review of Books* 27.6, 17 March.

Index